DELINEATION
OF PROGRESSIONS

Sophia Mason

ISBN: 0-86690-280-5
LCC:84-71624

First Printing: 1985
Seventh Printing: 1998

Cover Deisgn: Mary Martha Rader

Published by:
American Federation of Astrologers, Inc.
PO Box 22040
6535 S. Rural Road
Tempe, AZ 85285-2040

Printed in the United States of America

IN APPRECIATION

This book is dedicated to my many students who willingly gave of their charts so that we could share and learn through their experiences.

Many thanks to my dear friend and astrologer, Gladys Maruschke, for her assistance with the charts.

And above all, a special thanks to my two students, Marcia Kompier and Jerry Gallagher for their valuable time and assistance. Their continual aid and encouragement in the compiling of this text book were the essence of its actual completion.

TABLE OF CONTENTS

PROGRESSIONS

The formation of our physical body are concerned with natal planets only for these are what we were born with. Progressions reveal the unfoldment of life and the changes that may alter or otherwise affect our physical body as we begin to evolve. Progressions will show how the native has changed characteristically. How many times have you said "I used to be that way."

The natal chart and planets will always continue their hold on us, just as we keep our same physical body. A chart is like a play on a Broadway stage. The progressions and slow moving planets give the index of our natal chart a chance to unfold and reveal the details of each act as each curtain of life is lifted.

As a realist, this writer has always viewed the Houses in a Natal Chart as one's Destiny. The planets in the Houses are the Fate of one's Destiny. The sign position of the planets reveal how the Fate of one's Destiny will be utilized. It is for this very reason that a separate progressed chart is advocated. As the slower planets change Houses, they also alter the course of our Destiny. Fate, according to the sign position of the progressed planet takes us into new realms of experience. New endeavors and new individuals who may help to mold our way of thinking and our actions.

No one thinks the same way when they are 10 years of age, or 30 years old or even at age 60. Through progression, the sign on the 3rd House Cusp will change, adding a new dimensional coloring to the natal sign position of the 3rd. The progressed ruler of the progressed 3rd House Cusp also adds another touch to our manner of speaking, writing and inter-reaction with brothers and sisters.

Each and every house in the Natal Chart will undergo a subtle change. Contacts with people of different backgrounds, additional education, health setbacks and emotional upheavals will all play a role in altering our approach and conditioning with parental attitudes, vocation, money, children, friendships and other major factors that will have a bearing on our lives.

Progressions operate quite differently in the charts of children than they would for adults. Children are controlled and limited in their scope of expression and activities by parents, grandparents, teachers and other authoritive figures. However, their basic characteristics can still be molded and changed for they

1

are in a very vulnerable age. Planets progressing into the First House can strongly color their general attitude and approach to life. For example, Saturn by progression entering the First House can instill a serious disposition. Perhaps a grandparent is now residing with the family and may try to repress or restrict the child's mode of expression and activities. Responsibility of younger siblings due to both parents having to work may add a bit of resentment. Dental problems and braces on the teeth or skin problems in adolescence is not uncommon.

The planet Mars on the other hand, progressing in a child's First House can change a quiet, subdued personality to one of rebellion and aggression. Sudden flare up of temper, coupled with an independent streak that was not in evidence before. Accidents and fevers may become more pronounced in this young individual's life.

By the time adulthood is reached, one's identity and basic characteristics are already established. Major planets progressing in the First House are more likely to affect the adult through outside influences. Saturn for example, progressing into the First, may instill a readiness to accept more responsibility. Sometimes there is the desire for marriage, a willingness to work hard for some major goal or career change. Depending upon other aspects in force at the time, one may be assuming the additional burden of a live-in parent or perhaps the loss of one through death or divorce of one's parents. In many cases, I have seen individuals taken on insurmountable tasks that I would have felt they were incapable of in the past.

This would also hold true for progressed planets entering the Progressed Tenth. In the life of a child, it is more apt to affect the affairs of a parent or grandparent or those in authority that have bearing on the child's future. Concerning the chart of an adult, they are more inclined to make major changes affecting their own personal goal in life. Some graduate from college, still others may return to adult classes. Some seek a promotion in their job while others may seek a completely different line of work.

Planets progressing into the 7th House of a young child may bring individuals into the child's life that he must learn to contend with. A new brother or sister he doesn't get along with. A teacher whom the child thinks is picking on him. A school counselor that the child feels is forcing him to take school subjects of no personal interest.

Planets by progression in the 7th House after one has reached adulthood is more apt to take on a personal interest in forming of partnerships or entering into marriage. If already married at that time, one may change their feelings about their present spouse or marital status.

2

As a planet progresses into the 4th House during one's early years, the home base and affairs of parents become important. A parent becomes ill, or may decide it is time to move to a new location. If the parents are no longer married, one may re-marry and a step-parent becomes the dominant factor. An adult looks at his home base from different eyes. This may well be when they leave the nest and go on their own. Some take on a live-in relationship while others may share their apartment or home with a roommate. The purchase or sales of a home or land may interest others.

It is imperative in the judgment of progressions to take into effect the age and environmental factor of the individual in question.

Are they old enough to make serious decisions concerning important factors of their lives? Of, will their charts have more bearing upon the affairs of parents and those in their immediate surroundings?

Progressions open the door to future possibilities of marriage, relocation, career changes or health setbacks. Or, perhaps, guide one into a new outlet to fill the void of time during retirement years.

What is ripe to transpire is revealed through progressions. The role of the major transits and Solar or Lunar Eclipse is to assist the promised event through their encouragement with favorable aspects. Or, to hinder, with unfavorable aspects, resulting in setbacks, delays and obstacles.

MATHEMATICS AND
TIMING OF PROGRESSIONS

It was not this writer's intention to include a chapter on the mathematics of progressions due to the easy accessibility of computerized charts and the availability of many fine instructors.

The many requests from individuals whom I met while on lecture tours, convinced me, that there were still many who preferred to hand calculate either the Natal or Progressed Charts.

The mathematics of progressions, which is Secondary Progressions, commonly known as a "Day for a Year" method, is illustrated in the final chapter. The progressed MC, Ascendant and progressed House Cusp is achieved by subtracting the Natal Sun's position as it appears in the Ephemeris for the day of birth, from the Progressed Sun's position as it appears in the Ephemeris on the Progressed Birth Date.

Although this has been completely covered in the last chapter, one more note of caution should be heeded. Do NOT use the Natal Sun's position from a computerized chart and attempt to subtract its position from the noon position of a Progressed Sun. This has become a common error among beginning astrologers with a computerized Natal Chart. They frequently forget that their Natal Sun has been adjusted by a computer to their precise time of birth. Always return to the Ephemeris for the year of birth and take the noon position of the Natal Sun and only then, subtract it from the noon position of the Progressed Sun. The difference between the two Sun's position is added to the Natal 10th House Cusp. Once the Progressed 10th House Cusp has been calculated, it is a simple matter to go to the Table of Houses for the Latitude of birth and find the Progressed MC. You now have the Progressed Ascendant and Progressed House Cusp.

Converse Progressions are merely erecting a chart for the same number of years as the Progressed Chart, except one would use the planets prior to birth. Converse Progressions are an excellent means of providing additional insight to the present aspects that are operating in the Progressed Chart. Details for erecting the Conversed Progressed Chart is fully illustrated in the last chapter of

4

this text. The astute astrologer, equipped with a Natal Chart, an up-to-date Progressed and Conversed Chart, the current major transits and the present Solar and Lunar Eclipse has the best working tools at his finger tips.

For the sake of simplicity in working with Progressed Charts, this writer has purposely omitted the use of Conversed Progressed Charts in every case except one, that should serve as an excellent example. A separate Conversed Chart is used as with the Progressed Chart, however, less emphasis is placed on the effects of the Ascendant sign characteristically. The most important feature being the aspects that the Conversed planets make to one's Natal planets and of course to the Conversed and Natal Angular House Cusps.

Timing of the events promised by aspects occurring in the Progressed Chart, are generally set off by Solar and Lunar Eclipse and the slower transits (i.e. Jupiter, Saturn, Uranus, Neptune and Pluto). It may help to view the astrological chart somewhat like the face of a clock. The Hour Hand would be the Progressed aspects, ticking off an important event that is about to transpite within the coming year. The Minute Hand would be the Eclipses and major transiting planets linking the Natal and Progressed aspects along with the Progressed Moon towards an important event. The Second Hand would be the New or Full Moon and daily transits linking all of the elements together in the selection of a given date.

STEPS TO FOLLOW
WITH A PROGRESSED CHART

Equipped with one's Natal Chart and an up-to-date Progressed Chart, we will begin looking for the following features that may indicate an eventful period ahead. Give consideration to the following configurations:

1. Progressed Sun, Mercury, Venus or Mars in aspect with the Natal planets.
2. Progressed planets in aspect with an Angular House Cusp of the Natal Chart (i.e. 1st, 4th, 7th & 10th).
3. Progressed planets in aspect with an Angular House Cusp of the Progressed Chart (i.e. 1st, 4th, 7th & 10th).
4. Natal planets in aspect with an Angular House Cusp of the Progressed Chart.
5. Progressed planets in aspect to one another.
6. Do not discount the slow moving planets (i.e. Jupiter, Saturn, Uranus, Neptune and Pluto) that through progression have formed an exact aspect with one another (i.e. Progressed Saturn exactly sextile Natal Neptune). While it is true that such an aspect can remain in force for many years, it can however, act as a catalyst when activated by heavy transits. Glance through each present year Ephemeris and note if an Eclipse will favorably aspect these two planets. Note also if there are any major transiting planets assisting in its influence while the Eclipse is in force. For example, transiting Saturn sextile or trine a Natal or Progressed planet.
7. Progressed Moon in aspect with Natal and Progressed planets.
8. Progressed Moon in aspect with Angular House Cusp of both Natal and Progressed Charts.
9. Major transits and Solar or Lunar Eclipse in aspect with Natal Planets.
10. Major transits and Solar or Lunar Eclipse in aspect with Progressed planets and Progressed Moon.

ORB OF INFLUENCE

Progressed Sun, Venus, Mercury and Mars have a three year span of effectiveness while aspecting a Natal or Progressed planet. The 1st year while the Progressed planet is within 1° orb of applying in exactitude. The second year for when the degree of the aspect becomes exact. A third year for the 1° allowable orb in separating.

During the three year span that this Progressed/Natal aspect is in force, one should make it a general practice to check the current year Ephemeris for additional re-enforcement. Will an Eclipse or a major transit provide the necessary additional energy to promote this Progressed/Natal aspect into action?

The Sun and Moon are illuminaries and never retrograde in motion. Mercury, Venus or Mars can turn Stationary Direct or Stationary Retrograde during progressions. The year that either of these three planets change direction will be one of importance. During that time (SR or SD in motion) it is possible for one of them to remain in the same degree for a longer period. Mercury for example, can remain in one degree for as long as six days, in progressions, this would be equal to six years. It is most important to note whether such a planet would form an aspect with a Natal or Progressed planet favorable or unfavorably.

For example, Venus turning Retrograde in motion may remain in the same degree approximately six to eight years. If, during that time span, Progressed Venus should also happen to sextile or trine a natal planet such as the Moon, this individual can develop great rapport with the general public (Progressed Venus favorably aspected with Natal Moon). This aspect could enhance one's public image, self-esteem and general expansion in business. Not without some drawbacks however, due to the fact that Venus is now in retrograde motion. The favorable build-up of one's reputation would have a longer lasting affect due to the continuous, favorable reaction of Progressed Venus upon the Natal Moon. The same would apply towards the mental application of Mercury of the energy level of Mars. Naturally, the unfavorable aspects may produce disparaging results, such a prolonged, drawn out aspect may delay a new business or enterprise from getting off the ground floor.

The Progressed Moon is treated differently due to the faster rate of motion. Remaining in one sign or one house only two and one half years, the length of influence is three months. One degree while the Progressed Moon is applying, one degree while exact and one degree while separating from the aspect.

Do not bother with Progressed Jupiter, Saturn, Uranus, Neptune or Pluto in relation to their own Natal position. They seldom progress more than a few degrees in one life time.

Aspects between Progressed Sun, Venus, Mercury and Mars along with those they make to the slower progressed planets have the same orb of influence as the Progressed planets to Natal planets. One year while applying, one while exact and another while separating.

The first and foremost important feature in progression is an aspect from a Natal or Progressed planet to an Angular House Cusp. If the native has a Natal Chart proven to be accurate from past experiences or has been rectified by a qualified astrologer, then he may consider the following pertinent features:

1. Aspects between Natal planets and Progressed Angular House Cusps.
2. Aspects between Progressed planets and Progressed Angular House Cusps.
3. Aspects between Progressed Planets and Natal Angular House Cusps.

ASPECTS

PARALLEL — / / or P
Parallel aspect are two planets having the same declination. A passive aspect by itself, but one that can add more power to the planets if they are also in Zodical aspect to one another.

CONJUNCTION — ☌
Two planets in the same longitude. One of the most important aspects in Progressions. They are emphasizing a definite state of affairs an individual or new circumstances. For example, Progressed Mars to the conjunction of Natal Sun in Leo can be productive of an injury, infection or surgery to the eyes, heart or back, if major transits should afflict the conjunction while in effect.

SEMI-SEXTILE — 30° or one sign apart — ⚹
Slightly harmonious. Can be important as a sort of linkage in progressions, tying together two planets to indicate a certain event or individual. Does not work well by itself but needs assistance from other progressed aspects to add more force.

SEXTILE — 60° or 2 signs apart — ✳
Another harmonious aspect of attraction and opportunity. Indicates favorable events that can help to soften any unfavorable aspect also in force at the same time.

SEMI-SQUARE — 45° One and a half signs apart — ∠
SQUARE — 90° Three signs apart — ☐
SESQUIQUADRATE — 135° Four and half signs apart — ⛫
All three are very similar in their abrasive quality when applied with progressions. They generally denote problematic conditions and obstacles that will have to be overcome. Changes in present conditions or required adjustments are the rule. This is a time for one to be realistic and not attempt to over estimate their capabilities beyond their capacity. Depending upon the nature of the

planet and house position, there is a possibility of loss through death or separation through others. Health may pose a problem requiring medication, treatments or surgery. These are aspects of high nervous tension that generates a feeling one is being pushed beyond their limit.

TRINE — 120° Four signs apart — △

The most favored aspect for beneficial gain, successful enterprise, freedom from restrictions or limitations and generally very protective of health. Marriages, new advancements in career, birth, inheritance or other monetary gains are often required with progressed trines. If the individual applies proper usage of this aspect, whatever he desires can be obtained with the least amount of effort on his part. The effects of a progressed trine can be permanent if used wisely and handled properly.

QUINCUNX-INCONJUNCT — 150° Five signs apart — ⚻

This is an aspect of having to provide a service to someone. As in the health and care of another who may be ill. Or, having to care for someone's child while they work. Sometimes you have to give more of yourself than what you are getting in return. Or, others often expect more of your services for the same amount of pay, or a lesser amount. Situations arise in which one is pulled in many different directions and the person is unable to cope with all these demands made at once. Changes in relationships to others, separation or death is possible. Monetary gains through the resources of another will not be forthcoming or will be of a lesser amount than was normally expected. Talk of money will arise as a rule through some kind of situation in which you will be forced to make an adjustment, not necessarily to your own advantage.

OPPOSITION — 180° Six signs apart — ☍

A time of great distress, strain, antagonism, separation, delays, doubt, disappointments and possible slander. This is a time for compromise, to reach out and meet the other party half way. A friendship, partnership or close relationship can turn into enmity if one is not careful. If major transits assist, loss of someone through death is possible.

IMPORTANT FEATURES
IN A PROGRESSED CHART

One looks at a Progressed Chart and asks "Where do I begin?", or "What changes should I note?". The following should act as a guideline directing your attention to the most important features in a Progressed Chart.

#1. Note whether the Ascendant Sign is one of Long Ascension (i.e. Cancer, Leo, Virgo, Libra, Scorpio or Sagittarius), or of Short Ascension (i.e. Capricorn, Aquarius, Pisces, Aries, Taurus and Gemini).

#2. Individuals born with Short Ascension rising undergo far more changes in life and of direction than those born under signs of Long Ascension. Natives with Short Ascension rising often feel as though they have lived many different lives in their one lifetime.

#3. Pick up your own Table of Houses and look under the Aries Ascendant Sign for 41° Latitude. Note that it is quite possibly 16 lines in length equalling to 16 years of life. As you can see, once an individual progresses into the Ascendant Sign of Aries, he will remain under the rulership of the Arian planet Mars for approximately 16 years. Now look under the same Latitude for Libra Rising and again count the rows under the Libra Ascendant and it should come close to 36 lines. This is equal to almost 36 years of age. It is easy to see how one with a high degree of Aquarius Rising may progress through another four signs before he reaches the end of his life.

#4. Each time your ascendant changes signs through progressions, you also change rulers. You will always maintain the coloring of your Natal Ascendant sign and ruler, however, the house and sign position of your progressed ruler will add a new dimension to your characteristics and your destiny.

#5. Those born with the sign Cancer on the Natal Ascendant, will run the gamut of emotions and moods until their Ascendant changes to

11

the sign of Leo. Natal Cancerians and progressed Cancerians should use, not only their Natal Moon as their Ascendant Ruler but also Progressed Moon as it changes signs and Houses every two and one half years. Natives with Cancer on the Ascendant by progression will experience these extreme changes of moods for approximately 30 years or more.

#6. The Natal Sun will eventually change signs by progression. However, the Sun will rarely change houses, unless very close to a Natal House Cusp. The 10th House Cusp and some of the other house cusps advances through the Zodiac at approximately the same rate of speed as the Sun. In other words, the progressed Midheaven will always be at the same Zodiacal distance from the progressed Sun as the natal Midheaven is from the Natal Sun.

#7. Both Venus and Mercury vary in Speed. They will not only change signs by progression but can enter into the next adjoining house.

#8. The slower planets, Jupiter, Saturn, Uranus, Neptune and Pluto can advance through as many as three houses in one lifetime and possibly four if the planet in question is very close to a House Cusp at birth.

#9. The most important feature to watch, is when planets by progressions become angular, entering the 1st, 4th, 7th or 10th. When considering the slower planets, one should be able to judge the approximate age. This is achieved by subtracting the longitudinal difference between the planet and the House Cusp of which it is positioned. This is illustrated on Chart #1.

#10. A slow planet in the 2nd House will eventually progress into the First House, bringing with it new self-centered interests.

#11. A slow planet in the Natal 9th House will eventually progress into the 10th House altering one's goal in life.

#12. A slow planet in the Natal 8th House will eventually progress into the 7th House creating new interests in others.

#13. A slow planet in the Natal 5th House will eventually progress into the 4th House instilling changes in one's home base.

#14. Note the possibility of any major slow planet in a high degree of a sign and through progression it changes into the next sign. Also, pay close attention to the slow planets in a very low degree of a sign and through progression and retrograde motion, revert back to the previous sign (i.e. Progressed Retrograde Jupiter in 0° Aries revert to 29° Pisces). Either of these two incidents can bring about a major change of attitude, general mode of expression and according to the house position, new experiences and circumstances. For example, an unmarried person born with Saturn in 29° Virgo advancing into

0° Libra through progression can experience an altering of interest in what they formerly expected or wanted of a marriage partner. Many with such an aspect, may begin to think seriously of marriage (progressed Saturn in Libra) and welcome the responsibility that it may bring. The individual may select for a marriage partner, one of a strong Capricorn coloring, with perhaps Capricorn Rising, Sun or Moon in Capricorn or Saturn natally in the First House. Should Saturn receive unfavorable aspects and the individual is already married, they may be chafing at the bit, regarding marriage as being too restrictive or confining. Again, much depends upon the aspects that progressed Saturn in Libra receives from other planets at that time.

#15. Bear in mind, that any major transit leaving a natal house, will very shortly re-enter that same house in the progressed chart. The only difference may be the sign position of the transiting planet. (Chart #2)

#16. Bear in mind that a slow moving transit (i.e. Jupiter, Saturn, Uranus, Neptune and Pluto), in aspect with a Natal planet will in due time also aspect the same progressed planet. For example, transiting Jupiter in 24° Sagittarius trining Natal Neptune in 24° Leo will, in a matter of a few weeks also trine Progressed Neptune in 27° or 28° Leo, depending upon the native's age.

#17. As the Progressed Moon changes into a new sign, make it a rule to keep a close watch on the planet that governs its sign position. For example, when Progressed Moon enters 0° of Gemini, the condition of Natal and Progressed Mercury should be carefully scrutinized. Will a progressed planet aspect either Natal or Progressed Mercury? Note any aspect from the major transits or an Eclipse. All these insights will re-enforce the activity of Progressed Moon in Gemini. Especially, if the Progressed Moon is also actively involved with aspects either to Natal or Progressed planets, major transits or an Eclipse.

#18. Anytime a sign changes on any house cusp through progression, you will change your mode of expression and attitude towards that particular area of life. The following are some of the ways in which we may alter the situations of the houses in question:

1st House: A new sign on the First House will change one's mode of expression, hair style, general attitude and in some cases, a new different vocational interest. A major change is generally in store for the native. Much depends upon the sign that is rising on the progressed chart.

13

2nd House: Our manner of savings or earnings. Gemini for example progressing on the 2nd may indicate more than one checking account, saving account or outlet for personal, monetary gain.

3rd House: One's mental attitude and expression, both in speaking and writing. Changing relations with siblings. Scorpio for example, progressed on the 3rd House Cusp, may alter one's thinking concerning death or sex due to an upsetting experience through either.

4th House: Changes in the Home base. Children move in or out. One shares the home or apartment with a love relationship or a roommate. There is the possibility of change in the health of a parent.

5th House: Children, if not your own, than of others, play a prominent role. Some may marry an individual with children, others become teachers or work with gifted children. This is also the House of creativity and hobbies and latent abilities can become activated.

6th House: A flare up of a different kind of health problem. For example, an individual may suddenly develop kidney stones due to Progressed Libra on the 6th. There were heavy transits in Libra in the Porgressed 6th, such as Pluto and Saturn or Venus, ruler of the Progressed Sixth received difficult aspects. Signs changing on the Progressed 6th may indicate new work related duties. Dealings with Aunts and Uncles and domestic pets.

7th House: A change of attitude towards the present spouse, either for the better or the opposite. Some take on a partner, others may marry.

8th House: Changes concerning one's sexual attitude. Some make permanent arrangements to avoid having children through surgery. If one has not dealt with insurance companies previously, they may do so during the coming years.

9th House: In-laws may play an important role. Travel or higher education come to the fore. Others take an interest in sports or a health spa. Legal or religious matters may become activated.

10th House: One begins looking for new goals in life. A possible change of vocation or a change of department in the company of their employ. New bosses are introduced.

14

Inter-reactions with parents change. Some graduate from high school, others from college, while others may join the armed forces.

11th House: Friends take on new perspectives. Some join clubs and organizations or become an elected officer of an association.

12th House: The changing role of secret enemies. Whom do you find you can no longer confide in. What have you become sensitive to in the way of drugs or medication? What are your latest secret fears? What do you now use as a means of escapism from troubled times? Whom will be hospitzlied or imprisoned, if anyone?

We have just covered most of the "Important Features" of a Progressed Chart. The basic changes that may affect one's attitude, mode of expression, circumstances and general environment.

The following chapter will cover the "Crucial Indicators" that help to reveal major events or trends that may alter the life of the native or those within his immediate surroundings.

CRUCIAL INDICATORS
IN THE PROGRESSED
CHART

Important events are always accompanied by aspects that involve both Natal and Progressed Charts, Planets and Angular House Cusps. The following guidelines are just a few of the various configurations to help one to recognize the major trends or changes about to take place in one's life.

#1. Progressed aspects take precedence over the heavy major transits. For example, should the Progressed Sun form a square aspect with Natal Saturn in the Second House of Money and perhaps, transiting Jupiter, Saturn or Pluto are trining that same Natal Saturn, the monetary depletion and restriction will prevail. The major transits may assist in preventing bankruptcy or provide some kind of help from other sources, but not enough to offset the heavy financial drain. This aspect will stay in force until Progressed Sun has left the aspect to both Natal and Progressed Saturn. (Chart #3).

#2. One, two or three progressed aspects does not indicate a major crisis, even if all three are semi-squares or squares. It takes at least five and generally more progressed aspects to create a serious trend. Such as, a heart attack, discovery of cancer, car accident or the loss or illness of someone close to the native. The three progressed square aspects may indicate mental depression due to slow-down in business or loss of job or responsibilities of a parent.

#3. I would look deeper into the Progressed Chart if two of those three progressed aspects afflicted either the Natal or Progressed Ascendant's degree or the Natal or Progressed MC's degree.

#4. It is of this writer's opinion that aspects to either the Midheaven (10th House Cusp) or the Ascendant's degree, do not individually specify an event. But rather, either one may do so. It is as though, their main role in Progression were to provide the triggering effect for other progressed aspects in force at the same time.

#5. If the Natal Chart has been rectified or proven accurate through past

16

events, the following four points should be given more strength in comparison with progressed aspects between planets. Aspects involving the following:

Natal Ascendant's degree
Progressed Ascendant's degree
Natal Midheaven's degree (10th House Cusp)
Progressed Midheaven's degree (10th House Cusp)

The more aspects that are formed with the above four major points, the more active the year ahead will be. For example, a progressed planet in sextile aspect with the Natal Ascendant while the Progressed MC forms a trine aspect with a Natal planet indicates a very promising, successful year ahead. And, should offset or cushion any major squares forming between progressed and natal planets.

#6. Important events often occur when two planets, one Natal and one Progressed are within 1° or exact in aspect with one another, and both rule the same house. One in the Natal and the other in the Progressed. (Chart #4)

Judge according to aspect. If square, semi-square or opposition, a difficult problem will have to be overcome. Sextiles and trines bring an easy flow of conditions and beneficial events.

#7. Important events occur when two planets rule the same house and are in the same degree, but do not aspect each other. Generally an Eclipse, Lunation or major transit may adversely aspect one planet while favorably aspecting the other. Bestowing the ability to overcome the problem in relation to the House in question. (Chart #5)

#8. Important events occur when two planets rule the same house, again, one Natal and one Progressed and two different major transits aspect both. Judge accordingly. For example, this native may have Aries on his Second House of money with Natal Mars in 12° Leo and transiting Uranus in 12° Sagittarius is trining the ruler of his Natal Second. His progressed Second House of money has the sign Taurus with progressed Venus in 15° Virgo and transiting Saturn in 15° Scorpio is in sextile aspect with the ruler of the Progressed Second. This native will have more than one outlet for financial gain and through diversified areas, due to the Uranus and Saturn transiting aspects.

#9. Watch for an Eclipse, Lunation or major transit to occupy a House, Natal or Progressed, and in turn aspect the ruler of the other chart. For example, an Eclipse takes place in the Natal Sixth and squares the ruler of the Progressed Sixth. This is a verification of a Sixth House event. Job loss or health set-backs are possible.

17

#10. The Progressed Sun moves at a steady rate of 1° per year. Conjunction to Natal Moon, Venus, Mercury and Jupiter or Progressed thereof, is not altogether dangerous. The Progressed Mercury or Venus may conjoin the Natal Sun, Moon or Jupiter. This linkage of two planets are coloring one another and emphasizing a condition. One has to logically look ahead in the present year Ephemeris for any Solar or Lunar Eclipse or major transit that may affect this conjunction, favorably or unfavorably. (Chart #6)

#11. The Sun and Moon often act as spring boards, so to speak. If the Progressed Ascendant or Midheaven forms an aspect with the Natal or Progressed Sun or Moon and the luminaries receive an aspect from other planets, Progressed, Natal or Transiting, these can be reflected directly to the Progressed Ascendant or Midheaven.

#12. The Progressed Sun's mean motion is approximately 1° per year. At the age of 45, the Progressed Sun will semi-square its own natal position. It is for this reason that very few individuals pass their 45th year of birth without some major crisis touching their life. If not personally, through surgery, or accident, then perhaps to a close member of the family. The balance of the chart, at the Progressed 45th year, should be taken into consideration to disclose whom it may involve. Pay close attention to any other progressed aspects that may be in force at that time and particularly note the major transits in close aspect to the natal or progressed planets. Weigh carefully any Solar or Lunar Eclipse during that year for possible re-enforcement.

#13. The Sun is an illuminary and never Retrogrades, therefore, we can count on its mean motion of 1° per year to semi-square its own position at age 45.

Progressed Venus, Mercury or Mars can also semi-square its own natal position, but an exact age cannot be so easily determined. This is due to the variation of speed of these three planets. There is also the possibility of their turning Retrograde in motion which can deny the remote possibility of a semi-square aspect to itself.

The easiest way to determine whether any of these planets will semi-square themselves is to add 45° to their Natal position. If for example, Natal Venus is position in 18° Leo, she will semi-square her own position when she progresses into 3° Libra. Glance into the Ephemeris for the native's year of birth and note when Progressed Venus will reach 3° Libra. Should Progressed Venus turn SR, before she reaches the sign of Libra, she may never semi-square her own natal position.

#14. The periods in which Progressed Venus, Mercury or Mars turns Stationary Direct or Stationary Retrograde is most important. It is during this time that they will remain at the same degree for a prolonged stay. If for example, Progressed Venus turns Retrograde (SR) at 23° Virgo and in turn should trine Natal Moon in 23° Taurus, this type of aspect can last as long as 8 to 10 years. The trine aspect may bring the native to the Public's notice and keep it there indefinitely, but not without some drawbacks due to the Retrograde motion of Progressed Venus. The same would hold true for the mental application of Progressed Mercury and the energy level of Progressed Mars.

#15. What constitutes the danger of a possible accident or surgery, to the native, is having Progressed Mercury or Mars Retrograde back to its own Natal position and at that particular time, receive difficult aspects from Progressed Ascendant, MC, Sun or Progressed Moon. For example, Natal Mars may be in 12° Gemini and progresses into 15° Gemini at which time Progressed Mars turns SR. Fifteen to twenty years later, depending upon the Retrograde motion of Progressed Mars, it returns to its own Natal position of 12° Gemini. This may be the year in which the Progressed Ascendant reaches 12° Virgo or the Solar Eclipse is in 12° Sagittarius, either one afflicting both Natal and Progressed Mars.

#16. Major transits, Eclipse and Lunations should be applied to one's Progressed Chart at the same time that they are being under consideration with the Natal Chart. A New Moon may trine a planet in the Natal Second and bring a forgotten refund check. However, if that same New Moon happens to square the Progressed Ruler of the Progressed Second, or a planet therein, your automotive transmission or other major appliance can break down, taking that beautiful check right out the door as fast as it came in. (See Chart #7)

#17. Some individuals seem to achieve "Public Recognition" and remain in the limelight for a longer span of time than others. This often results from the Progressed 10th House Cusp favorably aspecting a slow Natal planet and then in turn aspects the progressed position of that same slow planet. For example, Progressed MC in 6° Aquarius applying to a sextile aspect with Natal Uranus in 7° Aries. By itself this would be a three year trend of career advancement and job potential. One degree while applying, one while exact and another in separating. However, should the native be matured in years, it is possible that his Natal Uranus has advanced to 9° Aries. This would

19

extend his remaining in the public's limelight for several more years while Progressed MC reaches 8° Aquarius and applies to the sextile aspect of Progressed Uranus. By the time Progressed MC leaves the separating aspect with Progressed Uranus, his career potential would have had a better than average chance of becoming well established, due to the prolonged favorable aspects. (See Chart #8)

#18. Just as the Progressed 10th House Cusp can stretch the career peak of an individual, so can the major transits. Have you ever noticed the comeback of an older stage or screen star who remains in the public's eye for a longer period of time. With older individuals, the 10th House Cusp progresses further into the Zodiac, thereby holding the major transits at the Midheaven for a greater span of time.

For example, one with 10° Sagittarius on the MC Natally and transiting Jupiter in Sagittarius along with transiting Uranus also in Sagittarius can give a tremendous boost or lift to one's career.

If through progression this native has 6° Aquarius on his Progressed 10th House, his career and public image will be enhanced and remain intact from the time transiting Uranus reaches Natal 10th House Cusp until it leaves his progressed 10th House Cusp in Aquarius. This is equivalent to approximately 13 years for Uranus. The four years of Sagittarius on the Natal 10th, seven years while in the Progressed 9th and finally the two years that it enters the Progressed 10th. This transit of Uranus will culminate the career which has more than adequate time to become established. Transiting Jupiter on the other hand, will enhance this native's career for a three year span. One year while in the Natal 10th House of Sagittarius, one year while transiting in the Progressed 9th in Capricorn and finally reaching its peak when entering the Progressed 10th House in the sign Aquarius. (Chart #8)

#19. A stressful condition or one that can be gainful depending upon the aspects, occurs when two different planets ruling the same house are highlighted during the progressed year by both being in aspect with other planets simultaneously. For example, the Natal ruler of the 6th is aspected by a Progressed planet while the Progressed ruler of the Progressed Sixth is aspected by a different planet, Natal or Progressed. (Chart #9 is a good example of the above configuration.)

#20. The role of the Progressed Moon is to time the events promised by the other Progressed aspects in force, during the same progressed year. A Solar or Lunar Eclipse conjoined with the Progressed Moon is an important configuration. Give serious consideration to all aspects, Natal, Progressed and the transiting planets that this conjunction may aspect. (Chart #10)

#21. Personal involvements in which the individual is directly or indirectly affected, generally include more than one aspect to the following points:

Aspects to the Natal Ascendant's degree
Aspects to the Progressed Ascendant's degree
Aspects to the Natal MC's degree
Aspects to the Progressed MC's degree

Afflicting aspects to several of these four main points, require careful study and consideration of both Natal and Progressed Chart for the year ahead.

#22. Other configurations that may affect the individual directly would be the Progressed Ascendant in semi-square aspect with the Natal Ascendant's degree. In the case of Short Ascension on the Eastern Horizon, it is possible for the Progressed Ascendant to square the Natal Ascendant's position somewhere between the ages of 50 to 60. If Long Ascension is Rising, the Progressed Ascendant will not square its Natal position until after the individual is 90 years of age.

#23. Look also for the Midheaven to semi-square or square the Natal or Progressed Ascendant. Or, the Natal or Progressed Ascendant to semi-square or square the Natal or Progressed Midheaven. Sextiles and trines are of course very beneficial in their nature and help to soften the hard aspects.

#24. Keep a weather eye on the possibility of the Progressed Ascendant adversely aspecting its own ruler, Natal or Progressed. For example, Progressed Ascendant in 18° Libra in square aspect with Natal Venus in 18° Cancer, ruler of the Progressed Ascendant. Should the aspect be a sextile or trine, it can be most beneficial. A gentleman with Progressed Ascendant in 24° Taurus was in trine aspect with his Natal Venus in 24° Virgo, ruler of the Progressed Ascendant. He came into a large sum of money that year.

#25. The Progressed Midheaven in an afflicting aspect with its own ruler is just as devastating as if it were the Ascendant Sign and just as beneficial with the favorable aspects.

#26. A Progressed planet in aspect with either the Natal Ascendant or the Natal Midheaven and rules its sign position, will produce the same results and the previous mentioned aspects.

21

The Chapter on "Important Features" discloses the basic changes occurring in one's Progressed Chart that could affect the general environment and mode of expression.

The "Crucial Indicators" reveal major events governing, marriage, birth, surgery, vocation, finances and in some cases, the loss of a close member of the family.

ASCENDANT SIGN

The Natal Ascendant Sign marks the impression you are likely to create and the mask you wear through life or your approach to things. Whether they are your actual feelings and emotions or not.

Your Natal Ascendant and its ruler will always remain a part of your make-up, for this is what you were born with. Progressed Ascendants add a touch of new dimensional colorings to our natal impressions and outward expressions. Various incidents, experiences and individuals, who may enter our life from time to time, help to alter and change our emotional and intellectual outlook.

Each Ascendant Sign is sub-divided into three decanates of 10° each. The sign and house position and aspects to the progressed decanate ruler will provide additional insight to our constant changing attitudes. New individuals and various circumstances will be introduced into our everyday existence that would otherwise go unnoticed, should we not take into consideration the Progressed decanate ruler.

Planets, both natal and progressed, are motivated by their sign position and in turn act through the house, representing the environment or circumstances. As the Ascendant Sign changes through progressions, a new ruler becomes the dominant factor. The sign influence of the progressed ruler has a deeper significance than house influence and denotes a more lasting effect.

A progressed ruler in a favorable sign and an unfavorable house is an individual who has a well defined character trait and ideas, but is struggling against difficult odds in a bad environment.

For example, a native has progressed into the positive, mental sign of 0° Gemini. The progressed ruler, Mercury is positioned in the sign Leo. Both planetary Ascendant ruler and sign position are well suited characteristically.

However, Progressed Mercury in Leo is not well positioned in the negative 4th House. The expansive mentality of Mercury in Leo, ruler of the Progressed Ascendant, may desire to write, teach or take some new commanding, important position, but feels hindered or restricted by his environment (House position). He may feel a pull between his own set of goals and his

23

emotional (4th House) bond and responsibility towards the rearing of children or the maintaining of a stable home life. There will be a constant struggle to achieve recognition but may not want to do so at the expense of his family, or what he feels is his sense of duty to maintain security in the home base. If a new advancement were proffered that would require him to be a good deal away from home, this native may decline. He may be at the age of life where he feels his children need the presence of a father (or mother) image.

A Progressed Ascendant ruler in an unfavorable sign and an unfavorable house produces conflicts. Both within and without and against the environment that tends to make that period of time in life a constant struggle.

For example, a native with Cancer Rising on his Progressed Ascendant has Progressed Moon in his Progressed 9th House in the sign of Aquarius. The Air sign (Aquarius) blends well with a Fire House (9th House environment) however, the Moon is not well suited either in Aquarius or in the environment (9th House). There may be erratic behavior in seeking personal independence (Aquarius) to seek higher education or travel (9th House environment), but emotional ties, responsibilities or restrictions in the rearing of children may hinder this desire. The native feels an inner conflict that dictates what she should do in opposition to what she wants to do. Invariably, he or she may lash out against those she loves, periodically in retaliation.

A Progressed ruler in an unfavorable sign but in a favorable house has inner conflicts that prevents him from successfully handling the affairs of the environment or circumstances (House position). For example, a native with Capricorn on the Progressed Ascendant and progressed ruler Saturn is position in the progressed 6th House. Saturn is an earthy planet and is very well placed in an earthy Virgo/6th House. This native may be given a position of responsibility and trust because his boss recognizes the fact that he has the capabilities to work well alone. He may be a good organizer of details and patient with those whom he comes in contact with. However, Saturn is position in the Air sign of Aquarius. An Air sign and an Earthy House does not blend well. This individual may experience some problem in coping with the introduction of new equipment, theories or machinery in his line of work. Saturn in the Sixth prefers a methodical manner in the work related details. New and unique ideas or unexpected and spontaneous introduction of new systems can throw these natives out of sorts very easily. They prefer the tried and the true and abhor unexpected visits in their office or shop that creates distraction. It is difficult for these natives to speak before large groups, unless they have a well-laid out lecture format.

Before discussing the Ascendant Signs and decanates, we should acquaint ourselves with the Table of Houses to determine the length of time each will be rising on the Eastern Horizon.

24

For better comprehension and clarity in dealing with Progressed Ascendants and decanates, the Latitude of 40N43 for the city of New York is used for illustrating purposes. The common use of one particular Latitude will serve as an excellent guide in the understanding of the time spans. As you glance through your own Table of Houses, locate the Latitude for New York City and the sign Aries on the Ascendant.

Aries Ascendant

Ruler: Mars

When someone has progressed into the sign of Aries, they have just emerged from the negative sign of Pisces. Depending upon the native's age, there will be a gradual, noticeable change in the personality. A striving for independence. The reaching out towards new and different experiences. One looks forward to the challenging aspects of new endeavors and enterprises. They slowly creep out of their cocoon, now seeking new roles. Some may go about it aggressively with impatience. Much depends upon the condition of Natal and Progressed Mars.

A child Arian by progression, requires firm handling and discipline. They can become overly pushy with a "I want it now" attitude. If with a playmate who won't give the Arian child the truck, the Arian will probably throw a toy block at the playmate in retaliation. The parent should watch for sudden flare up of high fevers that can damage ears or eyesight. In older individuals, accidents, surgery, sinus conditions, headaches and allergies spring up.

(Chart #11 is an example of one progressing from Pisces to Aries.)

New York City — Latitude 40N43

If each row in the Table of Houses represents, approximately one year of life, then we are to assume that an individual born in New York City entering the Progressed Ascendant Sign of 0° Aries will remain an Arian for 17 years.

During these 17 years, note the condition of Natal and Progressed Mars.

Will Natal Mars form an aspect with Progressed Ascendant or MC?

Will Progressed Mars form an aspect with Natal or Progressed Ascendant or MC?

Are there any progressed planets aspecting Natal or Progressed Mars?

Will an Eclipse or a major transiting planet (i.e. Jupiter, Saturn, Uranus, Neptune and Pluto) aspect Natal or Progressed Mars? If so, what is the condition of transiting Mars at that time?

Use the same technique with the decanate ruler.

25

All these factors will react upon the native internally (sign position) and through the environment (house position). The sign and house position of both Natal and Progressed Mars will reveal new motivating interests and circumstances that will have bearing on personal affairs.

Should Natal or Progressed Mars change signs while the native has Progressed Aries on the Ascendant, there will be a gradual re-routing of personal aims and goals into new fields of endeavors according to the house position.

0° to 10° Aries is the first decanate ruled by Mars/Aries.
This decanate will remain in effect a little under 6 years.

These natives have recently emerged from the withdrawn, confused sign of Pisces. They are feeling an urge to accomplish something. To become independent, use aggressive actions if necessary to achieve their freedom. They welcome new challenges, new enterprises and new lines of thought. Because they have been held back in the past, they may feel overly impulsive and impatient in wanting to take an active role, even if they know nothing of the subject presented them at the time. Mars is the planet of accidents and surgery, it is possible that someone or the native may encounter these problems during this six year period.

10° to 20° Aries is the second decanate ruled by the Sun/Leo.
This decanate will remain in effect a little under 6 years.

As adults, we lead such diversified lives with many different individuals touching us and creating new experiences. Decanate rulers, their sign and house position and aspects thereto, can enable us to be aware of these new inroads entering our life. The Natal and Progressed Sun's position will introduce a subtle touch to our make-up. We become more determined to finish our projects. We have more pride in our accomplishments and want others to notice them. Hobbies, new creative projects may interest us. Children, our own, or those of others become a part of our everyday existence. We may decide to have a child, become a teacher, join the PTA or other school programs. The Sun is exalted in Aries and gives a love of pleasures and dramatic ability but needs emotional control.

Leo and the Sun rules the heart, eyes and back. If both Mars and the Sun are afflicted through Progressed aspects, Eclipse or major transits, the native, or someone in the immediate environment may undergo surgery (Mars) on the heart, eyes or back (Leo/Sun).

20° to 30° Aries is the third decanate ruled by Jupiter/Sagittarius.
This decanate will remain in effect a little under 6 years.

As we leave the Fixed sign of the Leo decanate to enter the Mutable sign of Sagittarius, it becomes increasingly difficult to finish certain tasks. The Arian sign loves the challenge of new projects and creative hobbies, but unless it is kept stimulated, the Sagittarius decanate may become bored. There is the possibility of spreading oneself too thin with various projects during this six year span, making the native highly nervous. There is a natural concern for the welfare of others. A possible interest in returning to college or night school. Travel becomes interesting or situations arise concerned with matters in distant cities. New sports are introduced or the joining of a health spa.

Should Mars, the Progressed Ascendant ruler, and Jupiter, the decanate ruler become highlighted during this six year span, accidents or disputes over mechanical defects may produce legal action, especially if both are afflicted.

Taurus Ascendant

Ruler: Venus

At first, the transition, from Progressed Aries to Progressed Taurus is met with mixed emotions. There may be a lashing out in anger over frustrating developments, the native realizes is necessary, yet feels is too restrictive. There may be a yielding of personal independence. Perhaps a new job in which the native no longer has control of his own sense of freedom and movement or actions. A slow, methodical, steady routine takes over the daily duties. In some cases, a working gal gets married. Others begin a family. Thoughts of working towards some future goal or security may necessitate the boring routines.

In viewing the Taurus Ascendant for New York City's Latitutde, one can see that our native will have Taurus rising on the Progressed Ascendant approximately 20 years.

During these 20 years, note the condition of Natal and Progressed Venus.

Will Natal Venus possibly change signs during this time span?

Will Natal Venus form an aspect with Progressed Ascendant or MC?

Will Progressed Venus form an aspect with Natal or Progressed Ascendant or MC?

Are there any progressed planets in aspect with Natal or Progressed Venus?

Will an Eclipse or a major transiting planet aspect Natal or Progressed Venus? If so, what is the condition of transiting Venus at that time.

Use the same technique with the decanate ruler.

All these factors will react upon the native internally (sign position) and through the environment (house position). The sign and house position of both

Natal and Progressed Venus will reveal new motivating interests and circumstances that will have bearing on personal affairs during the 20 years that Taurus is on the Progressed Ascendant.

0° to 10° Taurus is the first decanate ruled by Venus/Taurus.
This decanate will remain in effect a little under 7 years.
The individual becomes more fixed in his views and objectives. A very determined sign that dislikes all matters that is unpleasant or painful. To escape from these uncomfortable conditions, the native may use such means of escapism as profuse reading, music, over-indulgence in TV viewing or radio listening. The accumulation of money or personal possessions may become a dominate factor during this seven year span. A possessive streak in the nature can create problems in romantic or marital relationships.

Parents of Taurean children by progression may soon feel that their young offspring is becoming lazy and only motivated into action with the promise of monetary gain. Suspect areas of health problems lie with the throat and neck. Throat infections with the very young can be a serious hazard. Also guard for the croup and mumps. In adults, there may be problems with the thyroid gland, goiter, or frequent sore throats.

10° to 20° Taurus is the second decanate ruled by Mercury/Virgo.
This decanate will remain in effect a little under 7 years.
It is during this period that the native will apply a more analytical approach in the achieving of financial security. The care of one's health takes on a new meaning. It appears easier to lose weight and to approach a diet program with realistic goals. Some may indulge in health foods or begin taking vitamins.

Should Mercury and Venus be activated during this seven year span, it is possible to gain or lose financially through work and health benefits. For example, shop unions (Virgo) decide to go on strike and you suffer the financial loss as a result, for you must picket. Accidents at work bring possible affiliation with workers' compensation. One may undergo surgery and depend upon sick benefits. Others may get laid off from work and begin collecting Unemployment Compensation.

Note all progressed aspects with Venus and Mercury as well as the major transits and Eclipse.

20° to 30° Taurus is the third decanate ruled by Saturn/Capricorn.
This decanate will remain in effect a little under 7 years.
The analytical approach that was presented during the second decanate of Taurus begins to pay off through hard work and advancements. Many individuals begin establishing their careers during this decanate. Government agencies or

police and community affairs may touch one's life. There is the desire to achieve power, prestige and mastership over some situation.

Older people such as parents, grandparents, aunt or uncle or an old friend may be a source for concern or present themselves as a burden. The main theme of this decanate is hard work and a dogmatic attitude towards the accomplishment of a desired goal.

Watch for other progressed planets, an Eclipse or major transits as they aspect either Natal or Progressed Venus and Saturn.

Gemini Ascendant

Ruler: Mercury

Gone are the tranquil days of the Taurus Ascendant sign, as one now enters the highly nervous, mutable sign of Gemini. You used to sleep like a baby before, now you may have trouble turning your brain off at night. One gets involved in several projects at the same time. Several individuals seem to pull at you and make inroads on your valuable time. Projects that you had no trouble finishing in the past tend to elude you now. The phone never stops ringing, you finally relent and purchase an answering device.

If you are a matured adult, there may be trouble with bursitis of the shoulders or arthritis in the hands. The affairs of one's brother or sister may become a source for concern during this 30 year span of time.

In viewing the Gemini Ascendant for New York City's Latitude, one can see that this native will have Gemini rising on the Progressed Ascendant approximately 30 years.

The planet Mercury becomes the new ruler as the Progressed Ascendant Sign changes to Gemini and should be used in collaboration with the Natal Ascendant and ruler.

During the 30 year span, note the condition of Natal and Progressed Mercury.

Will Natal Mercury possibly change signs during this time span? Thereby integrating new avenues in which the native will seek to expand his mentality or make positive use of his nervous energy.

Will Natal Mercury form an aspect with Progressed Ascendant or MC?

Will Progressed Mercury form an aspect with Natal or Progressed Ascendant or MC?

Will any progressed planet form an aspect with Natal or Progressed Mercury?

Will an Eclipse or a major transiting planet aspect Natal or Progressed Mercury? If so, what is the condition of transiting Mercury at that time.

Use the same technique with the decanate ruler.

All these factors will react upon the native internally (sign position) and through the environment (House position). The sign and house position of both Natal and Progressed Mercury will reveal new motivating interests and circumstances that will have bearing on personal affairs during the 30 years that Gemini is on the Progressed Ascendant.

0° to 10° Gemini is the first decanate ruled by Mercury/Gemini.
This decanate will remain in effect approximately 10 years.

As this decanate of Gemini is solely ruled by Mercury, the native tends to lose some of his fixity of purpose. May develop excellent intuition but does experience difficulty in completion of tasks. A diversified and dualistic mentality that may need direction for they may not be very discriminative during this 10 year span. One must learn not to permit everyday insignificant matters to prevail over important issues. The communication field may become important as an interest builds up for writing, speaking, appearing on TV, radio or lecturing. The nervous energy requires an outlet and golfing or an an exercise program may be undertaken.

Parents of Gemini Progressed Ascendant children have to teach these children consistency. Also to avoid indecision and frequent changing of issues.

The vulnerable areas for health are the lungs, shoulders, arms and hands.

10° to 20° Gemini is the second decanate ruled by Venus/Libra.
This decanate will remain in effect approximately 10 years.

This is the marriage and partnership decanate and representative of fidelity. Not the type of marriage that will be swayed by sentiment, more of the mental or objective type. During this period of time, there may be thoughts of getting married or entering into a partnership. New creative and artistic pursuits, such as painting, dancing or music lessons may be undertaken. Engagements and marriages become activated within the family circle.

Should, either Natal or Progressed Mercury and Venus, receive afflicting aspects during this time span, there may be concerns of relatives of the marriage partner. Their siblings may require hospitalization, possibly surgery or perhaps have marital problems.

Note all progressed aspects with Mercury and Venus as well as the major transits and Eclipse.

20° to 30° Gemini is the third decanate ruled by Uranus/Aquarius.
This decanate will remain in effect approximately 10 years.

This is one of the most interesting and exciting of the three decanates in which life takes on many new changes in the most unexpected manner.

New and unique fields of communications take an active role with this decanate. Purchase of CB's, home base radio transmitters, computers and new electronic games are par for the course. Group activities and possible joining of clubs and organizations. Others become interested in airplane model building with gas engines. Some join a bowling league or take up golfing, the study of astrology or a computer course.

Should Natal or Progressed Mercury and Uranus be afflicted during this time, there can be sudden loss or separation from siblings or close friends.

Note all progressed aspects to both Natal and Progressed Mercury and Uranus. Take into effect the major transits and Eclipse aspects.

Cancer Ascendant

Ruler: Moon

It is a difficult sign to have on the progressed Ascendant as one's mood and temperament tends to change every two and one half years. This is the average allotted time that their ruling planet, Moon, will remain in one sign or one house. The emotions and feelings undergo a constant change as well as the circumstances and environment surrounding their life. They may feel as though they are on a never ending treadmill. A native born with the sign Cancer rising Natally must watch the aspects to both Natal Moon as well as Progressed Moon.

In viewing the Cancer Ascendant for New York City's Latitutde, one can see that this native will have Cancer rising on the Progressed Ascendant approximately 38 years.

Each time that the Progressed Moon emerges into a new House, different circumstances, situations and individuals are introduced. The native tends to run the gamut of emotions and temperament each time the Progressed Moon changes signs. A complete chapter covers the transition of Progressed Moon through the signs and houses. The Cancerian Rising, Natally and Progressed, should study this Chapter carefully and apply it to their charts. They should also watch all major transits and Eclipse to both Natal and Progressed Moon.

0° to 10° Cancer is the first decanate ruled by Moon/Cancer.

This decanate will remain in effect a little under 13 years.

The native becomes more involved with family projects. Enlarging, buying or selling of the home or property is probable. As this is a Cardinal sign, the native becomes interested in achieving personal recognition and independence. Many embark upon a professional career, however, there is always the underlying, psychological fear that the family life may suffer or become neglected if a career is pursued too heavily. This is especially true in the case of

31

a married woman with young children. The male Cancerian, for the first time, may want to take a birthday cake in for a fellow employee. They may develop a maternal instinct towards fellow employees and show concern when one becomes ill. Food interests develop, growing of a garden, canning vegetables. The Male Cancerian may take a personal interest in building a miniature doll house for his daughter. The female Cancerian may start collecting doll house items if they cannot afford to purchase an actual house.

Should an Eclipse conjunct either Natal or Progressed Moon, or other major transits afflict, there may be concern for an aging member of the family.

10° to 20° Cancer is the second decanate ruled by Pluto/Scorpio.

This decanate will remain in effect a little under 13 years.

This is one of the most intense of decanates and the emotions and desires should not be repressed but diverted into new and constructive outlets, or these desires will express themselves in the most undesirable ways. This may be at an age when the native marries, but to a partner who is divorced. Alimony and child support payments or medical payments will then play the most dominant role during this decanate.

A female Cancerian may develop a sensitivity to birth control pills and sees medical attention. Others require surgical treatments for female disorders. The male Cancerian may have problems with prostate glands.

The Pluto/Scorpio decanate can produce birth and death within the immediate family. Insurance, unemployment funds, income tax and mortgage payments plus other joint finances may require adjustments or altering.

Watch for other progressed planets, an Eclipse or major transits to aspect either Natal or Progressed Moon and Pluto.

20° to 30° Cancer is the third decanate ruled by Neptune/Pisces.

This decanate will remain in effect a little under 13 years.

The most sensitive of decanates in which the native can easily lose self control. The psychic ability becomes pronounced. Some develop a creative flair resulting in an unusual object or hobby that can be productive and operative from the home. The native may want to seek seclusion but through some strange twist of events, will have to deal with the public at large.

Some find that they are constantly running back and forth to the hospital or institution visiting a close member of the family.

Experiences with ghosts or other forms of apparitional appearances are not impossible. Both the second and third decanate can produce events in which one may hear or feel the presence of another being that is supernatural.

Watch for other progressed planets, an Eclipse or major transits to aspect either Natal or Progressed Moon and Neptune.

Leo Ascendant

Ruler: Sun

As this native makes the transition from the Progressed Cancerian Ascendant to the Progressed Leo, something changes in the native's family background. The situation that existed while he was a Cancerian will no longer affect him in the same manner now. Either his parents have moved to a distant state or have deceased. Personal achievements, a desire to attain recognition in a prominent field and becoming the central figure is important. These natives may seek a position in which they will hold a manager of supervisory status.

Children, if not your own, then those of others come into your life and dominant the scene. Creative hobbies, showmanship and the theater comes to the fore.

In viewing the Leo Ascendant for New York City's Latitude, one can see that our native will have Leo Rising on the Progressed Ascendant approximately 40 years.

During these 40 years, note the condition of Natal and Progressed Sun.

Will Natal or Progressed Sun change signs during this time span?

Will Natal Sun form an aspect with Progressed Ascendant or MC?

Will Progressed Sun form an aspect with Natal or Progressed Ascendant or MC?

Are there any progressed planets in aspect with Natal or Progressed Sun?

Will an Eclipse or a major transiting planet aspect Natal or Progressed Sun? If so, what is the condition of transiting Sun at that time.

Use the same technique with the decanate ruler.

All these factors will react upon the native internally (sign position) and through the environment (house position). The sign and house position of both Natal and Progressed Sun will reveal new motivating interests and circumstances that will have bearing on personal affairs during the 40 years that Leo is on the Progressed Ascendant.

0° to 10° Leo is the first decanate ruled by Sun/Leo.

This decanate will remain in effect approximately 13 years.

There is self-assurance, self-confidence and self-esteem, or lack of it. Good recuperative powers and vitality. A desire for recognition, honor and success and the will to achieve such a position. Can be generous with gifts or their valuable time, but requires praise in return for this generosity. May develop a natural ability to get along well with children and be able to converse with them at their own level. Can become dramatic when the occasion calls for it. It may reveal itself in one's speech, actions or gestures. A possible advancement to a position of trust or supervisor.

10° to 20° Leo is the second decanate ruled by Jupiter/Sagittarius.

This decanate will remain in effect approximately 13 years.

It is possible that the native may become involved in a large, expansive and important enterprise. The native may develop an interest in writing, others may deal with printing material that produce items for games of chance. As in the printing or sales of lottery tickets, bingo cards or racing forms.

This is an overly optimistic decanate in which one's generosity may exceed the ability to fulfill the promises one makes to others.

Legal affairs may come to the fore concerning one of your children or you become entangled in a lawsuit with a young person.

One of your children may enter college, travel considerably or relocate.

Should Natal or Progressed Sun and Jupiter become afflicted through other progressed planets, an Eclipse or a major transit, it is possible that someone at a distance or an in-law may have a health problem with the eyes, heart or back.

20° to 30° Leo is the third decanate ruled by Mars/Aries.

This decanate will remain in effect approximately 13 years.

This is a strong competitive decanate. The native seeks a new enterprise and has the fixity of purpose to see them through to completion.

The desire to work for oneself or enter a vocation in which they hold a supervisory position may become prominent in the make-up.

Others may become involved in the mechanics of a game room, operation or repairs of electronic game machines.

One of the native's children may decide to enter the armed forces, join the police force or the native himself may be interested in these new vocations.

Should Natal or Progressed Sun and Mars become afflicted through other progressed planets an Eclipse or major transits, an accident is possible involving a child. Or, surgery may be required on the native's eyes or back. Much depends upon the sign and house position of Natal and Progress Sun and Mars, and the condition of transiting Mars at the time that either are receiving afflicting aspects.

Virgo Ascendant

Ruler: Mercury

Virgo on the Progressed Ascendant can bring changes in one's vocation. If you have not handled detailed work before, you may have to do so now. Record keeping of one's mileage, time or various equipment may be required by one's employer. Not formerly having to work so heavily with such precision and specialized records or methods, can be unnerving for the previous Leo Ascendant who detests detailed work.

This is the decanate in which the individual requires certain skills that teach the native how to better organize their time. Changes in their vocation in which practical methods are introduced in the handling of various endeavors. This newly acquired practical knowledge insures future job security and professional expertise. The practical skills that are accumulated during this decanate are later seen as financially rewarding due to the acquisition of a highly specialized technical knowledge or training.

The Virgo trait of perfection can overdo the details and result in digestive disorders, nervous conditions and ulcers.

In viewing the Virgo Ascendant for New York City's Latitude, one can see that our native will have Virgo rising on the Progressed Ascendant approximately 35 years.

During these 35 years, note the condition of Natal and Progressed Mercury.

Will Natal Mercury possibly change signs during this time span, thereby integrating new avenues in which the native will apply their new found practical and methodical expertise?

Will Natal Mercury form an aspect with Progressed Ascendant or MC?

Will Progressed Mercury form an aspect with Natal or Progressed Ascendant or MC?

Will any progressed planet form an aspect with Natal or Progressed Mercury?

Will an Eclipse or a major transiting planet aspect Natal or Progressed Mercury? If so, what is the condition of transiting Mercury at that time.

Use the same technique with the decanate ruler.

0° to 10° Virgo is the first decanate ruled by Mercury/Virgo.
This decanate will remain in effect a little under 12 years.

As one emerges from the dramatic sign of Leo Ascendant to the quiet sign of Virgo, the native becomes less flamboyant and more discriminative.

If he hated the handling of detailed work in the past, he may be forced to work with it now. For example, the native becomes employed by a company who requires a detailed account of all travel time, gas and mileage that is spent on the road.

The native becomes active with the police department or with health and welfare agencies, nursing or the medical fields.

Critical tendencies start to develop. The native begins to find fault with others.

One may be required to handle a large amount of paper work and detailed information in securing sick benefits, workmen's compensation, disability pension or Social Security. If not for the native himself, then perhaps for some close member of the family.

Should Natal or Progressed Mercury receive afflicting aspects from other progressed planets, an Eclipse or major transits, there may be concerns with the health of aunts and uncles or small pets.

10° to 20° Virgo is the second decanate ruled by Saturn/Capricorn.
This decanate will remain in effect a little under 12 years.

This is the decanate in which the native develops good organizing ability. He begins to recognize the fact that the acceptance of responsibility and hard work will eventually lead him to the road of success.

If in the age bracket of retirement, one may do so during this second decanate due to Saturn's rulership of secured pensions.

Others may seek more responsibility in their present job situation. Still others apply for an advancement for a position of authority.

This can be a depressing time of life should Natal or transiting Saturn receive afflicting aspects. One's credit rating due to pay garnishment may cause loss of reputation, either to the native or a close member of the family. One may have difficulty holding a permanent position, collecting unemployment benefits from time to time. Much depends upon the position of Natal and Progressed Saturn and aspects thereto, before one can determine whether it would affect the native or someone close.

Should Natal or Progressed Mercury and Saturn be afflicted by other progressed planets, an Eclipse of major transits, an older member of the family may be ill or require personal health care.

(Chart #12 is a native with Progressed second decanate of Virgo.)

20° to 30° Virgo is the third decanate ruled by Venus/Taurus.
This decanate will remain in effect a little under 12 years.

The obtaining of financial assistance through a health benefit program such as Social Security Disability for oneself or a close member of the family.

One may be required to handle books, records or reports concerning financial matters, a checking account or sales account.

A female may play an important role in financial gain or loss through work or business dealings.

If you have maintained good health and food habits in the second decanate, you may have difficulty in keeping up your dietary program in this decanate. Venus being the ruler, often instills a desire for rich foods and slows down the energy a bit. Much of this can result in gradual weight gain before one leaves and emerges into the Libra Ascendant.

Libra Ascendant

Ruler: Venus

A transition from a Virgo Progressed Ascendant to a Progressed Libra endows a gradual relaxing of the meticulous side of life. The individual is still concerned with personal hygiene and good housekeeping, but not to the point that it affects their health creating nervous tension and ulcers.

A child's coat, formerly thrown on a chair, would have upset the previous Virgo rising because it made the house look messy. "No more, the nagging is not worth the nervous tension that it creates," says the native with Libra now on the progressed Ascendant.

Social functions, getting together with groups of people or friends for exchange of ideas on a mental level takes precedence over insignificant daily tasks.

Parents of children progressing into the Libra sign should strive to maintain peace and harmony in the family circle. Arguments or violent actions between husband and wife should be avoided in the presence of the child. This youngster can become emotionally upset and distributed to the point of becoming violently ill, when such situations exist.

In viewing the Libra Ascendant for New York City's Latitude, one can see that our native will have Libra Rising on the Progressed Ascendant approximately 36 years.

During these 36 years, note the condition of Natal and Progressed Venus.

Will Natal or Progressed Venus change signs during this time span? Thereby integrating new avenues in which the native will apply their new found sense of balance and good judgment coupled with tact.

Will Natal Venus form an aspect with Progressed Ascendant or MC?

Progressed Venus form an aspect with Natal or Progressed Ascendant or MC?

Will any progressed planet form an aspect with Natal or Progressed Venus?

Will an Eclipse or a major transiting planet aspect Natal or Progressed Venus? If so, what is the condition of transiting Venus at that time.

Use the same technique with the decanate ruler.

All these factors will react upon the native internally (sign position) and through the environment (house position). The sign and house position of both Natal and Progressed Venus will reveal new motivating interests and circumstances that will have bearing on personal affairs during the 36 years that Libra is on the Progressed Ascendant.

0° to 10° Libra is the first decanate ruled by Venus/Libra.

This decanate will remain in effect approximately 13 years.

This is the marriage and partnership decanate. Some individuals marry when the sign Libra progresses on the Ascendant. Others enter into a business partnership.

It is not unheard of for some individuals to have an intimate affair in which one of the two parties, or perhaps both, may be married at the time.

A complaisant attitude takes hold where the individual has difficulty in making decisions. Some hope the problem will resolve itself, thereby eliminating the necessary task.

The energy span runs in spurts. Either the native is very, very lazy or very, very active. When he is in his relaxed state, he prefers others to join him and gets annoyed when there is much activity surrounding him. Should the native be in his active state, he prefers others to hop right in and join the work force.

The native should drink plenty of fluids during this decanate to maintain balance in the system, thereby alleviating the possibility of kidney ailments.

10° to 20° Libra is the second decanate ruled by Uranus/Aquarius.

This decanate will remain in effect approximately 13 years.

Independence is the keyword for this decanate. This can prove disruptive in the marriage where formerly the native was content to remain the loving husband or wife.

A rebellious streak now prevails. One decides marriage is wonderful, but no longer the all consuming relationship it once was. The native feels an urge, a desire to spread their wings. To explore new horizons. Seek new friendships. Join a club or organization where they can participate in group activities and discussions.

Both single and married second decanate Librans may take up the study of astrology, computer programming or attend astrological conventions.

Single Librans may meet interesting, exciting and stimulating new friends. However, one of these new found relationships may slowly develop into a love relation.

Note all progressed aspects with Venus and Uranus as well as the major transits and Eclipse.

20° to 30° Libra is the third decanate ruled by Mercury/Gemini.

This decanate will remain in effect approximately 13 years.

The native seeks more intellectual pursuits. Some may be interested in writing, lecturing, teaching or learning new creative hobbies. Others take up the study of court reporting, or becoming a beautician, an attorney, a marriage or school counselor. Much depends upon the placement of progressed Venus and Mercury.

New vocational interests in which the female native may be the hostess in a night club or a better restaurant, sell cosmetics or arrange social functions for corporations.

These natives learn how to subtly manipulate others as they develop the art of passive resistance. A shrewd mind, one with an iron fist in a velvet glove.

Should Natal and Progressed Venus and Mercury be afflicted by other progressed planets, major transits or an Eclipse, there may be concerns of relatives through marriage, such as the marriage partner of one's brother or sister.

Note all progressed aspects with Venus and Mercury as well as the major transits and Eclipse.

Scorpio Ascendant

Ruler: Pluto

As the sign Scorpio emerges on the Progressed Ascendant, the native becomes aware that a major change in life is about to take place.

They begin to take stock of oneself. A new hair style, change of attire, possible face lift or removal of facial scars or moles. Some change vocations or may completely relocate to another state.

There is deep intensity of emotions. An intuitive insight that one must prepare themselves physically, emotionally and mentally for the eminent changes that lie ahead.

Depending upon the age factor, there is a strong inclination for sexual interests and responses. In some cases a change of sexual attitude or standards.

Parents with children progressing into the sign of Scorpio should take the time to discuss the changes that will take place within the youngster's body, both physically and emotionally. The child may not bring up this topic with the parent, but they are well aware of the strong intense desires building up within. Self exploration and masturbation are common as a child seeks to investigate the mystery of sex. A wise parent does not let this type of incident upset them, but realizes that some signs are more prone to wonder on matters of sex.

Death is another hang up that some children may experience. The parent should not force this child to attend a funeral if they display an aversion to do so.

Possible health areas lie with bladder disorders and infections. The sexual organs of both male and female may need correcting, or require surgery. Hemorrhoids are often more common and constipation.

In viewing the Scorpio Ascendant for New York City's Latitude, one can see that our native will have Scorpio Rising on the Progressed Ascendant approximately 40 years.

During these 40 years, note the condition of Natal and Progressed Pluto.

Seldom does Natal Pluto change signs in anyone's lifetime, unless Pluto is position in a very high degree of a sign, such as 29 degrees of Cancer and progressed into 0° Leo. Or, Pluto is position in a very low degree of a sign and retrogrades back to the previous sign. For example, Natal Pluto in 0° Virgo and due to retrograde motion, returns to 29° Leo.

These are turning points in a person's life. One does not need to have Scorpio on the Natal or Progressed Ascendant to feel the change, however, it will have more impact if Pluto is the Ascendant's ruler. New avenues of resourceful enterprising will be introduced according to the house position.

The faster moving planets, Sun, Mercury, Venus and Mars change degrees almost as fast as the house cusp of which they are positioned. Therefore, as the house cusp progresses a degree, so do these faster planets, indicating that they seldom move to far away from their Natal house position. In other words, these planets will huddle pretty close to the same houses in the Progressed Chart as they are positioned in the Natal Chart.

NOT SO, with Natal Pluto. Why? Because Natal Pluto will only progress a few degrees at the very most in one life time. Therefore, the Progressed House position of progressed Pluto will carry more weight. As the house cusp containing the sign position of Pluto advances to the left in the Progressed Chart, Pluto will move right along with that sign. It is possible for Progressed Pluto to advance through three or more houses depending upon one's length of life.

As progressed planets aspect Natal Pluto, the effect will last until the progressed planet has passed the aspect to the degree of Progressed Pluto. Link together the Natal House position of Pluto and the Progressed House position of Progressed Pluto. For example, a Progressed planet is applying to an aspect with Natal Pluto in the Natal 4th House and to Progressed Pluto presently positioned in the Progressed 3rd. Depending upon the tone of the aspect involved, the native may have to collaborate with a brother or sister (3rd House) possibly to do with wills, inheritance or insurance (Pluto) of a parent, or perhaps settlement of property (Pluto in Natal 4th).

Note if Natal or Progressed Pluto will form an aspect with Progressed Ascendant or MC.

Will any progressed planet form an aspect with Natal or Progressed Pluto?

Will an Eclipse or a major transiting planet aspect Natal or Progressed Pluto? If so, what is the condition of transiting Pluto at that time.

Use the same technique with the decanate ruler.

0° to 10° Scorpio is the first decanate ruled by Pluto/Scorpio.
This decanate will remain in effect approximately 13 years.
The decanate of possessiveness, jealousy and strong desires with intense emotions.

A fixed sign instilling a strong will power. Can be very uncompromising and dogmatic in their views, whether they be right or wrong. A relentless opponent. Their outward calm appearance belies the inner turmoil that prevails. An air of secrecy colors their manner of speech and mental expression. They detest the airing of personal family affairs and will hastily reprimand family members or close friends who do so.

10° to 20° Scorpio is the second decanate ruled by Neptune/Pisces.
This decanate will remain in effect approximately 13 years.
This is the decanate of psychic healing if the native's chart is so inclined. Others may experience the phenomenal happenings of ghosts or other apparitions.

A strong intuitive, almost magical, ability to detect deceit and deception in others. A far more sensitive decanate than the first, yet, can become thoroughly annoyed should the person they assist, refuse to fend for themselves.

Possible dealings with hospitalization insurance or settlements. Should guard against confusing elements in matters to do with car insurance, fire insurance, alimony or sick benefits.

One should question the offer of goods being sold at a lesser value that might suggest it could be stolen.

Note all progressed planets in aspect with Natal or Progressed Pluto and Neptune as well as the major transits and Eclipse.

20° to 30° Scorpio is the third decanate ruled by Moon/Cancer.
This decanate will remain in effect approximately 13 years.
This is the security/financially astute decanate. Money, investments, purchase or sale of a home or property and business enterprises may become an all consuming pastime.

The native can become protective and possessive of family ties. May overly react through emotional flare-up at the first sign of rejection or criticism. May forgive but will not forget a personal affront or injury.

As with the second decanate, one's psychic ability may be enhanced. Possible communications with deceased members of the family.

During this time span with the third decanate of Scorpio Rising, the native may inherit, property or land or handle family disputes concerning these matters.

There may be alimony payments or possible parental financial assistance and support.

Should Natal and Progressed Pluto and Moon receive afflicting aspects from other progressed planets, an Eclipse or major transits, there is the possibility of loss of an older member of the family. A parent, grandparent or aunt and uncle.

Sagittarius Ascendant

Ruler: Jupiter

Parents of children emerging from the secretive sign of Scorpio to Progressed Sagittarius will be pleased to find their youngster becoming more relaxed and outgoing. The child may become interested in sports or other school scholastic activities. They appear easier to converse with and are more apt to share some of their personal experiences and feelings.

The adult, depending upon age factor, may enter college or return to adult evening classes for further studies. Others may take on-the-job training programs.

Travel, contacts with individuals who have a strong foreign accent, in-laws or legal situations such as law suits or jury duty become pronounced with Sagittarius on the Progressed Ascendant.

In viewing the Sagittarius Ascendant for New York City's Latitude, one can see that our native will have Sagittarius Rising on the Progressed Ascendant approximately 39 years.

During these 39 years, note the condition of Natal and Progressed Jupiter.

It is unlikely that Jupiter will change signs while the native has Sagittarius on the Progressed Ascendant, but certainly not impossible. Should Jupiter change signs, the native will experience a new motivating interest leaning towards a new direction in travel, law, religion and publications.

Although the mean motion of Jupiter is faster than Pluto's, it still is not able to keep up with the degrees as they change on the house cusp. Therefore, Jupiter is apt to move right along as its sign containment moves and progresses. As with Pluto, Jupiter may enter as many as three or four houses in one life time.

Note if Natal or Progressed Jupiter will form an aspect with Progressed Ascendant or MC.

Will any progressed planet form an aspect with Natal or Progressed Jupiter?

Will an Eclipse or a major transiting planet aspect Natal or Progressed Jupiter? If so, what is the condition of transiting Jupiter at that time. Use the same technique with the decanate ruler.

0° to 10° Jupiter is the first decanate ruled by Jupiter/Sagittarius.
This decanate will remain in effect approximately 13 years.

Contacts with people of all walks of life and different backgrounds. A greater desire to work independently at a vocation where there is personal freedom of action and decision. Outdoor work, published material on a grand scale or field of communications may draw an interest. Others may be required to wear a uniform with their job or come in contact with individuals who may deal with handling of uniforms.

Whatever episode touches the native's life during this decanate, is sure to be on a grander scale. For example, the native or his family member seldom enters an ordinary local hospital, the illness involved may call for a stay in a well known clinic or the Veterans hospital.

If dealing with publications, one may handle out of state mailing rather than local; in communications, long distance phone calls rather than local. Male Sagittarians are inclined to work with larger equipment, such as a large printing press, drive a semi-truck or work at the airport.

Much of course depends upon the condition of Natal and Progressed Jupiter.

10° to 20° Sagittarius is the second decanate ruled by Mars/Aries.
This decanate will remain in effect approximately 13 years.

An impulsive, impetuous and impatient decanate. Will travel independently if necessary to expand one's knowledge in any chosen field of endeavor. The native no longer concerns himself with having to travel if he must. Should a seminar or convention offer a topic of which the native holds an interest, it matters not how far it may be, but whether it will satisfy his thirst for the knowledge he seeks.

New enterprise on a grand scale may be introduced. The native may personally embark on a new project concerning publications, communications, radio, TV, lecturing, law, religion, travel or sports.

Should Natal or Progressed Jupiter and Mars be afflicted by other progressed planets, an Eclipse or major transits, an in-law may have an accident or require surgery. Possible lawsuits over personal injury or job discrimination.

20° to 30° Sagittarius is the third decanate ruled by Sun/Leo.
This decanate will remain in effect approximately 13 years.

The native develops a more frank and expansive manner of speaking. Excellent vitality and recuperative powers. May instill a dramatic flair to whatever confronts the native at this point of life. It may reveal itself in the native's manner of lecturing, through his published material or some creative hobby.

The native may strive with earnest, to achieve public recognition and honors in some particular field. Will not be content until he has received the highest approbation for his efforts.

Influential or professional people may be of fortunate assistance. Leo is a fixed sign. This decanate is more likely to complete new projects or enterprises entered into. Remarkable luck is possible through investments or games of chance. Such as, bingo, lottery, races and football pools.

In a female's chart, a possible romantic attraction to a professional man or one in good financial situation. Some may meet the love relation at a distant city or he may be of a different background.

Children progressing into the third decanate of Sagittarius may be able to achieve a scholarship program or excel in a school scholastic activity.

Should Natal or Progressed Jupiter and Sun be afflicted by other progressed planets, an Eclipse or major transits, an in-law or someone residing at a distance may suffer a heart ailment. Possible lawsuits involving a young person. Possible legal entanglements surrounding the affairs of one's children. It is likely that one of your children may move to a distant city.

Capricorn Ascendant

Ruler: Saturn

As a child progresses from Sagittarius to the negative Capricorn Ascendant, the parent is the first to notice the difference in the child's attitude. At times the child seems to be his or her outgoing self and yet at other times, quiet, secluded, serious and desirous of wanting to be alone. They begin to half self-doubts about themselves. An inferiority complex.

Their health may be troubled with chronic colds and the typical childhood ailments as chicken pox, mumps and measles. Others require corrective braces on their teeth.

Responsibility is the keyword for Capricorn on the Progressed Ascendant. Depending upon the native's age at this time, some may consider retirement, while others are becoming serious about establishing a foothold in a business or a better position in their job.

It is time to settle down and plan what to do with the remaining balance of one's life. Some think seriously about getting married, they seem ready and eager to commit themselves now. Others want to plan and organize their future for better security. A well defined goal for material status and financial independence.

In viewing the Capricorn Ascendant for New York City's Latitude, one can see that our native will have Capricorn Rising on the Progressed Ascendant approximately 30 years.

During these 30 years, note the condition of Natal and Progressed Saturn.

It is unlikely that Saturn will change signs while the native has Capricorn on the Progressed Ascendant, but certainly not impossible. This can happen if Natal Saturn is position in a high degree of a sign, such as 28° or 29° and progresses into the next sign. Or, if Natal Saturn should be, perhaps in a low degree, such as 0° Virgo and retrogrades back into 29° Leo. Should this change occur, Saturn will instill a new and different responsible attitude within the native's make-up.

Although the mean motion of Saturn is faster than Pluto's, it still is not able to keep up with the degrees as they change on the various house cusps. Therefore, Saturn is apt to move right along as the sign containment moves and progresses. As with Pluto, Saturn may enter as many as three or four houses in one life time.

Note if Natal or Progressed Saturn will form an aspect with Progressed Ascendant or MC.

Will any progressed planets form an aspect with Natal or Progressed Saturn?

Will an Eclipse or a major transiting planet aspect Natal or Progressed Saturn? If so, what is the condition of transiting Saturn at that time.

Use the same technique with the decanate ruler.

0° to 10° Capricorn is the first decanate ruled by Saturn/Capricorn.

This decanate will remain in effect approximately 10 years.

The native gradually develops a serious outlook upon life. They may become easily depressed and discouraged with a sense of deep anxiety. At times, they can be thoughtful, protective and considerate for the welfare of others. The native may be misunderstood for others will tend to see them as unfriendly and cold. The native's attitude of personal reserve and aloofness masks in reality, a deep sensitive, shy nature.

At times, the native seems always to be placed on "HOLD," so to speak. They make a purchase, the shipment is delayed or lost. They seek a job that really interests them and find the company is moving or re-arranging their departments and the hiring of future employees is delayed.

Whatever the native attempts, they feel as though, the project will in some way, be hindered or restricted. It is as if, they have to put in more time and harder labor to achieve the same degree of success that others obtain with far less effort.

It is not uncommon for many natives of this decanate to work nights or alternate shifts in their place of employment.

Although progress and success may be slow, the steady persistence and continual efforts do pay off in the long run.

These natives will develop a reputation for reliability, practical ability, careful handling of task and duties and capable of considerable responsibility without supervision.

10° to 20° Capricorn is the second decanate ruled by Venus/Taurus.
This decanate will remain in effect approximately 10 years.

Due to the fixed sign of this decanate, these natives will be capable of overcoming obstacles by sheer determination. They can be thoughtful, quiet and kind, but at times, short tempered, stubborn and resentful and not easily appeased.

This decanate instills a prudent attitude with forethought in the capacity of savings and handling of personal funds. However, there seems to be a periodical drain on finances. Just when a bank account is building up and everything looks great, something takes a turn for the worse. The car breaks down and requires expensive repairs. Or, perhaps some forgotten bill comes due, at the time you are thinking of replacing your TV set. Just when you spend a little of that reserved fund on something nice for the home, your family or yourself, a bill confronts you.

This can be a time in life when one clears up a heavy mortgage. Or, pays off a long drawn past due account. Financial gain or assistance may come from a parent or other figure of authority.

Should Natal or Progressed Saturn and Venus be afflicted by other progressed planets, an Eclipse or major transits, it is possible one may lose an older member of the family who has a Venus/Taurus coloring (Taurus Sun, Taurus Rising. Taurus Moon or Venus natally in the older person's first house horoscope).

20° to 30° Capricorn is the third decanate ruled by Mercury/Virgo.
This decanate will remain in effect approximately 10 years.

These natives become adept in organizing good work procedures and efficiency programs. It gives an orderly, analytical and critical mind. Will weigh decisions carefully to reach a practical solution.

An excellent decanate for anyone in a business or vocation where one must deal with weighty details and handle heavy analytical tasks.

There is mental strength and stability and leadership qualities. Also good for vocations in which the native may have to work alone as an insurance salesman or a manufacturing representative.

A possibility of involvement with political government or work with unions. As, in becoming a union President, Secretary or perhaps serve on the grievance committee for one's local union.

There is more concern with one's manner of dress. This decanate is more clothes conscious than the other two. The native believes in elegance in styling and at least one or two well tailored and expensive outfits. They are knowledgeable in the fact that simplicity coupled with good taste will make a lasting impression upon others.

May work for a parent or an older person.

Should Natal or Progressed Saturn and Mercury be afflicted by other progressed planets, an Eclipse or major transits, an old health problem may return. Some difficulties are experienced in achieving steady employment. A possible loss of an aunt or uncle.

Aquarius Ascendant

Ruler: Uranus

As one emerges from the negative sign of Capricorn to the Progressed and positive sign of Aquarius, there is a remarkable change in the personality. It appears as though the native has come out of a shell. They become more animated in their speech. A curiosity in learning what makes other people tick eventually may lead them to the study of astrology and the occult subjects.

The native feels as though he has been restricted and hindered in the past with much responsibility. Now he feels an urge and a desire to be free to explore new horizons. Care must be taken so as not to upset the marriage state by being overly rebellious. Doing one's own thing is fine, but not at the cost of family life.

They will talk more and express themselves more openly than they have in the past. They are friendly and will cooperate willingly as long as no one dictates to them, for they will no longer submit to authority of any kind.

Friends, clubs and organizations and associations with others will be pronounced during this decanate.

In viewing the Aquarius Ascendant for New York City's Latitude, one can see that our native will have Aquarius Rising on the Progressed Ascendant approximately 20 years.

During these 20 years, note the condition of Natal and Progressed Uranus.

It is unlikely that Uranus will change signs while the native has Aquarius on the Progressed Ascendant, but certainly not impossible should Uranus be placed in a high degree and progress to the following sign. Or, perhaps be situated in a very low degree and due to retrograde motion, regresses back to the former sign.

Uranus is considered one of the major planets, and should it change signs, whether one has Aquarius Rising or not, it will mark an important change of motivation according to Uranus's sign and house position.

Although the mean motion of Uranus is faster than Pluto's, it still is not able to keep up with the degrees as they change on the house cusp. Therefore, Uranus is apt to move right along as its sign containment moves and progresses. As with Pluto, Uranus may enter as many as three or four houses in one life time.

Note if Natal or Progressed Uranus will form an aspect with Progressed Ascendant or MC.

Will any progressed planet form an aspect with Natal or Progressed Uranus?

Will an Eclipse or a major transiting planet aspect Natal or Progressed Uranus? Of so, what is the condition of transiting Uranus at that time.

Use the same technique with the decanate ruler.

0° to 10° Aquarius is the first decanate ruled by Uranus/Aquarius.

This decanate will remain in effect approximately 7 years.

The native may become intense in demanding one's personal sense of freedom. It would be unwise to rebelliously seek to attain this new found taste for freedom. Disruptions in the marriage state or family life could well be the result.

There is the possibility of making new and unusual friends. Many of whom will be totally different from the friends he has been accustomed to in the past. The joining of clubs and organizations may provide the backdrop for the meeting of these new acquaintances.

The native may develop a witty, sometimes a far out sort of crazy sense of humor that close friends and family members may say "It is so unlike him."

New, exciting and unexpected circumstances and events will occur. Many of these incidents will take the native into different paths than those he had originally chosen to follow.

New inventive and imaginative tools may be incorporated into his everyday life or vocation. Such as, computers, bio-rhythm, astrology or the occult in general.

10° to 20° Aquarius is the second decanate ruled by Mercury/Gemini.

This decanate will remain in effect approximately 7 years.

Although the Aquarian Ascendant is a fixed sign, the Gemini decanate is mutable and changeable. Should Natal or Progressed Mercury be placed in a fixed sign also, the native will have no difficulty with deep concentration matters. Otherwise, they may attempt too many projects, becoming a master of none.

This decanate can be unique in ideas, writing, lecturing, speaking, publicity, correspondence and any type of advance mental work. The native may be drawn into the study of electronics, aeronautics, astrology, metaphysics and other scientific interests.

There will be much activity in short distance travels and local fields of communication. Letters received will arrive unexpected, or contain surprising news. The mail will come in spurts, in large quantities at one time, and none at others.

Relatives, neighbors or those whom one meets in a classroom, may bring about sudden changes in the native's life. Or, perhaps change the native's course of direction through an unusual set of circumstances.

Should Natal and Progressed Uranus and Mercury be afflicted, one should guard against unexpected accidents. There may be sudden separation through brothers and sisters or other close relatives.

20° to 30° Aquarius is the third decanate ruled by Venus/Libra.

This decanate will remain in effect approximately 7 years.

This is the decanate of balance and personal magnetism. The native develops good reasoning powers in so far as decisions concerning the matters of others are involved. However, in the making of decisions that affect the native's personal life, it becomes very difficult.

The native may be inclined to form a business partnership in some totally new and different field of endeavor. In some cases, the native's partner will experience strange and peculiar events and may be pulled into unusual and remarkable situations.

There is an inner longing for a close, romantic attachment. Although, the relationship may not always be conventional, it should be most inspirational.

Should Natal and Progressed Uranus and Venus be afflicted through progressed planets, an Eclipse or a major transit, there can be some disruption in the marriage state or through partnerships. This can result in a sudden divorce or a dissolving of an association. Generally, the action leading to the breakup is originated through the partner.

Pisces Ascendant

Ruler: Neptune

This is the sign of escapism. Some individuals find their escape from reality through music, learning to play the organ or guitar. Others through personal expression in art, flower arranging, poetry, dancing lessons, photography and other creative outlets.

Should Neptune, ruler of the Progressed Ascendant sign Pisces, receive afflicting aspects, the individual may seek escapism through the wrong channels. Abuse of drugs or medication, intoxicating liquor, clanedestine romances or merely through hiding under the beddings in an attempt to escape from reality in the coma stage of sleep.

The native may come in contact with hospitals, institutions or prisons during the short time he has Progressed Pisces on the Ascendant.

They should not permit themselves to be exploited by others who will use the native for their own selfish purpose. This can be prevented if the native would heed his own psychic and intuitive insight. If tuned in properly, they can detect deceit and deception very easily in others.

Parents of children progressing into the Progressed Ascendant sign of Pisces should find positive outlets for their child's active and highly developed imagination. Otherwise, the child may regress into a fantasy world of its own. It may be difficult after a time for the child to break the habit of constant escapism through daydreaming. Respect the child's desire for quiet periods of solitude. However, do try to regulate the amount of time spent alone and in seclusion, so that it does not become a common past time. Also be very selective of your child's choice of friends. These Piscean Progressed children can be easily influenced, led and exploited by others.

Expect some kind of allergy problem to arise or a sensitivity to a certain type of medication or drug. Always keep a close watch on your child anytime a new drug is administered.

In viewing the Pisces Ascendant for New York City's Latitude, one can see that our native will have Pisces Rising on the Progressed Ascendant approximately 16 years.

During these 16 years, note the condition of Natal and Progressed Neptune.

It is unlikely that Neptune will change signs while the native has Pisces on the Progressed Ascendant. This can only be possible if Natal Neptune is in 29° of a sign and by progression advances into the next sign. Or, in 0° of a sign and due to retrograde motion, regresses back to its former sign.

Although the mean motion of Neptune is faster than Pluto's, it still is not able to keep up with the degrees as they change on the progressed house cusp.

Therefore, Neptune is apt to move right along as its sign containment moves and progresses. As with Pluto, Neptune may enter as many as three or four houses in one life time.

Note if Natal or Progressed Neptune will form an aspect with Progressed Ascendant or MC.

Will any progressed planet form an aspect with Natal or Progressed Neptune?

Will an Eclipse or a major transiting planet aspect Natal or Progressed Neptune? If so, what is the condition of transiting Neptune at that time.

Use the same technique with the decanate ruler.

0° to 10° Pisces is the first decanate ruled by Neptune/Pisces.
This decanate will remain in effect a little under 6 years.

The psychic and intuitive decanate. Many are extremely artistic and creative. Should guard against the possibility of becoming dominated or subjected to the influence of other people.

The native develops a subtle, but charming personality with a certain degree of magnetism that others find fascinating. This could bestow a somewhat false impression, leading the opposite sex to believe that the native is eager for a clandestine affair.

There may be many contacts with strange or peculiar people. Some may be emotionally, physically or mentally handicapped. Contacts with hospitals, institutions, welfare agencies, charitable organizations, police or prison are also possible.

Be alert to allergies or sensitivity to certain drugs and medication. Always seek a second medical opinion with this decanate rising, to eliminate any possibility that the physician may have misunderstood or perhaps became confused concerning the nature of the native's illness.

Should Natal or Progress Neptune receive afflicting aspects from progressed planets, an Eclipse or a major transit, one may develop trouble with the feet, be given the wrong medication or overly sensitive to the prescribed drug. Others may experience difficulty with gas appliances, auto oil leaks, fume seepage or gas odors.

10° to 20° Pisces is the second decanate ruled by the Moon/Cancer.
This decanate will remain in effect a little under 6 years.

This is the decanate of emotional sensitivity and mediumistic or psychic ability. The native develops a susceptibility to impressions in the surrounding environment.

Some strange conditions or developments surrounding the home life. One of the parents may be consistently ill or have an illness that requires a daily dosage of certain medication. Or, a parent may have a drinking problem.

Some acquire a step-parent during this decanate or if the native is very young, he may be raised by someone other than his own parent. Perhaps, his parents have to both work and his grandparent is responsible for his upbringing.

There may be some hidden secrets in regards the home life or family affairs.

Some natives develop sewer problems, leaky roof or basement, plumbing or trouble with hot water tank, septic tank or gas leakage.

Use care in the purchase of a home to be certain that the deed and transfer papers are clear. Sometimes there may be hidden clauses in the apartment rental contract.

One should cut back on table salt to avoid water retention. Avoid alcoholic beverages to prevent bloating and sudden weight gains.

Take only the medication that is prescribed for you by your physician. Refuse all others from well meaning friends. The drugs they take may work in reverse for you.

Should Natal or Progressed Neptune and Moon be afflicted by progressed planets, an Eclipse or a major transit, it is possible an older member of the family may have to be placed in a nursing home, an institution or hospitalized. The native may lose one's home or have difficulty in securing ownership due to confused and deceptive conditions.

20° to 30° Pisces is the third decante ruled by Pluto/Scorpio.

This decanate will remain in effect a little under 6 years.

The decanate of secrecy. The Scorpio decanate adds persistency to the Piscean mutable nature. The native is more apt to finish creative and unusual projects that produce results through financial gains.

Possible financial windfall through unusual or hidden resources not directly earned by the native. Such as, profit sharing, paid hospitalization, Christmas bonus, church bingo winnings, lottery winnings, income tax refunds, investments or an inheritance.

Should Natal or Progressed Neptune and Pluto be afflicted by progressed planets an Eclipse or a major transit, there is the possibility of fraud and deception resulting through loss of such matters as insurance settlements, alimony or injury claims.

One should always read the fine print on all documents involving joint finances, mortgages and monetary agreements before signing.

LONG AND SHORT ASCENSION

It was previously stated that Libra was the longest of Ascension signs and Aries was the shortest. While this holds true for Greenwich, England's 0° Longitude, the Ascension sign will lower one whole sign for every two hours that we move west of 0° Longitude.

New York City is approximately 5 hours West of Greenwich, England. If we were to lower the Zodiac approximately two signs, we would have Leo as the longest of Ascension signs and Pisces as the shortest. Look into your own Table of Houses and view this for yourself.

An additional two hours further west, a total of 7 hours, would probably have the sign Cancer as the sign of long Ascension and Aquarius as the shortest.

One must be aware, that the length of time that any Zodiacal sign will be Rising on the Natal or Progressed Ascendant, depends upon where the native was born.

INTERCEPTIONS

In the Natal Chart, intercepted houses are very important. These areas of life will become more activated than the others whether or not they contain a planet. **First,** everytime you judge the condition of that intercepted house, you must weigh both rulers. The planet ruling the house cusp and the planet ruling the intercepted sign. **Second,** there are three modes of expression coloring that house, the sign on the house cusp, the intercepted sign and the few degrees of the sign on the following house cusp. **Third,** when a major transit (Jupiter, Saturn, Uranus, Neptune or Pluto) enters an intercepted house, the planet's energy will first be motivated by the sign on the house cusp and then carry over into the sign that is intercepted and lastly the sign on the adjoining house cusp. **Fourth,** this is the largest house in the Natal Chart along with the opposite house. When a major transit enters an intercepted house, it stays there for a longer span of time. The slow planet can make many more aspects to Natal planets and of course, during its stay, receive a better than average share of aspects from the faster transiting planets and Lunations. Thus, these two intercepted houses make more demands upon our life, create more circumstances to occur and bring additional individuals for us to contend with. Planets in intercepted houses can overly tax our energy and strength when they become activated through progressions or the major transits.

Should there be no intercepted houses in the Natal Chart, but through progressions, intercepted houses are created, then one must look closely to the two rulers in the Progressed Chart. Progressed intercepted houses are saying that there are several avenues in one's life that are becoming activated. The native will be pulled into several different areas at one time. Should a progressed planet or a major transit square the ruler of the house cusp and on the other hand favorably aspect the ruler of the intercepted sign, the native wants desperately to accomplish something but is hindered or blocked by someone or something.

Sometimes two major transits will highlight both rulers of an intercepted house, one may afflict and the other transit may sextile or trine. In order to succed with this type of situation, one must deal with a responsible attitude the nature of the afflicted planet and the house in which the transiting planet is positioned. Only after the native has removed the obstacle to the best of his nature, can he truly forge ahead into the area of which the favorable planet wants to take him.

PLANETARY ASPECTS

Progressed aspects between Natal and Progressed planets and Natal and Progressed Angular House Cusp are one of the most sensitive points to consider.

Angular House Cusps and aspects thereto, represent one of the dominant factors in timing of major events. This is followed by aspects between Progressed planets and Natal planets.

Free will verses Fate is the determining and contributing element in delineation of progressions.

An individual who can remain "calm and collected," in the face of an unexpected crisis is less likely to permit outside influence to dictate to him.

Controlled emotions and re-actions generally give the attitude of "Let's wait and see what happens next," or, "I'll flow with the tide until I know the direction it is taking me."

However, when other individuals step into the picture, the matter of Free Will is minimized. Free Will can be our own choice but Fate is the intervention of others over whom we have no control.

PROGRESSED MOON

Progressed Moon governs women in general, the mother, grandmother, an aunt or in a male's chart, a young female who is already a mother of a child. The Progressed Moon also governs one's emotions, sense of security, land and property. It is one of the prime factors in acting as a catalysis for other progressed aspects in force at the same time.

Both the condition of the Progressed Moon and Natal Moon, with aspects thereto, should be the prime consideration for natives with the sign Cancer on the Natal or Progressed Ascendant.

PROGRESSED MOON THROUGH SIGNS AND HOUSES

The Progressed Moon is another major factor in the timing of events. The following points should be given careful consideration:

1. Whenever one or more of the slower transiting planets (i.e. Jupiter, Saturn, Uranus, Neptune or Pluto) aspect a Natal or Progressed planet, the Progressed Moon may add the necessary force to set that major aspect into action.

   For example, transiting Neptune in 25° Sagittarius squaring Natal Venus in 25° Pisces can remain in effect over a period of two years when one considers the slow action of Neptune's retrograde motion. Should this be the year that the Progressed Moon be in a high degree of Gemini (or any mutable sign joining in with this heavy square between transiting Neptune and Natal Venus), the month that the Progressed Moon reaches 25° and should Neptune still remain within 1° orb of Natal Venus, this will mark the month for the action to transpire. The Progressed Moon can be the catalysis in setting off slow transiting aspects.

2. The Progressed Moon does not have to directly aspect the Natal, Progressed or Transiting planet to be effective. Whenever a Natal or Progressed planet is aspected by a major transiting planet or an Eclipse, look to the position of the Progressed Moon. Is the Progressed Moon located in the sign position or the house ruled by that Natal or Progressed planet? If so, watch for an Eclipse to aspect the Progressed Moon or perhaps another major transit while the Natal planet is still under the influence of its own aspect. For example, during the time that transiting Pluto was 27° Libra and squaring Natal Mercury in 28° Cancer, the native's Progressed Moon was position in 17° Gemini (ruled by Mercury), and conjoined by a Solar Eclipse in the summer of '83 in 20° Gemini. The native lost her brother.

3. Make it a rule to watch the major transits or Eclipse as they aspect the Natal or Progressed planet ruling the sign position of the Progressed Moon.

4. The effective time for the Progressed Moon is three months. One month while applying to an aspect, another month while exact and a third month in separating. If, during this time the Progressed Moon should aspect a Natal or Progressed planet, and the ruler of the Moon's sign position is also involved in a progressed aspect, it has all the earmarks of an important event. For example, Progressed Moon in 5° Capricorn inconjunct Natal Venus in 5° Leo. Natal or Progressed Saturn is squaring the Progressed 10th House Cusp. This native lost her mother, through a heart attack.

5. The Progressed Moon can act as a transmitter sort to speak. If the Progressed Moon conjuncts, afflicts or favorably aspects an angular house cusp and in turn also aspects a transiting, natal or progressed planet, the energy of that planet will be reflected by the Progressed Moon and carried over to the angular house cusp.

6. A native born with Cancer Rising on the Natal Ascendant, will have the Moon as it's ruler. The Natal position of the Moon marks the starting point for the native at birth. On approaching 28 years of age, the Progressed Moon will return to its natal sign and house position.
The average mean motion of the Progressed Moon is 1°5' per month. The average speed of travel for the Progressed Moon is two and one half years in one sign or one house. It takes approximately 28 years for the Progressed Moon to tenant the entire chart.

MOON IN
SIGNS AND HOUSES

Progressed Moon in Aries: Note the position of Natal and Progressed Mars and aspects thereto from progressed planets and the major transits, to confirm the Arian action of the Progressed Moon's position.

Progressed Moon in First House: (Natal or Progressed Chart) Note the ruler of the Moon's sign position by sign, house position and aspects thereto, for it may help to determine what the Progressed Moon is trying to convey.

This is a Cardinal sign and an angular house representing action and ambition.

Either position of the Progressed Moon will instigate a change in vocation, location or the beginning of a new enterprise. The native may develop a more positive attitude and leadership qualities. There is the feeling that one must take the initiative in certain matters whether they wish to or not. Much of the activities in the forthcoming two and one half years will be centered around oneself.

Health problems may crop up along the lines of headaches, sinus, allergy, high fevers, infections, inflammations and possible accidents or surgery.

Progressed Moon in Taurus: Note the position of natal and progressed Venus and aspects thereto. This may help to confirm monetary issues.

Progressed Moon in Second House: (Natal or Progressed Chart) Note the ruler of the Moon's sign position by sign, house and aspects thereto. This will clarify possible financial gains or losses or one's stubborn resistance to change.

This is a fixed sign position and a fixed house.

Money spent is more likely to be on objects that will enhance one's surrounding, as in new furnishings or home decorating.

Financial loss and gains will be activated according to the aspects the Progressed Moon makes to Natal, Progressed and Transiting planets. Decisions in regards monetary matters, loans, checking accounts or savings accounts may be affected through the action of another person.

It will be more difficult for the native to adapt to new surroundings or developments, for they will find these changes upsetting to their nature.

Health problems may crop up along the lines of throat infections, goiter problems, and vocal cords.

Progressed Moon in Gemini: Note the position of Natal and Progressed Mercury for additional actions with siblings and close family members.

Progressed Moon in Third House: (Natal or Progressed Chart) Note the ruler of the Moon's sign position by sign, house and aspects thereto for clarification of a busy two and one half years ahead.

A mutable sign and a mutable house, can bring about many changes in direction.

The native becomes involved in many various projects. If one avenue does not suit your purpose, you may well venture into another. The Gemini nature does not like to put all "His eggs into one basket," so to speak. There'll be many diversified areas touching your life; for example, more than one checking or savings account, or a full time job and a possible part-time job. This is generally considered to be a very busy period with much running about and answering or letters or making phone calls. There will be contacts with brothers and sisters and close family ties.

Study courses may be undertaken, an exercise program or perhaps golfing. More than one individual will make inroads on your valuable time. You will have to determine your priorities and consider what is best for you.

Health problems can be nervous exhaustion from trying to tackle too many projects at one time. Learn to turn your mind off at night so that you can get your proper rest. Ailments of the bronchial tubes and pleurisy should be guarded. Above all, try to avoid stress and worry to prevent nervous conditions.

Progressed Moon in Cancer: Note the position of Natal Moon for additional insight pertaining to family affairs.

Progressed Moon in Fourth House: (Natal or Progressed Chart) Note the ruler of the Moon's sign position by sign, house and aspects thereto for clarification of buying or selling of property or parental concerns.

The sign Cancer and the Fourth House are Cardinal in nature, stressing ambition and action. However the nurturing nature of the Cancerian sign does not want to achieve success at the expense of their family. Therefore, a business enterprise is possible, but one that will fit in with family schedules.

Old, pending matters are often resolved and come to an end, making way for new beginnings, when the Progressed Moon enters the 4th House or the sign of Cancer.

All matters pertaining to domestic affairs, a parent and property are activated. Moving to a new location is possible, while others may enlarge or redecorate the present home. There is a change of moods and temperament, causing the emotions to undergo a very trying period.

Water retention, salt intake and obesity are three major factors in guarding one's health.

Progressed Moon in Leo: Note the position of Natal and Progressed Sun for additional insight in dealings with children, romance or investments.

Progressed Moon in Fifth House: (Natal or Progressed Chart) Note the ruler of the Moon's sign position by sign, house and aspects thereto for clarification of investments, schools or in dealings with games of chance.

The sign Leo, is Fixed; and the Fifth House is also Fixed by nature. Creative hobbies begun when the Progressed Moon enters this sign or the 5th House, are more likely to develop into money making projects.

Affairs of children (not necessarily your own), schools, romance and investments are highlighted. It is imperative that the condition of Natal and Progressed Sun be carefully scrutinized during this two and one half year period.

Favorable aspects between the Progressed Moon and Natal, Progressed and Transiting planets can bring about a pregnancy if one is in that age bracket or is trying to have a child. This can be a time in which one of your children may be awarded a scholastic achievement. Fifth House also governs games of chance. The possibility of winning through football pools, lottery and bingo games are increased.

Should the majority of the heavy transits be in the sign of Scorpio or unfavorably aspect the Progressed Moon in Leo, much trouble can be brewing. Perhaps alimony payments (Scorpio) are difficult to collect. A possible auto accident involving a young person and the insurance (Scorpio) company balks at the payment. Or, perhaps one of your children will be experiencing heavy financial stress and you may have to assist with personal monetary funds.

Health should be guarded surrounding the eyes and the back. Undo stress should be avoided to prevent tightening in the chest area. Someone in the immediate family may have a health problem with high blood pressure, a stroke, heart attack, eye surgery or suffer a back injury.

Progressed Moon in Virgo: Note the position of Natal and Progressed Mercury for additional insight dealing with co-workers and vocation.

Progressed Moon in Sixth House: (Natal or Progressed Chart) Note the ruler of the Moon's sign position by sign, house and aspects, thereto for clarification of possible changes involving one's vocation and health.

The sign Virgo, is Mutable, and the Sixth House is Mutable by nature. One can expect major chances in vocation, dealings with co-workers, aunts and uncles and health within the following two and one half years.

Working conditions and employees or co-workers will be of prime interest. Detailed procedures may have to be dealt with in the handling of one's daily tasks. You may be constantly imposed upon by others who seek your services. Supervisors may place extra burdens of responsibilities upon your shoulders often with no compensation of extra pay incentive.

Special clothing or uniforms may be required or you will come in contact with these items in your line of work. Possible dealings with police department, or security work, airport personnel, restaurant or perhaps working in a dry cleaning/laundry establishment.

You may become more conscious of your health and weight. Progressed Moon in Virgo can provide the excellent incentive for beginning a diet and weight loss program.

Affairs of aunts and uncles and dealings with domestic pets become pronounced.

Progressed Moon in Libra: Note the position of Natal and Progressed Venus for additional insight dealing with close relationships and partners.
Progressed Moon in Seventh House: (Natal or Progressed Chart) Note the ruler of the Moon's sign position by sign, house and aspects thereto for clarification of possible marriage, dealings with partners and litigation.

The sign Libra is Cardinal and the Seventh House is Cardinal by nature.

Cardinal signs tend to initiate personal action. There is generally a ridding of an old standing issue before they feel like venturing into a new one. A heavy emphasis on First House, Aries or Mars, leans towards a challenging new enterprise on a personal level after they have discarded an old problem that has proven to be no longer feasible. The emphasis on the sign Cancer, Fourth House or Moon, must resolve old issues with a parent, family member, land or property or with someone who is sharing their living quarters before they can venture into new territory. The Libra Cardinal sign must let go of an old relationship to make way for new individuals who may enter their life, while there is a heavy emphasis on the Seventh House and Venus.

The Libra sign is associated with business and marriage partnerships. Many individuals get married or enter a partnership while their Progressed Moon advances into the sign of Libra.

Expect many social affairs, parties or functions to have a marked influence upon your life. Some of these will bring new persons into your sphere of activities. Choose your companions wisely, if you are a young gal, the men may be married (Libra).

63

The sign Libra spurs up wedding bells and showers surrounding the immediate family or friends.

Should the native be single, it is possible that he or she can find the marriage partner of their choice during this two and one half year span.

Should Natal or Progressed Venus or the depositor of the Progressed Moon's become afflicted through other progressed planets or heavy transits, the native may get involved with people of questionable background. Or, the person they fall in love with may be presently married or involve the native in a messy divorce case.

Be sure to drink plenty of fluid to avoid the possibility of bladder or kidney infections. Watch your weight. What was lost while your Progressed Moon was in Virgo can be regained and more during its stay in Libra. Libra loves its candy, cake and cookies.

Progressed Moon in Scorpio: Note the position of Natal and Progressed Pluto for additional insight dealing with alimony, insurance and joint finances.

Progressed Moon in Eighth House: (Natal or Progressed Chart) Note the ruler of the Moon's sign position by sign, house and aspects thereto for clarification of possible mortgage, IRS, alimony, insurance problems.

The sign Scorpio is Fixed, and the Eighth House is Fixed by nature. Whatever change is made during the two and one half year span, will have a lasting quality to it.

Any altering of the sexual parts of the body should be undertaken after careful and serious consideration. Unnecessary sterilization may be regretted at a later time. Be careful of contraceptive medication, it is possible you may be allergic to them. Corrective surgery may be required on the sexual parts of the body, such as a hysterectomy or perhaps a male member of the family may require surgery on the prostate glands.

On the positive side, this Moon's placement in Scorpio can be an excellent incentive for eliminating old, unwanted and bad habits. You can develop enough control to stop smoking, drinking or lose weight. Possible gain through inheritance; the final payment of a mortgage on a home; the final payment of alimony for a child that has become of age. If you have not had hospitalization or dental plan with your company, this insurance benefit may be started by your company. Some decide to retire and collect Social Security benefits and others may apply for disability compensation.

You may begin thinking about new investment programs to enhance your future savings, such as purchasing multiple housing units.

Progressed Moon in Sagittarius: Note the position of Natal and Progressed Jupiter for additional insight for an interest in higher education and travel.

Progressed Moon in Ninth House: (Natal or Progressed Chart) Note the ruler of the Moon's sign position by sign, house and aspects thereto for clarification of possible legal matters, travel, dealings with in-laws.

The sign Sagittarius is a Mutable sign, and the Ninth House is Mutable by nature. Both represent the element of one's future outlook. Mutable signs bring about major changes in one's habits, job, health or environment. The native is inclined to return to school, college or take additional technical courses that may enhance future growth and advancement.

The native may have plans and thoughts of savings now for what he hopes to build or purchase in the future (a new car or a home).

Mutable signs bring more than one outlet of interests. Care should be taken not to promise more than one can deliver. The intentions are honorable and good, but one gets too involved and think they have more time than they actually have.

All affairs may become activated during the coming two and one half years surrounding publications, religion, matters at a distance, legal entanglements, possible jury duty, in-laws and travel.

The sign Sagittarius is a nervous sign and the native should take time out for relaxation and see to it that they get a good nights sleep.

Progressed Moon in Capricorn: Note the position of Natal and Progressed Saturn for additional insight dealing with career and public recognition.

Progressed Moon in Tenth House: (Natal or Progressed Chart) Note the ruler of the Moon's sign position by sign, house and aspects thereto for clarification of career changes, political affiliation and authoritative figures.

The sign Capricorn is Cardinal; and the Tenth House is Cardinal by nature. Prestige and success is important. This is a period of time in which one should lay a solid foundation for future advancement. Plan carefully for a desired goal. Be ready to assume additional responsibilities. Even if you are not being compensated with extra pay, you are learning a new facet of information that can make you an invaluable employee later.

Some natives take the Progressed Moon in Capricorn as a very dismal, restrictive period. It appears that everytime they try to accomplish something, they are beset by delays and restrictions. For example, a new job is presented to them, but, they must wait until the new office building is completed. Or, they are just ready to return to a career of their own when their daughter has a baby and in serious financial trouble, so you baby sit.

Others are burdened with additional responsibilities of a parent. Or the husband is on strike and the funds are dwindling, so you can't purchase that new car. The sign Capricorn tends to make one worry consistently or to take life seriously. It can become a gloom and doom period if one is not careful to try and be more optimistic.

What one wants to do seems to be hindered by what "one feels compelled to do through a burdened sense of responsibility."

This is a "see your dentist" time for possible teeth problems or the requirement of dentures. Skin problems are not uncommon and expect aching knees whenever it looks like rain. Avoid drafts, keep warm and drink plenty of hot fluids.

Progressed Moon in Aquarius: Note the position of Natal and Progressed Uranus for additional insight dealing with friends and organizations.

Progressed Moon in Eleventh House: (Natal or Progressed Chart) Note the ruler of the Moon's sign position by sign, house and aspects thereto for clarification of clubs, associations and friends.

The sign Aquarius is Fixed, and the Eleventh House is Fixed by nature. Sometimes rebellion against past restrictions crop up.

One must use care in the selection of new friends and acquaintances. It is possible they can create a favorable or unfavorable effect upon personal affairs or future aspirations.

During these two and one half years, the native may encounter an unusual set of circumstances that can completely change a certain facet of his lifestyle.

It may be difficult for concrete plans to formulate at first, due to last minute intervention. The sign Aquarius is abruptive and unexpected. One never knows for sure which way the wind will blow. Very often these sudden interruptions seem to alternate the situation into new channels of expression.

The native may become interested in joining various clubs and organizations. Others may take an interest in the study of Astrology, the scientific fields or perhaps desire to own a computer.

These two and one half years will prove to be both interesting and exhilarating with many unexpected events occurring. A most unpredictable period.

In cold weather, it is a good idea to wear leg warmers to prevent muscle cramps. Be careful not to sit too long on hard chairs where the possibility for circulation to the legs may be cut down.

Progressed Moon in Pisces: Note the position of Natal and Progressed Neptune for additional insight dealing with hidden matters and emotionally sensitive people.

Progressed Moon in Twelfth House: (Natal or Progressed Chart) Note the ruler of the Moon's sign position by sign, house and aspects thereto for clarification of secrets, hospitals and hard to detect illness.

Pisces is a Mutable sign, and the Twelfth House is Mutable by nature. Changes are generally in store for the native. However, these two elements

(Moon in Pisces or in the Twelfth) tend to keep the native in the dark while others enforce the change.

Very often the native does not detect the situation which is developing around him until it is too late for a reversal; so they learn to adapt and accept, whether they like it or not.

There may be contacts with an individual or a family member who may develop a physical, mental or emotional handicap. Perhaps an illness that is hard to define, or they cannot tolerate a certain drug that can be of benefit to them.

Others may come in contact with drug abusers, schemers, con artists, or someone who drinks too heavily.

The native must use care in the handling of prescription drugs. Take only those prescribed by the family physician. Re-check your prescription given to you by the pharmacist for possible error.

If hospitalized, notify the head nurse and your physician of any sensitivity to certain medication. Repeat this last instruction again, for Pisces often causes confusion where the medication may not be noted on your record. Take the time to talk with your physician about the pills and shots you will be given during your stay. Refuse all others, that do not conform to your physician's instructions.

You will be going through a difficult transition period in which others will take advantage of your good nature. If this should occur, it is because you have permitted it to happen by not paying attention to what is going on about you. Each time that you are used and abused, your subconscious mind is storing this experience. In due time you will have learned a valuable lesson and say, ''It will never happen to me again.''

There will be contacts with various institutions, hospitals, charitable organizations, jails and police departments.

Invest in good quality and proper fitting shoes. You don't need problems with your feet, such as: spurs, ingrown toe nails, bunions or painful corns.

Should you feel a need to escape from the harshness and reality of life, take up guitar or organ lessons, belly dancing, yoga, painting or photography, even if you don't have an ounce of talent. Fishing, music and the study of psychology are other unlimited outlets.

Above all, Pisces can be self-destructive. Avoid harboring thoughts of self pity, lack of self worth and suicide. The unfavorable aspects can be difficult, especially for the Piscean sign. However, once the Progressed Moon has moved onto the sign of Aries, the native wonders how they could have possibly felt the way they did.

MOON ASPECTS

There are two distinct differences between the length of time the Progressed Moon and Natal Moon are in effect while in aspect with a Progressed angular house cusp.

The Natal Moon does not alter its longitude position at birth. It is for this reason that the Natal Moon will remain in effect for a three year span. One year while applying to the degree of the house cusp, a second year while exact and a third in separating.

The Progressed Moon, on the other hand, is in effect for three months. The Progressed Moon's mean motion is approximately 1°5' per month. Therefore, as it aspects an angular house cusp (Natal or Progressed house cusp), it will remain effective for three months while applying, exact and in separating. The Progressed Moon is often referred to as, "Minor Progressions." The Progressed Moon has a lesser impact on personal affairs and events than the Natal Moon. Unless of course, other major transits or progressed aspects are in force at the same time.

The following points should make for easier understanding:
1. Aspects between Progressed Angular House Cusp and the Natal Moon are considered in the same manner as the rest of the Natal planets.
2. The Natal Moon does not aspect progressed planets. It receives aspects from progressed planets.
3. Due to the rapid motion of the Progressed Moon, we consider the aspects to both the Natal and Progressed Angular House Cusp.
4. The Progressed Moon also aspects both Natal and Progressed planets and receives aspects from the major transiting planets and Eclipses.

Moon conjunct Ascendant: The Natal Moon being of three year endurance, may create emotional flare-ups. The native is likely to feel very sensitive to the environment. Should the native move, which is possible, to a new location, the native may have trouble adjusting. Their emotions become unstable so to speak and the individual cannot determine the cause of it.

Many changes are in store. If single and good aspects prevail, the person may marry. Whether it is the Natal or Progressed Moon, there is a likelihood of increase in family, either through marriages or birth. An excellent time for anyone who deals and works with the general public. When the aspects with the Progressed or Natal Moon are favorable, others see the native as a warm, sensitive and caring person. Possible benefits through older women or a parent.

Difficult aspects produce unstable emotions, tears and over-reactions to statements of others. The demise of another person, a grandmother or grandfather (should he be a Cancer Sun, have Moon in Cancer or Cancer Rising or Moon in the grandfather's first house), a mother-in-law or possibly an aunt. Much depends upon the tone of the progressed and natal chart.

Moon conjunct Midheaven: The influence of the Natal or Progressed Moon to the M.C. is more fatalistic than those to the Ascendant. The native has less chance of free will in affairs surrounding him. This is due to the personal sacrifices, restrictions and self control that one will undergo to obtain one's ambitions and success.

This is an excellent time for seeking a public service vocation, for the native is sensitive to the public needs and requirements.

A change in one's vocation is possible. There are usually other indications in both the natal and progressed chart to warrant the change.

Should unfavorable aspects afflict with the Natal or Progressed Moon, a female member of the family may pass away. Generally a Solar or Lunar Eclipse will conjunct or square the conjunction of the Moon and the M.C. position to produce such a serious event. Or, possibly several major transiting planets in adverse aspect with the Moon/MC conjunction.

Marriage is also possible should the Moon be in favorable aspect with the ruler of the Natal or Progressed 7th house cusp or Venus.

Moon conjuncts Seventh House Cusp: The Moon represents one's mother. Should the Moon in conjunction with the 7th House Cusp receive difficult aspects, one's mother may not approve of your lifestyle. She may disapprove of your boyfriend or the way you earn your money. Whatever, there is an opposing force from an older woman. In some cases it can be a mother-in-law or a sister-in-law. Perhaps someone you are in partnership with.

You may come in contact with older women more than average in your daily activities. The sign position should disclose what type of women one will encounter. If in Sagittarius, perhaps a foreigner or one of a different color or background. Cancer and Capricorn signs deal more with grandmothers who may pass away, or older women one may work with, whom you feel is trying to boss you unnecessarily.

In a male's chart, the Moon in Leo crossing over the 7th House Cusp, may indicate a female who already has a child. Yet, the attraction is there and could possibly lead to marriage.

69

Should a woman get married at this time, it indicates that her mate might be on the sensitive side. Domesticated and a homebody, who may love to cook. Heavy afflictions may indicate that he still has his mother living with him who has not yet cut the umbilical cord.

Progressed Moon conjunct Fourth House Cusp: The Fourth House is the end of old, pending matters. Making way for new beginnings. This can mean the death of a parent who has been ailing for some time. The completion of a drawn out divorce. The final selling of one's home or property. There will be much activity with family members and perhaps a parent. Moving to a new location or changes with the home environment are probable, such as, the sharing of the apartment with another person or a lover. The Progressed Moon, after conjunction with the I. C., will remain in the Fourth House for two and one half years. It is during this time that these various transitions can take place.

If one does not move there may be an enlargement or redecorating of the present home. Or, perhaps a job that one will operate from the home base.

Young couples feel like starting a family. Others, who have formerly dined out quite a bit, may be more content to stay at home. The emotions are vulnerable and subjected to various moods.

Moon sextile or trine Ascendant: There is great rapport with the general public at large and through contacts with women. Should the Moon favorably aspect the Ascendant, it will naturally throw favorable lights upon the Decendant (7th House Cusp). Marriage is high on the agenda or increase in the family through birth.

An excellent time to buy, sell or enhance the property. Should the Natal Moon rather than the Progressed Moon be involved in the aspect, the public image is highly enhanced. Women in general will be of assistance. There is greater chances for marriage or birth of a child.

Due to the favorable response from the public, this is an excellent period for salespersons, speakers, bankers, real estate agents, insurance agents and anyone else who may have to work and deal mainly with the common people.

Moon square Ascendant and Decendant: Women in general will pose a problem. For example, you want to return to work, but your mother or mother-in-law will not babysit your child. You may have a female at work who is creating unnecessary details. Or, you may want to get married, but your mother or future mother-in-law doesn't think the time is feasible and are against the idea. Male natives may have problems with their wives, mother or perhaps get a domineering female for a boss. Whatever the problem, women will be the source of emotional and frustrating experiences. If one is running for re-election or any government office, the native will have to approach the public with kid gloves and use care in his speech. Those in business dealing with the general public may not fare too well during these three months or three years, depending upon which Moon is in aspect with the Ascendant.

Some difficulty in domestic situations or concerns of a family member, possible loss of an older female. Emotional depression and strain in the marriage state or with a close relationship.

(Consider the semi-square 45° and the sesqui-quadrate 135° aspect in the same vein as the square.)

Moon square M.C. and I. C. (10th and 4th House Cusp): There is stress in the career and home base. A loss of job creates emotional tension on financial upkeep of home and family.

Or, the breadwinner is offered a better position, but must relocate. This means uprooting the entire family, selling the home and taking the children out of their present school district. What one wants to do always seems to be restricted by what one is expected to do in the name of responsibility. A female native may want to return to work, but does not have the support of her husband and children. Creating stress in both areas of her life, career versus home.

Should the Progressed Moon (or Natal Moon) square the M.C. and I. C. from the left side of the chart, that is, possibly from the 12th, 1st or 2nd House, the native creates his own problem through poor judgment in the handling of business or family affairs. He makes unwise decisions without consulting others.

Should the Progressed Moon (or Natal Moon) square the M.C. and I. C. from the right side of the chart, that is, either the 6th, 7th or 8th House, the native has little choice in the matter. Others, parents, children or the marriage or business partner make inroads on his time and are the cause of the restrictions to his success.

Moon Inconjunct an Angular House Cusp: It has been this writer's experience with this aspect to give the keywork of "adaption." Invariably, the native will have to put his own personal plans aside for the care or service of another. The native will have to adapt his lifestyle to fit in the many inroads of activities and people who will make demands upon him. A high degree of stress is common due to the many pressures made upon the native's limited time factor. The native will feel emotionally and mentally drained. And yet, many of the matters involving the native may not be of his own personal doing, but through those in his immediate environment.

71

Progressed Moon conjunct Natal Moon: This occurs at the age of 28 and 56. For a female, this can be a dangerous aspect if the conjunction receives difficult aspects from other progressed planets or major transiting planets. This aspect will strongly react upon the house position of the Natal Moon and the House of which it rules in the Natal Chart. It does not have to concern the native, but rather a female relative in the immediate environment. Yet, one should not take a risk and seek a complete physical check-up.

In a male's chart it can be the wife or mother who will be of concern. Unless of course, the native has Cancer Natally on the Ascendant or by Progression. For example, this native has Natal Moon in 21° Scorpio and Progressed Moon conjoined at the same time as transiting Uranus in Scorpio. He was advised to seek a complete physical in the bowel section. An x-ray revealed a tumor the size of a baseball. The conjunction of both Natal and Progressed Moon also received favorable aspects from transiting Jupiter and Saturn at the same time. The tumor proved to be non-malignant.

Progressed Moon sextile, trine Natal Moon: Look to the Natal position of Natal Moon and Progressed Moon for beneficial responses from women in general. An aspect of well being, birth and possible marriage. If not to the native, then in the immediate family.

Progressed Moon square Natal Moon: In a female's chart, this is a three month period of emotional depression for no apparent reason. If Progressed Moon now be in the Sixth, trouble through women at work. Or, in the 7th, through women partners or female relatives of the husband. The sign and house position of Progressed Moon should reveal the female and problems thereto. In a male's chart, concerns of the wife's or mother's health. The break-up with a girl friend. Lack of communication with general public.

The Progressed Moon will square the Natal Moon at least 6 times during a life span. The first time at the age of 7.

First square — age 7: The child must leave the comfort of the home and enter school. If other squares enforce this aspect, the child may have difficulty adjusting to the outside world.

Second square — age 21: If the native has not established themselves in a career, or has entered college, there may be a desperate attempt to establish a goal. Natives should wait a while before deciding upon marriage. Squares at the age of 21, may be a parent who does not like the child's choice of love relationship, but the child persists to defy the parent.

3rd square — age 35: A desire to achieve something of a personal level, but may feel hindered through family restrictions. If dealing with the general public, best to think twice before speaking. Deal carefully with women.

4th square — age 49: A mid-life crises where one feels life is passing you by. May do something foolish unless self-control is exercised. Some women enter change of life at this time, which accounts for some health upsets. Men may have trouble understanding the wife, or foolishly become involved in a clandestine relationship.

5th square — age 63: If working, some may retire early. Some make the mistake of moving in with their children. Not the time for domestic changes or selling of property.

6th square — age 77: A period of emotional depression and sense of loneliness. One feels unwanted and unloved. The maintaining of one's health is extremely important at this square. This is not the time to sell one's property and uproot one's emotional security. The best time would have been at the previous sextile or trine to Natal Moon.

In all ages, the squares lessen the energy level and vitality. One must take it easy. Not push oneself beyond one's capacity. Always get complete physicals around these periods to make sure your health is up to par. Avoid confrontations with women in general. However, there may be some concerns with female relatives if the major transits at this time are afflicting or the progressed planets enforce the Progressed Moon.

Progressed Moon opposition Natal Moon: Personal confrontations with family members. Diplomacy is required in dealing with female relatives. These oppositions occur at age 14, 42 and 70.

1st opposition — age 14: The child, whether female or male, is maturing and feels the mother or a grandmother is inflicting their will upon him or her. There is a temporary "locking of the horns" so to speak. Where the child is trying to determine how far he can push that female relative and still get away with certain undesirable privileges. Sometimes it is not the mother or grandmother, but perhaps a school teacher or school principal who is taking sides against the child. It is an emotionally trying time for a child. They should be given both moral and emotional support.

The 2nd opposition — age 42: Another mid-life crises and the "empty nest" syndrome, or where children are pretty much on their own. The mother, mother-in-law or a female child may pose a problem. In a male's chart, the wife or mother may be a source for concern. Sometimes the male is inclined to lean towards an extra-marital affair.

The 3rd opposition — age 70: The retirement age. Opposing forces may be through a female child. Or, the decision to give up one's home and live in a Senior Citizens development. Can be an emotionally depressing period.

The opposition at age 14 and 42 can be a most devastating period. Especially if other major transiting planets or progressed planets are adding re-enforcement through afflictions of their own. Children feel as though too many adults are against them (their mother, school authorities), and as a result many run away in rebellion.

At age 42, opposition between the Progressed Moon and Natal Moon with heavy afflicting squares from transits or progressed planets can bring about the loss of a mother, a divorce or a break-up in the family ties. Health should be the prime concern and a physical check-up in order to prevent any serious illness from getting a firm hold.

Moon conjunct or parallel Sun: Progressed Moon conjunct Natal Sun is very similar to a New Moon effect. What major changes will the native encounter during the next 28 years? Look into the present year ephemeris for the planetary position of the transiting planets for the month that your Progressed Moon will conjoin your Natal Sun. Then, take the New Moon of that month and aspect all the transits to your natal planets. This should provide one with a preview of what events will transpire in the coming 28 years. For example, this native had Progressed Moon conjunct his Natal Sun, 27 years ago. Transiting Venus, ruler of his Natal Eighth, Trined his Natal Jupiter in his First House and he came into a large sum of money approximately five years later. Transiting Jupiter also Trined his Natal Moon in Taurus and again he came into another large sum of money through the lottery, about 15 years later. Transiting Uranus was in Leo also at that time, conjoined with his natal Mars within 3° in his 6th House of health and he had an accident resulting in back surgery some 20 years later. Check back into your own chart. When did your Progressed Moon conjunct your Natal Sun? What happened in your life during the 28 years following that conjunction?

The conjunction of Progressed Moon with Natal Sun can be of great importance and impart disturbing elements to the health. However, much depends upon the aspects that the major transits and other progressed planets are enforcing at that time.

This is a period of time in which the native should take stock of his professional career and personal affairs. He should decide where changes should be made, if any are in order. The opportunities will no doubt present themselves, and the aspects will determine whether they will be favorable or unfavorable.

Moon sextile or trine Sun: This has been a very beneficial effect upon the health and general well being. There is the possibility of gain through outside influence as from people in a higher position. Another aspect of possible marriage or birth in the family. Women who are professionally employed can safely take a chance with some new business or enterprise and succeed. This aspect makes for popularity with the opposite sex and the general public. If one is unemployed, it holds the promise of obtaining employment with a good salary. One finds it easier to bounce back to normal from any personal or financial difficulty.

Moon square, semi-square or sesqui-quadrate the Sun: An emotionally up-setting and trying period, where misjudged changes of plans take place.

There may be some domestic problems with family members, concerns of the mother or an older female relative. Danger of damage to the reputation.

Indication of quarrels, misunderstandings, differences, separation and estrangements through the marriage partner or business associate. Women may suffer difficulties with the father, a boy child or any male intimate relationship.

The situation is more intense if the Progressed Sun is squaring or otherwise afflicting the Natal Moon. There is less severity with the above indications with Progressed Moon in aspect with Natal Sun due to the minimizing effect of the three months of being in aspect. The Progressed Sun, on the other hand, naturally has a three year effect.

It was not intended to underestimate the Progressed Moon in dire aspect with Natal Sun. This can be a dangerous three month period if other transiting or progressed planets are heavily afflicted at the same time.

This aspect can be one of the main indicators of health problems. One should maintain good dietary habits. Get a complete physical check-up. Especially the eyes, heart and blood pressure. Above all, one must develop strength of character in the knowledge that this aspect will not last forever, and apply a positive attitude in the handling of everyday affairs.

Moon opposition Sun: Another difficult period. And, like the above aspect, it is more intense if the Progressed Sun is opposing the Natal Moon. A critical period in which one might be faced with an important decision that has been lingering for some time. Unless one seeks a compromise and cooperates through yielding to the wishes of another, this aspect can lead to a separation, divorce, sorrow or a serious confrontation. The opposition brings out into the open, enemies which may try to damage the native's reputation. Sometimes, one must accept the possibility of broken attachments through death, severing of relationships or the end of a business partnership.

Moon inconjunct the Sun: A male member of the family (husband, child or father), will require your services. They may be a source of worry and concern over their health. You may have to adapt to the needs of others. Possible death of someone through a heart attack or stroke.

Heavy work loads or money problems can be a source of stress.

Moon conjunct or parallel Mercury: A very active time of life in which there is much more movement and changes in general affairs. Phone calls, letter writing, and driving here and there will consume much of one's time. Should there be no square's to this conjunction, this can be beneficial in taking up new studies, opening a book store and salesmanship.

A time to renew strained relationship between brothers and sisters. Possible residential change. Good news according to the house that Mercury rules in the Natal Chart, unless this is Progressed Mercury, then look to the House of Gemini or Virgo in the Progressed Chart. Squares to this conjunction can bring dissipation of the energy from assuming too many projects. More than the native can handle, resulting in a high degree of emotional and nervous tension. Sometimes leading to gastric upsets or ulcers.

Moon sextile or trine Mercury: Native employed in the communication or transportation field can achieve a good deal of success in their vocation. As with auto salesman, or bicycle and motorcycle repair and sales shop. The printing industry or the writing, buying or selling of books as with authors and bookshops. Radio, TV, answering service and the telephone company.

Opportunities present themselves for travel or in making changes in the locality, that can prove beneficial. Those in the educational field, whether instructors or students, should have an easier time with vocation or studies. A new hobby such as golfing may be taken up, or perhaps writing of short stories or magazine articles.

Moon square, semi-square 45° or sesqui-quadrate 135° Mercury: The native goes through a period of constant worrying, either of unpaid bills, health or employment. They are beset by many, everyday, minor problems that are a source of constant aggravation. They must be careful and use good judgement in the signing of important papers or documents. Unpopularity and slander are possible features of this aspect. One must avoid acts of indiscretion that are likely to arouse adverse criticism. Difficulty in the rearing of a child or in dealings with a young person who may resent being under your control.

If the native is of school or college age, the studies may no longer hold an interest and become difficult. The native may want to quit school (if he or she is 16 years of age) or college. Some may change their majors right in mid-stream due to mental confusion.

Or, a parent may have trouble with a child and school authorities. One may feel that a teacher is bearing down unnecessarily on their child. This is an aspect of high nervous tension and mental stress. One should try to practice meditation during this period and strive for proper relaxation and self control.

Moon opposite Mercury: This is an aspect of confrontation with another. Unless the native applies tact and diplomacy in dealing with neighbors, brothers and sisters or close relatives, hard feelings and enmity will result.

The native may feel that others are infringing upon their personal affairs. This interference is apt to make the native feel resentful and result in a serious argument or separation.

Valuable time or money may be lost due to misinformation or misleading statements. One must be careful to double check all out-going and in-coming mail, phone calls and verbal instructions, in both personal affairs and in vocational duties.

Be careful of whom you employ in your place of business, a salesman or delivery person may confuse orders or incorrectly estimate the price for the job in mind.

Moon inconjunct Mercury: Someone in the native's immediate environment is causing a great deal of emotional and mental stress. If it be Natal Mercury, look to the House of Gemini and Virgo. Should Progressed Moon inconjunct Progressed Mercury, seek the houses of Gemini and Virgo in the Progressed Chart.

The native may experience difficulty in dealing with women in general. A neighbor, sister or co-worker who may misinterpret statements causing disagreements and arguments.

Moon conjunct or parallel Venus: Happiness in domestic life. Financial possibilities become increasingly good. An active period for social functions. Wedding invitations, baby showers and parties to attend. Also an aspect of possible marriage if the 7th House and other progressed aspects agree.

One feels romantic, may fall in love, is sentimental and inclined to receive gifts. A favorable aspect for women who wish to enter into the cosmetic or hair dressing business. The native experiences a good deal of popularity.

Moon sextile or trine Venus: A new creative or artistic endeavor that can bring financial increase. If other indications in the chart suggest financial hardships, this aspect should minimize some of the monetary stress. An excellent aspect for purchasing luxury items, jewelry or clothes and having one's hair styled. Social gatherings are high on the list of activities. Possible romance is in the air. The disposition is more outgoing and on a happier note. A good time to seek favors from women.

Moon square, semi-square 45° or sesqui-quadrate 135° Venus: Likely to bring about broken romantic attachments or engagements. Very emotional time where feelings are easily hurt. Should guard against extravagance in spending. Disagreements with a female child or family relations. Not the best time for having social functions or planning festivals, the attendance is poor or guests are unsociable.

Moon opposes Venus: The native will have to use tact and diplomacy in dealing with women due to the hypersensitivity that this aspect is likely to produce. Depending upon house and sign position, should either Venus or Moon be in Pisces, secret sorrow through a female. Or, deception and deceit through a female. If Moon or Venus be in Gemini, perhaps slander or gossip becomes troublesome, through a female. If Moon or Venus be in Leo, a female child may be a source of aggravation. One may break up with a love relationship, or a close female friend. It is a time that one should not force issues with those one cares about. Don't place someone in a position where they must take a stand, or an ultimatum. They may do just that.

Moon inconjunct Venus: For women, this can be an aspect of health problems relating to the menstrual period or the reproductive organs. The native must exercise good health habits and dietary control. It is possible to over-indulge and gain unnecessary weight.

Moon conjunct Mars: The native feels rather nervous, agitated and even eager for an argument. The temper is short. The native feels compelled to do something, yet lacks the patience to wait for projects to develop. One should use this excessive energy in working on the car, if a male, or cleaning or fixing the house exterior. A female can do some heavy house work that she has not had energy to do so before. Accidents are possible, so care is a must in driving a car and handling of tools and instruments. In a male's chart, he may argue with his girlfriend and regret it later. In a female's chart, possible arguments with a female. Emotional flare-ups are ever present and need controlling until this aspect has passed. Possible infections or inflammation in the area of the sign position. In Leo, guard the eyes and keep the contact lense clean from particles that can cause infections. Lift heavy objects with the knees bent, easing the burden on the back. In Capricorn, possible inflammation of the skin or around the knee area. In Gemini, protect hands and fingers when working with the lawn mower or other types of equipment with cutting blades. Use common sense and above all patience. The three months will soon be over.

Moon sextile or trine Mars: An excellent time for taking care of eye problems. More so, if the male is experiencing trouble with his left eye and the right eye in a female's chart.

There is a general increase in vitality and good health. An abundance of energy that dominates the native into taking forceful action in regards personal matters. An excellent time to begin new projects or enter into new enterprises.

Should the native be employed in a field in which he comes in contact with the general public, they will see him as a person who has the ability to make quick, accurate and common sense judgments. The general public will have more confidence and respect for this native during this period, excellent if he is running for public office.

As a lecturer, one would gain in respect and rapport through his attendees. Or, an auto mechanic would come across in sincerity with his customers who will feel they can rely on the mechanic's good judgment.

There is an increase in business largely due to the accomplished task of one's grasping opportunities through quick and decisive action and a resourceful attitude.

Moon square, semi-square 45°, or sesqui-quadrate 135° Mars: A time in which the native may have a auto accident or a series of constant, aggravating, mechanical, auto problems. The native takes the car in for a general repair, one week later, something else breaks down and so on until the native explodes and has a heated argument with the mechanic. This is a highly emotionally charged aspect in which one feels like fighting back, sometimes there are no causes for such action. Family squabbles are par for the course and much patience will be required.

Business ventures will not go as expected due to misunderstandings and disagreements. The native or someone in the immediate family may have to undergo surgery. Much depends upon the rest of the Natal and Progressed Chart.

In a male's chart, this could lead to arguments with wife or mother or mother-in-law. The health should be protected in regards sudden fevers and headaches.

Moon opposes Mars: Oppositions are an aspect of confrontations with another. Mars can create emotional flare ups between the native and his family or wife. Impulsive and inconsiderate behavior in dealing with others should be avoided, unless extreme patience, tact and diplomacy is used in the handling of women in general. There is the possibility of a severe break-up or separation in the relationship.

Hasty decisions concerning land, property and business dealings should be put aside until this Moon/Mars aspect has passed.

Moon inconjunct Mars: Hasty, impulsive behavior and the inability to control one's temper can lead to a possible accident or create a health problem. The native may feel resentful that another person is trying to boss him, and thus retalites in anger.

Moon conjunct or parallel Jupiter: A good time for business affairs and for negotiations with influential people, judges and civil authorities. A lucky streak prevails and the native feels pretty optimistic concerning personal affairs. A successful period for authors, magazine writers, TV and Radio personalities. A busy three months planning for future travels or promotional matters with the idea of future expansion.

Should the conjunction receive afflicting aspects from major transits or progressed planets, there is the possibility of law suits. Having to perform jury duty at a time when one is close to culminating a business contract. The native may experience a difficult time with a religious individual. Perhaps the native is divorced and wishes to marry in church and the minister fobids it. Should a child be in college, the tuition may be very expensive. Or, the native may have trouble with studies. One must be careful of legal documents they sign concerning land or property. An in-law may be a source of irritation or concern.

Moon sextile or trine Jupiter: One of the best times for business and financial success. Many opportunities bring benefits and advancements. If either Moon or Jupiter be in Taurus, the Second House, Scorpio or the Eighth House, possible luck through lottery, bingo games, raffles or football pools. Should Jupiter be in the 10th, the native may travel due to vocational interests with all expenses paid. This aspect produces opportunities that come to the native without too much effort on their part.

Moon square, semi-square or sesqui-quadrate Jupiter: This tends to create over optimism in affairs of the home and business. The native may foolishly enter into business without bothering to check the necessary facts and financial status. There is a lack of sound judgment which gives way to over-extension of expenditures. Trouble through matters surrounding religious organizations.

The native must use caution when entering into speculative deals and in promising far more than they can possibly deliver.

Moon oppose Jupiter: Travel plans go astray, or prove disappointing. Trouble brewing with in-laws, whereas an in-law may be seeking a divorce from a sibling. An unfavorable time for legal affairs. If the native is going to Las Vegas with the idea of winning at gambling, the trip may cost more than it was worth. This is a time for prudence in every day affairs, finances, dietary habits and family relations.

80

Moon inconjunct Jupiter: The native can undermine his health through over extending oneself through too many commitments that they are unable to handle. Family problems and possibly in-laws may create demands that keeps the native from handling his work related duties properly. There are too many people making too many inroads on the natives time and resources to the point of depletion.

Moon conjunct or parallel Saturn: A very heavy, restrictive period of time in which everything seems to be on "hold." No matter what one tries to accomplish, or how much effort the native may put forth, success and advancements seem to be hindered every step of the way. The native is bewildered, when others receive awards for far less efforts on their part. Responsibilities appear heavier than normal. Depression and a feeling that one is unloved or uncared for is common. Business does not thrive. Should the Second House receive favorable aspects, the conjunction of Moon and Saturn may require the native to work longer hours and harder in achieving that extra financial gain.

Patience and endurance are the two things that will help the native through this period.

Moon sextile or trine Saturn: A propitious time for resolving old issues. For settling matters of importance or negotiating with a figure of authority. This enables one to complete a task that requires solitude or deep concentration. The native realizes that to accomplish this worthwhile task, he must isolate himself until it is completed.

A government official, parent, someone out of the past, or a Capricorn type of individual (Capricorn Rising, Capricorn Sun, Moon or Saturn in the First House) may be of beneficial assistance to the native.

Moon square, semi-square 45° or sesqui-quadrate 135° Saturn: This aspect leaves the native with a feeling of melancholia mixed with period of emotional depression. There is a feeling of general inadequacy in respect to one's obligations and duties. The native feels as though everyone is against him, and that he is all alone. It is difficult to obtain emotional sensitivity, or an expression of love from another. One's lack of emotional and affectional responses may be due to the native's own making, for they FEEL as though the other person no longer loves them. They are so sure of this repression that they invariably turn others away from them.

Possible responsibilities or concerns of a parent. Loss of job, demotion, or cut in pay. The main effect is frustration or unrewarded efforts. The native is terribly ambitious and is earnest in his desire to be successful in his chosen field, but his plans seem to hit a delay and do not materialize as expected.

The native develops an inner intuitive feeling to be patient, to lay low, and endure the restrictions until the "monkey gets off his back," so to speak.

Moon opposes Saturn: The native is faced with heavy burdens, restrictions and the making of important decisions that lie heavily upon his shoulders.

As with the square, there is a good deal of repression. The native tends to give oneself and others unnecessary trouble with their constant emotional state of depression and discontent.

There is a lack of physical energy. The native may feel inadequate coupled with lack of self reliance that leads one to overlook their obligations and duties. Sometimes important tasks are permitted to slack, using every opportunity that presents itself as an excuse to put off the completion of it.

One must be careful in making statements for they may easily be misunderstood. Possible professional or domestic problems often add to the burdens. What one wants to achieve seems to be replaced by what one feels is his sense of responsibility.

Moon inconjunct Saturn: Mental depression plays an important role upon one's health. An optimistic outlook is required to overcome the feeling of neglect and being overworked. The native may drive others away from him with constant complaining, whining and a self-defeating attitude.

One may have to provide care and service to an ill parent. Your co-workers are older individuals or your work related duties are heavy. Sometimes one is used as a scape-goat for errors and mistakes that occur at work.

Moon conjunct or parallel Uranus: This aspect can produce unexpected, erratic and emotional outbursts. Should the conjunction receive unfavorable aspects, the native may experience trouble through a friend, group related projects, clubs or organizations and women in general. This may be a time in which the native begins having problems with electrical appliances, the TV, automatic dish washer or the starter and battery of the car.

The favorable aspects can bring unexpected opportunities for new and unique ideas that could develop into a money making project. New and sudden friendships are made with women of a unconventional background or with those in the occult and Astrology. This aspect may spur one into taking up the study of Astrology.

In general, Moon conjunct Uranus brings the element of unexpected happenings and conditions. Uranus rules "Acts of God," such as tornadoes, hurricanes, floods, mudslides, electrical storms and heavy windstorms. Care should be taken when the weather appears threatening.

Moon sextile or trine Uranus: The native takes an interest in joining various organizations; the golf club, parents without partners, weight watchers or bowling and other such group activities.

Opportunities appear to the native through unusual and unique happenings. Perhaps a chance acquaintance in an elevator leads to an unexpected job. Or, a wrong number dialed produces a new client.

This is an exciting, interesting time in which new female friends are made, who have unconventional backgrounds. Favorable for purchasing electrical appliances for the home, a computer, home base short wave radio or a new television set. This is a likely time for Cable TV to come into your neighborhood for hook up to your home.

If one is inventive, this may be a good time to promote one's new ideas.

Moon square, semi-square 45° or sesqui-quadrate 135° Uranus: Unexpected problems in the home. Electrical appliances may require costly repair. Not the best time to make major purchases, the native may be taking the item back several times for repairs.

One should not make irrational demands upon family members. Trouble may be brewing in the domestic sphere or with a parent.

Group activities that could bring unfavorable public opinion should be avoided. A female friend may be a source of conflict or develop into unexpected arguments leading to a separation. In general, this is a time when one should be careful in making erratic or shocking statements to female relatives that could provoke dissention.

Moon opposes Uranus: This is an aspect of confrontation with another that could lead to a separation should the native push the issue beyond the limits of tact and diplomacy.

Disagreements through a women's organization such as the PTA or a Secretarial Club could give way to a rift if the native does not compromise.

The native may develop a stubborn adherence to his ideas to the point of trying to push them onto others. The native should be careful in the handling of electrical appliances or the electrical parts of the automobile.

The events are likely to be of an unexpected quality that will force the native to take a stand or make an important decision that proves erroneous.

Moon inconjunct Uranus: Unusual, unreliable and eccentric behavior can react upon the health through misjudgment leading to accidents. The native must be careful that boring duties at work do not push him into doing foolish acts that can cause accidents.

This is an aspect of adaptation. Unexpected happenings can occur at work that may require the native to adapt to new work details or working different shifts at a last minute notice. Sometimes there is an uprising among the labor force or with a union and the native should avoid becoming involved because he is not thinking logically. Much to the family's despair, the native may go to the extreme in fighting for unions or causes in an erratic manner that could endanger his job.

Moon conjunct or parallel Neptune: As with all conjunctions, one must consider the aspects it is likely to receive from other planets. The favorable aspects promote an interest in taking dancing lessons, the creative arts, the purchase of a guitar or an organ or a camera and undertaking the study of photography for a possible hobby or new job interest. The intuitive faculties are tremendous. The native may come up with new and unusual ideas for a creative and profitable outlet through some artistic pursuit.

The unfavorable aspect to the conjunction of Moon and Neptune can cause confusion, gossip, rumors and backbiting among women within the native's circle of friends or domestic scene.

A possible hospitalization and illness of a family member that is difficult to diagnosis.

The temptation to escape from the harshness and reality of life through escapism such as going back to sleep after the children have left for school. Sleep is the coma state ruled by the planet Neptune, and some individuals find this method as their best means of isolating themselves from depression and difficult situations that the native feels he cannot cope with.

Moon sextile or trine Neptune: This is an aspect of reward for a past effort that the native asked nothing in return. In other words, the native may receive an unsuspecting gift from someone for whom he has provided a service or favor and charged nothing for his time. It is an aspect of appreciation for kindness shown.

The psychic ability is great, the intuitive ability may endow the native with the capacity to select the winning numbers for a lottery winning or feel they should attend a bingo game, for their chances of winning are enhanced.

Some take up the study of meditation, psychology, yoga or attend religious retreats.

Family members that are confined or ill may take an upward turn for the better. If the native has been having problems in the past with sensitivity to medication, this may be the time in which the physician may find the proper substitute.

84

Handle matters that require grace, charm and a persuasive personality. You will be at your very best these next three months, attracting attention in a quiet and unassuming manner.

Moon square, semi-square 45° or sesqui-quadrate 135° Neptune: The native discovers that women are becoming secret enemies. A conspiracy surrounds the native through vicious gossip, rumors and widespread deception. The native may be totally unaware this is happening until the situation has completely gotten out of hand, and then, he says, "How could they have done this to me?" The sign that the Progressed Moon is positioned, should provide the clue as to the coloring of the female involved. For example, Progressed Moon in Scorpio square Natal or Progressed Neptune in Leo, the female may be a Scorpio Rising, Scorpio Sun or Moon or have the planet Pluto in the First House. The issue may involve around the problem of the Scorpio's child.

This is a time when the native should be alert and observing. Do not be too trusting with new acquaintances or females who come on too strong. Keep your head out of the clouds and the feet firmly planted on the ground. Try to avoid impracticality in the handling of business and family affairs. You may feel a lot like daydreaming and goofing off, a short time is not harmful, but an extended period can be a detriment emotionally and financially.

The native may have to deal with overly emotional or highly overstrung women who may be on the verge of suicide or self destruction. The female may be a drug abuser, or an alcoholic and is having trouble with her marriage, family or a love relation that she wants you to help solve. The native can be easily drawn into this sticky situation if he permits the imposition upon his time.

Moon opposes Neptune: Avoid con artists and get rich schemes. Not the time to sign important documents. Things are not what they appear to be on the surface. Do not take the promises of others literally, what they say and what they actually deliver, will not be the same thing.

You may have to confront someone about their role in a deceptive act against you or your reputation.

Travel at this time may prove disappointing. You hit a detour and get lost or become ill through the drinking of well water that does not agree with you. Take care in all foods that you eat while traveling.

Your mother, mother-in-law or women in general may be opposed to your ideas or with something that you want to do.

Moon inconjunct Neptune: There is the urge to do something rather special or out of the ordinary. But, you feel cramped by a physical handicap or perhaps lack of ability and you find it difficult to accept these limitations. Rather than accept these hinderances, you may try to push further and further ahead until a state of complete frustration is reached. Then you give up in total despair.

Escapism may become the next route through self imposed isolation, tranquilizers, alcohol or the coma state of sleeping longer hours than the body requires.

Moon conjunct or parallel Pluto: A strong desire to be in control of one's environment. The emotions become deeply intense and there is extreme expressions of feeling. Both Moon and Pluto are psychic planets. The favorable aspects can bring about experiences with individuals who have previously passed away or the native may have pronounced psychometric gifts. The women that come into the life of this native are likely to be highly emotional and overly sensitive. If the native works with the general public, there is the ability to sway the masses with a powerful influence through their contacts.

The unfavorable aspects indicate a dictatorial influence through the mother or women in general. An inner sense that a female is trying to control you or change something of a personal habit or style of dress. A stubborn adherence to one's beliefs can cause upsets in one's environment or domestic relationships.

This aspect sometimes accompanies other progressed aspects in force that show a medical requirement for a "D & C," or a hysterectomy.

Moon sextile or trine Pluto: If this aspects is re-enforced by major transits or progressed planets involving the 5th, 1st and the 7th, pregnancy can result. There is unsurpassed energy and zeal in the desire to redecorate, enlarge or alter the present living arrangement. The native feels an urge to rid oneself of bills and loans and this aspect provides the necessary funds to do so. Sometimes, if other progressed aspects agree, the final mortgage payment on the home is completed.

Psychic ability becomes pronounced. Bad habits can be corrected. There can be gifts and monetary gains through women, the mother or in dealings with large groups of people.

Moon square, semi-square or sesqui-quadrate Pluto: A tendency for strong, violent and intense emotional outbursts of temper. Disagreements and arguments in the home due to an urge to control and manipulate family members or close associates and women whom the native is working with.

Money or possessions may be the cause of these disagreements and rifts. The native should try to avoid contacts with women and delay important monetary issues involving property, land and family relations.

Moon opposes Pluto: A serious confrontation with women. An agreement becomes a disagreement due to lack of understanding. Money may be the important issue, the native may feel he is not getting his fair share and stand firmly against the opposing party. The result can be a serious "locking of the horns" so to speak. Where neither party wishes to yield to the rights of the other. The native must use caution, words and expression will be used that will be regretted later after this aspect has passed. But, the emotional hurt will linger on due to the influence of the "vengeful" side of Pluto.

Deal cautiously with women who will conduct themselves in the most uncooperative manner. Any previously laid plans or agreements are likely to undergo an upsetting change. The native feels an unwarranted attack of aggression has been made against him. In retaliation, the native becomes hostile towards the other party.

Moon inconjunct Pluto: This aspect can react upon the health through serious, emotional outbursts and unyielding attitude in his own beliefs. They stubbornly insist they are right, even when proven wrong. High blood pressure can result when the native takes on a fanatical approach that he is absolutely right and becomes dogmatic towards any opposing forces that try to prove him wrong. The inner tension builds up and the emotions flare up through erratic behavior, resulting in extremes of blood pressure.

CHANGE OF FORMAT

It is a customary feature when writing about planets and aspects to begin with the most important illuminary, the Sun. This writer chose to be contrary in this respect, by beginning with the illuminary, the Moon.

The reasoning behind this change is elementary. The writer's research on both Progressed and Natal Moon led to many interesting factors which would not have served as well had the information been separated throughout the text. Thus, a very large chapter was born on the Progressed Moon. It was the writer's belief, that to place such a large chapter of the Moon between the Sun and Mercury, would break up the flow or one's train of thought.

THE SUN

The Sun is the physical body and its recuperative powers. It governs success, ambition, love of power, one's vitality and energy. The capacity to achieve honor and a desire to be in a position of authority. A supervisory position is high on their subconscious urge for personal attainment. The Sun ruled individual loves to delegate orders and is a natural born leader.

The Sun represents the father, the boss, a male authoritative figure, the husband and children, especially a male child. The Sun endows a creative flair, suitable for hobbies and the stage or screen. Sporting events, gambling, football pools, bingo games and horse racing are also ruled by the Sun.

In health, the physical body represents the eyes, heart and the back.

The Progressed Sun will never travel throughout the entire Progressed Chart as does the Progressed Moon. Armed with this foreknowledge, we know that the Progressed Sun will never conjunct its Natal position. There are only three possible aspects that the Progressed Sun can make to its Natal position; a semi-square (45°) at age 45; a sextile (60°) aspect at age 60; or a square aspect at age 90 (90°).

The Natal Sun will eventually change signs through progressions. However, it will rarely change houses, unless positioned natally very close to a house cusp. Why? Because the 10th House Cusp of the Natal Chart advances through the Zodiac sign almost at the same rate of speed as the Natal Sun. In other words, the Progressed 10th House Cusp will always be at the same Zodiacal distance from the Progressed Sun as the Natal 10th House Cusp is from the Natal Sun.

The Sun is the only illuminary (planet) with the steady mean motion of 1° per year. Therefore, it should be an easy task to determine the age when one's personality, ego and sense of pride will take on a new dimensional coloring. A native born with his Sun in 15° of a sign will undergo a change in attitude around the age of 15 to 16 when the Sun enters a new sign through Progression.

Sun conjunct the Ascendant: A conjunction between Progressed Ascendant and Natal Sun can only occur if the Natal Sun is positioned in the Natal First or Second House of the birth chart. As the Progressed Ascendant progresses, the

Natal Sun is drawn up towards the Ascendant's degree and a conjunction results. For example: a native with 15° Virgo on the Natal Ascendant and Natal Sun in 21° Virgo in the First House will experience a conjunction of Progressed Ascendant and Natal Sun around the age of seven (Virgo is one of the slower Ascensions). This is a three year effect and the conjunction should be given both a negative and a positive connotation. This is due to the many aspects the conjunction may receive from major transits, an Eclipse or other progressed planets.

In the positive sense, depending upon the age of the native, the conjunction of Natal Sun and Progressed Ascendant can enhance career potential, advancement and assistance from influential people. The father may obtain better employment. (In the case of a female's chart, possibly marriage or engagement.) The health sign is good and whatever the native undertakes, his line of endeavor should succeed.

On the negative side, there can be difficulty with men in general. Perhaps the planet squaring the conjunction rules the Third House, the concern may be of a brother or possible accident to the native. The father (or husband) may not fare well in his place of employment. Much depends upon the planet in question making the aspect and the house the planet rules. Should the chart be of a native in his early years, the child may experience the typical childhood illnesses. At any age, care should be taken with the hearing, sight and possible back injury or heart problem.

The Progressed Sun can form a conjunction with Natal Ascendant if the Natal Sun is positioned natally in the Eleventh or Twelfth House. As the Progressed Sun advances into the Zodiac, it will eventually reach the degree and sign on the Natal Ascendant. What has been stated previously would hold for this aspect as well.

Sun conjunct M.C.: The Natal Sun cannot form a conjunction with the Progressed Tenth House Cusp unless it is positioned natally in the Tenth or Eleventh House. As the M.C. advances in the Zodiac through progression, the Natal Sun will move towards the Tenth House Cusp.

The age factor should be taken into consideration. The Sun governs a child, and in conjunction with the M.C., a mother might be giving birth to a child if the native is rather young. Therefore, this could well indicate a birth of a brother or sister. The rest of the Progressed Chart should indicate the sex of the child. For example, should Progressed Mercury be in semi-sextile aspect with Natal Venus at the same time that the Progressed M.C. is in conjunction with Natal Sun, one can surmise it will be a female child (sister).

Should the native be of employable age, the conjunction of Progressed M.C. and Natal Sun can be excellent for job opportunities and advancements.

Some graduate from High School or College at this time, ready to enter the business world.

In a female's chart, the conjunction can indicate marriage, birth of a child or some successful dealing with men in general.

Naturally the afflictions to this conjunction requires caution in business affairs. One should not be hasty in forcing issues that involve authoritative figures and career. One's reputation should be protected. Avoid offers from well-meaning individuals who the native may suspect are not on the up and up.

The Progressed Sun can form a conjunction with Natal Midheaven if the Natal Sun is positioned natally in the Eighth or Ninth House. As the Progressed Sun advances into the Zodiac, it will eventually reach the degree and sign on the Natal M.C. What has been stated previously would hold for this aspect as well.

Sun conjunct Descendant: It is impossible for one to experience a conjunction between the Progressed Descendant and Natal Sun unless the Natal Sun is positioned nearby in the Seventh or Eighth House natally. As the Descendant's degree and sign advances in the Zodiac through progression, the Natal Sun will eventually be brought down to the Progressed Descendant House Cusp.

Again, the age factor must be taken into consideration. In a young child's chart, the conjunction between Progressed Seventh House Cusp and Natal Sun may indicate the affairs of a grandparent. The Seventh is the 4th of the 4th, thus having influence over grandparents. The father of this young child may form an important partnership.

The male adult may receive recognition from influential people. The possible forming of a partnership. Any afflicting aspects to the conjunction of the Natal Sun and Progressed Descendant may reflect upon the Ascendant. When the opposite person is in the Seventh House, it is possible that an influential person will be against the ideas that the native is presenting.

In a female's chart, this is one of the aspects of marriage. The sign position of the Progressed Sun in conjunction with Natal or Progressed Descendant should offer a clue as to the coloring and identity of the marriage partner. Afflicting aspects to this conjunction should indicate conflicting problems surrounding the marriage. For example, transiting or Progressed Jupiter in square aspect may bring dissension with a religious person who may not want to sanction the wedding due to religious differences. Or, if Saturn square, parental disapproval.

Sun conjunct I. C.: It is impossible for one to experience a conjunction between the Progressed Fourth House Cusp and Natal Sun unless the Natal Sun is positioned nearby in the Fourth or Fifth House natally. As the I. C.'s degree and sign advances in the Zodiac through progression, the Natal Sun will eventually be brought to the Progressed Fourth House Cusp.

The Progressed Sun can form a conjunction with Natal I. C. if the Natal Sun is positioned nearby, natally in the Second or Third House. As the Progressed Sun advances into the Zodiac, it will eventually reach the degree and sign on the Natal I. C.

In a child's chart, this may indicate possible purchase of property or home. Some advancement to a parent.

The adult may receive some type of recognition in his immediate environment. Possible gain through the purchase or sale of home or property. Possible inheritance of property.

In a female's chart, this is another aspect of marriage.

Any affliction to this conjunction can bring concerns of a parent. Possible difficulties with loss of property (as through divorce or bankruptcy). Many vexations in the family circle with a male member.

Sun sextile or trine Ascendant/Descendant: If through progression, the Sun should form a sextile aspect with the Ascendant, a trine aspect will result between the Sun and Descendant. Whatever aspects the one House Cusp, will in turn, aspect the other, as they are of the same quality and degree.

This aspect endows one with a strong sense of self-confidence while emotional balance for the ego is at its best. There is good organizing ability with the capacity to get along well with others. The desire to achieve personal importance or advancements. This aspect brings favorable dealings with men and those of authority.

In a woman's chart, if she is not married, this too is an aspect of marriage. If she is already married and does not work, this aspect will enhance her husband's vocation. Sometimes, if the Fifth House agrees, this may presage the birth of a male child.

Sun square, semi-square (45°) or sesqui-quadrate (135°) Ascendant: The Ascendant and the Sun are in conflict with one another. The native is unable to project himself in a likeable manner for he may appear to be too over-bearing, domineering or vain. Their pride has been hurt, perhaps through the loss of a job. The native feels let down, inferior and tries to cover up this feeling of lack of self-confidence.

Men pose a problem, either a parent or a figure of authority. Women may have difficulties with men in general — their husband, lover or a male parent. This is an aspect in which one feels as though others are totally against him or is trying to hold the native back from achieving success.

The vitality is poor and the energy span is low. Health problems can spring up, especially if Leo is on the Progressed Ascendant and the Sun is the ruler. One must watch the blood pressure, heart, eyes and back.

Sun sextile or trine M.C./I. C.: In a female's chart, this can be another aspect of marriage. In either male or female chart, it indicates public recognition for services attributed to the community. Advancement in one's career. Matters of a personal level of success are on an upward trend. Honors or awards through one's vocation or for services rendered the public is probable.

In a child's chart, this will affect job opportunities for a parent. Possible change of residence which proves beneficial.

Family ties are strengthened. A busy time within the family circle for marriage or births.

Sun square, semi-square or sesqui-quadrate the M.C./I. C.: Should this aspect occur during a time when the native is running for public office or re-election, it is possible the public will not vote in his favor. This is not necessarily limited to public officials, but can have bearing on individuals who are voted into various positions such as a union leader or the grievance committee.

This is a three year trend while the Progressed Sun is aspecting the Natal MC/IC, or the Progressed MC/IC is in aspect with Natal Sun. A difficult period for success in any enterprise. This may cause a slowing down period in sales. Loss through theft, fire or bankruptcy is possible. Assistance from influential men will not be forthcoming. One feels as though no one wants to help him out of a difficult situation.

In a child's chart, the father may have difficulty with his job. Perhaps he gets laid off, is on strike or gets demoted to a lesser rank.

On the whole, the achieving of one's aim in life is difficult and there is the general lack of interest in life. A sort of aimlessness in regards to one's aspirations and outlook on life.

Sun sextile Natal Sun: The Sun is the only planet that one can rely on to travel at the steady mean motion of 1° per year. Therefore, we can assume that at the approximate age of 60, the Progressed Sun will sextile Natal Sun. Naturally, both Natal and Progressed Sun will remain close to the Natal House position. The sign position should disclose, along with the rest of the progressed chart, the tone of this special event. If in a female's chart, this could bring the possibility of re-marriage (if widowed or divorced or has never married). In either male or female chart, an advancement in some business venture. Possible career promotion. Or, if one has children, a child may be the recipient of this aspect. The child receives an advancement in his career. Or, perhaps a grandchild is expected to be born.

Unless the balance of the progressed chart disagrees, this aspect should provide beneficial protection for health and vitality.

Sun semi-square (45°) Natal Sun: The Progressed Sun's mean motion is 1° per year, in 45 years it will semi-square its own natal position. In allowing 1° orb in applying, exact and separating, this aspect will remain in effect for 3 years. Therefore, the age span between 44 and 46 can be a stressful period.

One should make note of the major transiting planets during that time. What the Progressed Ascendant and M.C. along with the progressed planets are doing.

This is a mid-year crises. Individuals who feel they have not made any major breakthrough in their career may foolishly attempt to force changes at this time. Children leave home, join the service, or get married. The home is empty, the mother feels unwanted.

The house position of the Natal Sun (the Progressed Sun will naturally be in the same house position as the Natal Sun) should disclose the circumstances or individuals that will be a source of stress and concern. This may be the age in which one undergoes surgery for the first time. There may be separation or loss of a close family member. Divorce and disension are not uncommon among marriage or business partnerships.

It is a period of time in which good dietary habits are extremely important. Physical check-ups are a good idea.

Should the Natal Sun also semi-square a Natal planet, this will compound the situation at age 45. Not only will the Progressed Sun semi-square its Natal position but also afflict another natal planet at the same time.

Sun square Natal Sun: The Progressed Sun will square the Natal Sun at the approximate age of 90 years. The native is not going to feel at his level best. Health and finances may prove to be a difficult hardship. Changes may be forced upon the individual, such as pressure in moving in with a relative or to a nursing home.

Sun conjuncts Natal Moon: This can only occur in one's chart where the Moon is positioned natally in a higher Zodiac position than the Natal Sun, yet not too far away that the Progressed Sun cannot conjunct the Moon within a reasonable life time. For example, the native has Natal Sun in 24° Sagittarius and Natal Moon in 2° Capricorn. One can judge that the child will be eight years old when Progressed Sun advances to 2° Capricorn and conjoins Natal Moon.

This aspect can occur at any age depending upon the distance between the Natal Sun and Moon. The conjunction denotes a crisis in the life similar to a New Moon affect in which important changes lie ahead for the native.

This can bring relocation of the home and family due to one's vocation or company mergers. A possible increase in family through marriage of children

94

or birth of grandchildren. Favorable transits or progressed planets to this conjunction will enhance family affairs and career opportunities.

Under afflicting aspects, the conjunction of Progressed Sun and Natal Moon can be a serious indication of a health ailment. Strict dietary habits should be followed and a physical check-up. These are the two most important planets (illuminaries) in the universe. One planet affects the physical side while the other is functional. Under duress, the total body is under stress.

Sun sextile or trine Moon: Both home and career matters are functioning well. Life seems to be on a happier course in which trends are not upsetting. The health is good. There is new undertakings. Much depends upon the house position and sign placement of Progressed Sun and Natal Moon. Should one be positioned in Aquarius in the 9th, for example, one may decide to travel with a group of people. In Pisces, a cruise might be of interest. Should one be positioned in the eleventh, new friends can be influential in some way.

Men often marry under such a configuration. The Moon merely indicates a matured woman, one who may own property and possibly have a child by a previous marriage. In a male's chart, women in general will be beneficial or grant favors more readily.

Sun square, semi-square or sesqui-quadrate the Moon: Disharmony within the family circle. The health is not up to par. Children may be a source for concern. Business seems to be at a standstill.

Should a child marry, the native may not approve of the child's choice of partner. Generally, there is much emotional concern over family members, one's children and a parent.

This is a three year trend of emotional repression, difficulty in maintaining family harmony and often lack of funds for necessities. There is much inner tension and dissatisfaction with personal affairs.

Sun oppose Moon: Another difficult aspect involving a crisis possibly among family members. An opposition brings opposing forces, sometimes family ties are broken or there is separation through divorce or death. This aspect alone will not produce such drastic results, but will enforce other afflicting progressed aspects at the same time.

A female may become an open enemy. This could well be a friend, mother-in-law or distant relative.

Should there be no afflicting aspects to this opposition, the native may merely enter into a new phase of life. New goals for future expansion is possible. Sometimes a major decision is required as in re-location or change of vocation.

Sun inconjunct the Moon: Another aspect suggesting a health problem perhaps due to an emotional crisis. The sign and house position should provide some clue as to the person who may impose upon the native's time. One may have to adapt to changing family situations.

Sun conjunct or parallel Mercury: Mercury is a neutral planet and therefore has no sex. The planet Mercury requires another planet to give it sex. This may be an important year for a male member of the family. The conjunction of Sun and Mercury suggests a male individual. The native's brother, brother-in-law, uncle or perhaps a close neighbor. What is so important about this male individual? Look into the present day Ephemeris and note, if there is a major transiting planet that may be in favorable or unfavorable aspect to this conjunction. Perhaps the other progressed planets will afford a clue or an Eclipse.

Favorable aspects may bring a marriage for the brother, birth of a brother, or perhaps some kind of recognition that this family male member has deserved.

The afflicting aspects may caution the brother or male family member to exercise care in driving. Accidents, surgery and even the possibility of death or separation can happen.

Concerning the native's personal interests, this may be the time in which one returns to school to further one's education. Maybe the present job requires additional training.

This will be a rather busy time of life in which many duties and details will have to be handled. Much in the way of communications, short travels, letter writing and signing of important papers. The mind is constantly going, sometimes undue worry and concern over insignificant matters, keeps the mind from resting.

An excellent time with favorable aspects to return to the teaching profession, begin writing a book or magazine articles. One does not have to be a teacher to transmit knowledge, but perhaps an instructor will be an interesting role.

Sun sextile or trine Mercury: Another aspect that can indicate the birth of a brother. Or, the brother marries. New intellectual people will enter the native's life. Perhaps through returning to school, college or some technical training course.

This is an excellent aspect for mental aptitude required in handling of detailed work in connection with one's vocation. This is the time to conduct negotiations and seek contacts that will enhance one's success in business.

A sextile between Progressed Sun and Natal Mercury is possible, depending upon the distance between the two planets at birth.

A trine between Progressed Sun and Natal Mercury is not possible in every case, but is probable. Mercury and Sun would have to be far apart at birth and then the trine may only occur at age 90 or so.

Sun square or semi-square Mercury: This can indicate ill health of a brother, loss, separation or death thereto. Should either planet be in Pisces, perhaps death by drowning; or positioned in Aries, the brother may suffer an accident or shoot himself. These drastic indications are generally fortified by other major progressed planets. One should not take a dire view without first consulting the major transits, Eclipse, and other progressions in force at the same time.

The native should guard against signing important papers or documents involving a male individual. There is the possibility of misrepresentation or falsehood, and statements that do not ring clear in the small print.

The native is not at his best in clarity of thinking and good judgment. Errors are common, sometimes they can prove costly when occurring in business.

There are too many irons in the fire, this scatters the native's energies and may lead to nervous disorders, ulcers or high blood pressure.

The semi-square is likely to occur around the age of 40 and the square much later in life. This is merely an estimate and should not be taken as exact. The age factor depends upon the distance between Natal Sun and Natal Mercury at birth.

Sun opposition Mercury: This is not possible because the two planets are never that far apart at birth, and therefore impossible for Progressed Sun to ever oppose Natal Mercury.

Sun inconjunct Mercury: The Progressed Sun will never reach a 150° aspect from Natal Mercury. This too is impossible.

Sun conjunct or parallel Venus: The house rulership of Natal Venus should be taken into consideration, for this is an aspect of monetary gain. Possibly through inheritance, lottery, games of chance or football pools.

Social functions and affairs are enhanced. Marriages and birth take place within the family circle. There is an air of magnetic quality that draws the opposite sex into the picture. Love affairs and attachments are easily formed.

The native takes a personal interest in clothing and dietary habits for a better appearance.

This is generally considered an excellent aspect for all around attainment of success, parties, marriages, engagement and births. However, an afflicting aspects can be difficult. A possible change in the relationship between lovers, or health problems with the eye, back or kidneys.

Should Natal Venus be in the 6th, the conjunction (afflicted by major transits, an Eclipse or other progressed aspects) may indicate death or surgery of an aunt or uncle. Lower standards of one's sexual attitude and poor dietary habits can take its toil on the health. Under afflicting aspects, the type of individuals that will be drawn to the native will be of a lesser status, low character or have questionable backgrounds.

Sun sextile or trine Venus: The native has a powerful attractive quality that draws the opposite sex. This is an aspect of marriage, engagements and meeting a new love relationship.

One's sense of beauty is enhanced. There is a general interest in re-decorating the home or apartment. Some take up dancing, music or art lessons. Others take a new, personal interest in hair style, new attire and improving one's appearance.

This is one of the high points of life, bringing much happiness and contentment. Many social affairs or functions to attend. Increase in marriage or births in the family circle. The warmth that is generated towards others brings a return of gifts or monetary gain.

The trine is not impossible, however, it is likely to occur later in life when one is about to retire. The health is good and the finances are secured.

Sun square, semi-square Venus: This is likely to occur later in life where one may withdraw from social affairs and contacts with others. If married, possible separation, loss, grief or death through the partner. If one is seeking a second (or third) marriage, the native may find much dissatisfaction with the present suitor. Should Venus be in Leo, in the 5th house, or ruler of the 5th, a daughter may run away and get married or become pregnant while still single. The native's son may select a wife that is of low moral standards (if in Pisces), may be a heavy drinker or a drug abuser.

Sometimes, one's sense of values are temporarily misplaced; where one may give their love for all without considering future consequences.

Sun opposition Venus: This is not possible as these two planets are never that far apart at birth.

Sun inconjunct Venus: The Progressed Sun will never to a 150° aspect from Natal Venus.

Sun conjunct or parallel Mars: This is an aspect of hasty, impulsive and impetuous actions. The native feels aggressive and abrupt in his mannerism and sometimes for no apparent reason.

Should major transiting planets or other progressed aspects come in force at the same time, there is danger of accidents, fire or surgery. Bites from dogs and possible injury through firearms.

Decisions are made without proper forethought and later regretted. Temperance in all matters should be the key word. One must temper the urge to do something drastic when arguments or confrontations occur.

Depending upon the sign placement of Natal Mars, inflammation of the eyes or other inflammatory diseases are probable. One must also guard against scalds, burns and handling of sharp instruments or fireworks.

A male child may be creating much tension in the home, due to their desire for personal independence. Should this be the case, firm disciplinary action should be taken to keep the child in line until this aspect passes. Perhaps there is trouble with school authorities over the behavior of the child.

Sun sextile or trine Mars: In a female's chart, this can be birth of a boy child or if the native be single, possible marrige.

Those involved in business may feel the urge to tackle something new and different in their line of work. A challenging aspect towards some new line of endeavor. Possible gain or assistance from someone of Arian coloring (the person may have Aries Sun, Moon, Aries Rising or Mars positioned in the First House). The native will feel unusually active in wanting to achieve success. The energy span is at its highest peak. The recuperative powers are excellent and can aid a speedy recovery should surgery be necessary. There is the power and determination to attain something substantial. The desire to take the lead in certain matters.

This is an aspect in which one must put forth personal energy in order to reach top performance, and extraordinary achievements.

In a male's chart, there may be an interest in the Martial type of occupation as in joining the Armed Forces, the police or fire department, or learning a new mechanical trade.

Sun square, semi-square or sesqui-quadrate Mars: This is a crisis period indicating a critical and dangerous time. Arguments or serious confrontations may occur with a male individual, family member or a sibling.

Depending upon the age factor, in a young person's chart, the native may get involved with the wrong type of friends who will get them in trouble with the law enforcement agencies.

The native may feel a bit too sure of himself, carrying a chip on his shoulder where one is not needed. They may go in for rash behavior, fast cars, or desiring to own a motorcycle. Sometimes a dangerous love of speed creates a dangerous accident.

One must judge also the native's environment, for shooting, maiming, or a stabbing is possible.

In a female's chart, trouble with or through men in general, the husband, a male child or a father.

The judgment is bad, so one must not be pushed into making hasty decisions. Accidents, surgery, or cuts and burns, and inflammatory diseases or infections are possible. The sign position of Natal Mars should offer a clue, such as the eyes or back and heart if Mars be in Leo. Kidney or bladder infections if Mars be in Libra. Possible ulcers and gastric problems in Virgo, and so forth.

Sun opposition Mars: An opposition often indicates opposing forces between two persons. One may not see eye to eye with the other. The native may feel as though someone is making too many demands or inroads upon his personal affairs or time. This can lead to a direct confrontation with someone of an Arian coloring (the person may have Aries Sun, Moon, Rising Sign or Mars in the First House).

Someone may have suppressed anger that is welling up and ready to explode against the native. There are disputes with a male person in general. Other disputes can arise over mechanical defects as in the repair of a car. Injury through machinery.

Not the best time to seek favors from others, or to enter into a legal battle.

In a female's chart, this can be separation from a male child who has moved to another state or drafted into the Armed Forces. Separation from/or danger to the husband, father or a male child.

Premature actions, or hasty decisions, and impulsive behavior can be the native's downfall. One may feel a sense of personal failure due to the heavy demands they have made upon themselves. An aspect of strained relationships with others.

The health can suffer through a high degree of nervous intensity giving way to high blood pressure and cardiac problems.

Sun inconjunct Mars: This is an aspect of high intensity and emotional irritability. The native is not at his best in spanning his energy, and should take a calming attitude towards those who are demanding more of the native than is possible to give.

Arguments or dissension through others who want to enforce changes concerning the native's affairs. As in disagreements over working arrangements. A new co-worker that is constantly testing the native's temper, or perhaps a new supervisor demanding more work in the same amount of hours. This is also an aspect of health upsets through misuse of instruments or tools, leading to possible accidents. One must be constantly alert during this time span, and avoid rushing a certain job. The native should apply the use of all safety equipment as in eye protectors and hand guards.

Sun conjunct or parallel Jupiter: Depending upon the age factor, the conjunction of Sun and Natal Jupiter can be a scholastic award for a young native. Winning of a lawsuit. Beneficial gain or assistance from influential people, and those of a Jupiter coloring (Sun in Sagittarius, Moon or Rising Sign or Jupiter in the Natal First House). The favorable aspects to this conjunction is inclined towards marriage if single, or birth of a child, or grandchild. The general attitude and nature is one of optimism and enjoyment with life.

Success and advancement in one's place of employment is achieved with little effort. Favors and gifts seem to fall into the native's lap.

Afflicting aspects from major transiting planets, an Eclipse or other progressed aspects in force at the same time, can be devastating. Conflicts through law enforcement agencies, courts of law or a religious person.

An in-law may be a source for concern or perhaps someone who resides at a distance.

Individuals of foreign background or with a foreign accent may be a detriment to the native's reputation, or success.

One must guard against overindulgence in certain foods or drink to avoid possible health upsets with the gall-bladder or liver.

Sun sextile or trine Jupiter: A very prosperous and expansive period in which opportunities present themselves with ease. The native seeks new ways to achieve future growth in one's vocation. This is an aspect of general well-being and a happy state of mind.

If lawsuits are pending, this should bring it to a successful completion. The native may have an opportunity to return to college for another degree with all expenses paid by the present employer.

If one has formerly broken away from their religious beliefs, this aspect may re-enforce one's religious aspirations.

This is an aspect of marriage in a female's chart. In general, wealthy people, or those of prominence and persons higher up in the social circle than oneself, may be of tremendous assistance towards material or financial gain.

One should take advantage of all opportunities that present themselves. Avoid taking the easy way out of a difficult situation. And above all, one should not procrastinate, due to a somewhat lazy attitude. Any health problem should be easily dispensed with under this protective influence.

Sun square, semi-square or sesqui-quadrate Jupiter: Rash and impetuous actions can produce difficulties with the occupation, money, or those involving legal matters and religious orders.

Travel or published material may pose a problem. Or, one may have to re-locate to another state due to change in company status.

Procrastination should be avoided for failure in some project will make for strained relationships with others. The native may promise more than what can be produced, causing unsetting conditions with higher figures of authority, who will resent the native's lack of responsible actions.

Depending upon the age factor, some may desire to quit college or abruptly change their majors in mid-stream.

Litigations, legal affairs, travel, correspondences, printed material will all require care in handling. Carelessness under such an aspect can be disastrous on finances and occupation.

The native must use caution in signing of legal documents.

Overindulgence in food or bad habits are likely to take its toll upon the health.

This is an aspect of extravagance and the inclination to spend money unnecessarily.

Sun opposition Jupiter: The native is met with opposing forces in almost every course of action that could bring opportunities.

In-laws, persons of foreign background, or an influential person could put the native at a disadvantage, in any field of endeavor.

This is a dismal period for success, advancements or social contacts. Others try to undermine your ability. Others may seek to take your job away from you. Recognition and rewards will not be forthcoming. Lawsuits may have to be considered due to slanderous statements made by others against the native's integrity and honor.

This is a time to lay low and not push matters, for they will come to naught. Favorable aspects to this opposition can bring about a workable compromise in which the native will seek a better alternative route.

Sun inconjunct Jupiter: There is the tendency to take on too many projects, and promise others more than one can deliver. The native feels as though there is more time than actually is. This causes the native to put matters off until the last minute, then it is rush, rush, rush. Carelessness with details can result, and consequently others lose confidence in the native's ability to produce.

Litigations may result through what the native feels is job discrimination. Others getting the advancements that is due the native.

Nervous stress and tension may result through the possibility of trying to work full time, and seeking a college degree part time. Education may, in some way, have some hinderance or added burden upon one's ability to perform at work.

Sun conjunct or parallel Saturn: A three year trend in which the native feels as though he has assumed more than his share of heavy duties and responsibilities. The native develops a serious outlook on life. Friends may shy away from him due to his pessimistic attitude. This leaves the native to feel he has been abandoned by others. There is a withdrawal from social affairs. A desire to be left alone, and yet, feeling lost and lonely.

Occupational interests suffer unfavorable job change, or a position is lost. Adversities brought on by influential people or a government official.

A man, possibly a boss may be a source of friction, or there is anxiety and concern over the health of a parent.

Other people create frustrating delays, through their intolerant attitudes towards the native.

Major transits, an Eclipse or other progressed aspects afflicting this conjunction of Progressed Sun and Natal and Progressed Saturn, will increase the mental depression, anxiety and concern over one's reputation, career goals, government agencies and a parent.

Favorable aspects to this conjunction from major transits, an Eclipse or other progressed aspects, can bring about a just reward for past efforts and hard labor. Men in authority over the native will look upon his past work efforts with a possible job promotion. Generally, even with the favorable aspects, there is a certain amount of hard work, long hours, and much self sacrifice required to achieve desired results.

The one difficult problem with this aspect lies with the fact that soon after Progressed Sun conjoins Natal Saturn, it will soon conjunct Progressed Saturn. Depending upon the native's age, this may prolong the aspect in force should Progressed Saturn only be one degree away from Natal Saturn. In older nativities, there may be a year or two leeway between the conjunctions of Progressed Sun with Natal and Progressed Saturn.

As Progressed Sun conjoins Natal Saturn, one must look at the House position of Natal Saturn and the House containing the sign of Capricorn. The major transits and any Eclipse is likely to come from a different House natally when afflicting or otherwise favorably aspecting this conjunction.

103

Progressed Sun to Progressed Saturn should be considered with the Progressed Chart. Natal Saturn does not move too far from its Natal Longitudinal degree at birth. Therefore as the House Cusps advance in degrees, Progressed Saturn will be swept right along into a new house position. With this in mind, one must consider the House position of Progressed Saturn and the House containing the sign of Capricorn to determine the area of life most affected and the people most likely to be involved.

Sun sextile or trine Saturn: An excellent aspect for those interested in the political field and possibly running for office (not necessarily for the government, but perhaps as an official for a Labor Union, or a large organization such as the Veterans of Foreign Wars).

This is a beneficial three year trend and possibly longer, as the Progressed Sun will shortly aspect Progressed Saturn. The native gives more consideration for wise and well planned actions. There are still the heavy responsibilities involved, but the native seems ready and eager to assume them. Any job promotion or advancement in one's career will be as the direct result of past efforts, hard work and patience.

There is a greater ability to concentrate, appraise and organize one's time. The native develops a serious, yet considerate and sincere outlook, with much attention towards methodical and responsible actions.

The personality changes a little, the native will not be easily affected by the opinions of others. Emotional control is no longer lacking.

Influential people and an authoritative figure may be of assistance. In a female's chart, the husband gains a responsible position. If single, this is an aspect of marriage or a physical attraction to men who are older, matured for their years, and quite protective in every sense. While it is true that these men may not be as openly affectionate as the female native would like, but there is sincere loyalty and trust.

In general, this is an aspect of success in one's occupation. The developing of practical skills. Material or financial gain and assistance through a parent or a trusted individual. Excellent for long term investments.

The health is generally robust. This aspect can help overcome any previous illness with fortitude and strength and a determining willpower.

Sun square, semi-square or sesqui-quadrate Saturn: One of the most dismal periods in one's life. Personal and financial affairs appear to be at a standstill. The native places one foot forward, only to place three back.

This aspect may easily last longer than the three year span of time. After Progressed Sun has left the afflicting aspect with Natal Saturn, it soon heads toward Progressed Saturn. Around the ages of 20 or early 30's, there may be no brief respite, but merely an extension of time from three to perhaps four years. At a later age, Progressed Saturn may be 3 or more degrees away from Natal Saturn, the native gets a small break before plunging into another state of despair.

This is an aspect of hinderances, delays and restrictions. Everything the native touches seem to go awry. The effect is like having a "monkey on one's back" and not being able to shake him off.

One should not take on heavy obligations such as a heavily mortgaged home or a new car that one cannot afford. Changes in career should be avoided if possible. This is a contracting period, not an expanding phase.

The nature may be somewhat severe, depressed and even hostile towards those in authority. The inclination is towards pessimism.

The Sun governs men as a rule, in square or other afflicting aspects with Saturn, the father, grandfather or close male relations of a Capricorn coloring may be seriously ill. If other aspects in force agree, there is the possibility of loss, separation or death through a parent, especially the father.

In a female's chart, this may be serious cause for concern of the marriage partner. If single, the female native may come into contact with men of defective characters, stern and unemotional, or insensitive.

If the native is past 50 years of age, the aspect may affect the health through the aging process of the body. Rheumatism and problems with the arteries and other such aging illness. This is a detrimental period healthwise, and usually accompanied with loss of vitality, moodiness and severe depression.

Sun opposition Saturn: A depressive, restrictive period. Estrangements and separation or anxiety over a parent. Danger of damage to the reputation or credit rating. Occupational interests suffer through unfavorable job changes or loss of position. The native should not depend upon the promises of others to avoid upsetting disappointments. A boss or someone in authority may be a source of opposition and friction.

Health matters will require special attention. One should note the matters of the house position of Natal and Progressed Saturn through the consequences of the houses in both Natal and Progressed Chart that Saturn rules.

Sun inconjunct Saturn: There is frustration through delayed affairs. Other people impose upon the native creating additional responsibilities. A health defect or lack of physical stamina may prevent the native from realizing one's ambition. Job opportunities prove disappointing, and superiors or co-workers seem to disapprove of the native's actions or are an obstacle, causing difficulties at work.

In a female's chart, she may find herself in a position of having to care for an aging parent, an ill husband, or other aged members of the family.

Sun conjunct or parallel Uranus: This is an aspect of a high strung temperament that needs to be controlled. The native feels an urge for personal freedom and rebels against restrictive limitations. This new adventurous spirit may cost the native more than what he has bargained for, should he go about it in an agitated or rebellious manner.

Favorable aspects to the conjunction of Progressed Sun and Uranus can bring exciting events and circumstances into the native's life. New and unconventional friends are made. There may be the desire to become a part of a group activity or join an organization. Others become interested in the occult and Astrology. Electronics and computers enter the native's vocabulary.

Women under this aspect may meet new and exciting men. If married, the husband may undergo positive changes in his vocation, which was brought about through an unusual set of circumstances.

Changes, though favorable, are abrupt and unexpected in nature. For someone who has just undergone restrictive aspects from transiting or progressed Saturn, this can be a relief in breaking away from so-called bonds of inhibition and delays.

The unfavorable aspects from major transits, an Eclipse or other progressed planets, may result in a total upheaval of present conditions. The native may try to break away from restrictive bonds through the most erratic manner. Sudden loss of job or position is possible. Sudden separation through a male member of the family, through misunderstandings; or possible death, generally brought on by a heart attack or stroke.

In a female's chart, there is difficulty with the husband, giving way to separation or divorce. A child develops a rebellious attitude and is difficult to control. This is an aspect of sudden accidents and unexpected health problems.

Sun sextile or trine Uranus: A sudden interest in new fields of endeavors through Radio, TV, Hi-Fi equipment, short wave radios, electronics and computers. This is an opportunity to enter into new, exciting, and undeveloped territories never tried before.

The personality takes on a new, unique and magnetic quality that attracts others to him, enlarging his circle of newfound friends.

The native should take advantage of every opportunity that may present itself. The following three years, while Progressed Sun is applying, exact and leaving the favorable aspect with Uranus, will be one of the most exhilarating years. This trend may last even longer depending upon the distance in degrees from Natal and Progressed Uranus.

Should Natal Uranus be in 7° Aries for example, and Progressed Sun in 6° Leo, this aspect will take hold while applying at 6° with Natal Uranus, and remain in effect until Progressed Sun has left the separating degree of Progressed

Uranus, which may be in 9° Aries. Resulting in a five year period of excitement, new adventures and new circumstances. A sudden turn in events, and an improvement of living conditions through sudden opportunities or an advance in vocation.

Sun square, semi-square or sesqui-quadrate Uranus: Unconventionality and a stubborn attitude causes unpopularity with others. The native feels an urge to break the bonds of restrictions in such an erratic manner that becomes offensive to others.

There is a high degree of nervous tension and irritability within the system. There is often an attitude of impatience and intolerance with persons who do not agree with your irrational ideas.

The native becomes involved in unconventional situations, or with people of bizarre behavior, or environment.

Natives with many Fixed signs and a rather settled nature will find this aspect disturbing. A most upsetting period of time lasting from three to five years. There are unexpected adjustments to new conditions or circumstances in life, sudden setbacks and upsetting experiences.

This aspect is often connected with accidents or catastrophes. Sudden mishaps or unexpected and sudden health disturbances, as with a heart attack or stroke.

Possible, sudden separation or loss of a male member of the family (a father, son or uncle).

In a female's chart, loss of understanding in relationship with the husband leading to divorce or separation. If single, stormy relationships, and unexpected trouble through men. Not the time for marriage or cementing close relationships.

The sign position of these two planets, the matter of their house position through the consequences of the houses they rule, should be given serious consideration. For example, should the Sun be placed in the sign Leo, or perhaps Uranus governs the 5th House, then one can assume that a difficult period in regards to children will be most disturbing. Perhaps one has a young female child who gets pregnant, and an abortion is necessary. Or, she marries the boy and has the child, but no financial backing. The native is upset by the sudden developments of this child/boyfriend situation. Bitter arguments may ensue, or the native feels compelled to take the three of them into the home.

Whatever the situation, it is a most disturbing, upsetting and nerve-racking period.

Sun opposition Uranus: This is an aspect of sudden reversals and changes. However, should the opposition receive favorable aspects from major transits, an Eclipse or other progressed planets, this unexpected turn of events may well be for the better. Sometimes the native is caught in a rut, and such an aspect as this can force him out of it into new areas that would not have been considered previously.

A position is lost, but a new one springs up unexpectedly and for the better. A divorce is eminent, at first disturbing, but later one realizes it may have been for the best. Whatever the situation, it will occur through unusual and unexpected channels, and call for a compromise. A new avenue is opening up for the native, unfortunately it doesn't give much time for preparation.

Afflicting aspects to this opposition rejects the astounding and sudden or unforseen events. The native may experience complete failure in business or vocation. Loss of friends and separation from family. There is the making of impulsive, rash and unsound decisions. A divorce, which could possibly have been resolved, ends with sudden clashes of temper. Possible loss of separation from a child, who may be transferred to another sector of the country by his company. Or one who marries a wife that alienates the son against the native.

Whatever the situation, if the native does not control his emotions and rash behavior, separation through others will result.

Not the time to resolve legal cases or enter into litigations.

Sun inconjunct Uranus: There is difficulty in conforming to routine matters. This can be disturbing to co-workers who find the antics of the native upsetting and contrary to working conditions. The native may jeopardize his chances of success through irrational behavior. One should be careful in handling of electrical equipment and mechanical devices. This is an accident prone and health hazard aspect.

Sun conjuncts or parallel Neptune: The general trend appears to be remoteness from what is concrete, tangible or the ordinary. The tendency is towards depending upon unreliable or unstable people whom the native may take too seriously. May be easily influenced or led by others. Should avoid over-indulgence in drugs or alcohol.

This can be a powerful aspect and not necessarily negative. Much depends upon the major transits, Eclipse or other progressions, in force at the time. With favorable trends, a strong inspirational bent could lead to the study of music, joining with a band, art, creativity in some progressive form. An intuitive insight that is uncanny and borders on psychism. The native may work behind the scenes with someone in a new and unusual undertaking. The conjunction, in the sign Libra, could be a partnership in the owning of a bar or a carry out beverage store. Some take up the study of Astrology, the occult, psychology, or other scientific fields as in nursing and pharmacy.

With unfavorable aspects, the native must guard against deception during the three years ahead, and possibly longer should Progressed Neptune not be too far away. The native will be an easy prey for others to take advantage of, or mislead. Avoid doing underhanded or behind the scenes activities that are questionable, for one is likely to be the victim of false rumors and possible scandal.

Should Progressed Sun conjunct Neptune in Leo, it is possible that one of the children may come down with an unusual illness or one that is difficult to diagnose. Perhaps a daughter is having an affair with an unsavory character. The Sun also represents a parent, the father as a rule, who may have a strange illness or be involved in a mysterious situation.

The native should be careful of taking non-prescribed medication.

Sun sextile or trine Neptune: Endows the native with a spiritual or psychic ability, and the art of visualization. This can be a successful period of time, if the native can develop the art of formulating an imaginary picture of what he wants to do, then make an ideal pattern from which to work. The more he works on this art of visualization, the more it will draw the native on to its fulfillment.

This is a span of time in which ideas, inspirations and artistic potentials can be brought to successful fruitation.

There is a magnetic and charming quality about the native that draws others into his immediate social circle. There is the desire for lovely objects, dressing more attractively, taking up dancing or music lessons. Some purchase an organ, guitar or other musical instrument.

Natives in the writing field should experience a more visionary and active imagination that can enhance their skill.

Others may enter humanitarian fields as in nursing, X-Ray technician, orderly, psychology, or volunteer hospital work.

Photography, a swimming pool, or a boat may be a good source for relaxing inner tensions.

Possible hidden gains through speculation, games of chance or football pools.

Sun square, semi-square or sesqui-quadrate Neptune: The native should avoid schemes proposed by other people which may involve an element of deception, or holds a risk of getting involved in shady business transactions.

Care should be taken in whom one permits within the social circle, to avoid one's reputation from getting damaged through unreliable or questionable characters.

The native may be easily susceptible to impressions. A person who can be exploited by other people.

There may be much chaotic conditions, scandals or entanglements, and deception surrounding the affairs of the native.

Sometimes there is confusion or a feeling of hopelessness surrounding a health problem in which the doctor cannot find the cause or cure. A sudden or unexpected reaction to a drug or medication may occur.

In a male's chart, concern over the health of the father. Or, possible deception and deceit from other men through business dealings.

In a female's chart, confusing elements concerning the father or the husband's affairs or health. If single, deception through men who profess to be single, and later prove to be married. Or, are hidden drug abusers or heavy drinkers. Should either Progressed Sun or Natal or Progressed Neptune rule the 5th, be placed therein or be positioned in the sign Leo, the concern may be over a child. One may be involved in an act of theft, sales of drugs, or involved with dubious friends. The child may be ill and require hospitalization.

This is a period of time in which the native must be aware that others may try to undermine his reputation. To harm him through scandal whether deserved or not. The native will always have to guard his actions during this span of time, and be alert to the health conditions of close members of the family.

Sun opposition Neptune: Oppositions generally involve another person, and in the case of Neptune, this person may work behind the scenes trying hard to damage the reputation of the native. The native is totally unaware of what is happening until the situation is almost out of control. The native reacts with complete surprise that anyone could do this to him.

The native is much too gullible and trusting. Must learn to be more suspicious of others.

Sun inconjunct Neptune: The native wants desperately to achieve something out of the ordinary, but either ill health, a handicap, or lack of proper knowledge holds him back. The native continues to push himself until out of frustration, he gives up and goes into total isolation, resorts to drinking, drugs, or goes back to bed and tries to sleep away his inner sense of defeat.

This is another aspect of an illness that is difficult to diagnose. Extreme care in taking proper prescribed drugs and medication. Re-check prescriptive drugs administered through a pharmacy, or a nurse during a hospital stay.

Possible deception or confusion through co-workers who tend to blame the native for errors occurring at work. Difficult circumstances arise through chaotic and undisciplined situations, in which a supervisor may try to undermine the working condition or material of the native. Sometimes a theft occurring at work is unjustly blamed on the native.

The native will have to avoid daydreaming during working hours, and be alert to all possible confusing or mysterious situations that may occur in his place of employment.

Sun conjunct or parallel Pluto: This is a powerhouse aspect, but most important is the age factor at the time of the conjunction. In a young female child of 10 to 15 years of age, this can be an aspect of seduction. A parent would be wise to carefully guard this child's activity. Talk openly with this child of sexual matters and the possibility of overtures from males, or indecent exposure. Whether this be from a step-father, father, brother, neighbor or stranger.

In the charts of young boys, this can bring about an early awareness of sexual interest. Should their conjunction of Progressed Sun and Natal Pluto receive afflicting aspects, the parent should watch this child also against the possibility of sexual assault or perversity.

In adults, this conjunction can instill a high degree of hidden emotions that one would not expect exists until it is released with compelling power. For example, a woman may meet an attractive, sexually magnetic type of male, and submit herself to him with an all consuming love and devotion. Should she be betrayed by this man, the emotional outbursts of vengence will surprise even the native herself. She has experienced the ruthlessness of another, and now the crisis of self-preservation must be dealt with. Never before has she felt such hatred for anyone in her life.

In everyday matters this is an aspect that instigates changes. One feels compelled to get rid of the old, and make ready to begin the new. This can be the milestone of one's life. Where one opens a new door to a new direction of life, only to have to close the door to a former existence.

With favorable aspects in the chart of a married woman, this can be the possibility of a birth of a son. Or, perhaps the husband has been given an advancement in his career, in which he will be in control of a department, people, or machinery.

Sun sextile or trine Pluto: This is a powerful aspect for anyone who deals with the general public as with a public servant. Anyone running for re-election or a government office stands an excellent chance of winning. There are powerful people behind this native, who are eager and willing to assist him in new and daring enterprises.

There is an inner confidence to succeed and the self-discipline and determination to do so. The inner resources are tremendous.

Career advancements are possible. There is the realization of new ideas, with the ability to establish one's own position as a leader.

This is an aspect of birth of a child. It is also an aspect under which women decide on the best technique for sterilization. This favorable aspect releases the female from concern and worry of getting pregnant, if they did not wish to do so; thereby selecting surgery as a means of control, rather than undergoing surgery due to serious health problems. Male nativities with this aspect have also undergone similar choices for surgery as a means of birth control.

Sun square, semi-square or sesqui-quadrate Pluto: There is the tendency to overdo and to overestimate their own ability as to what is possible for them to do. Some natives may place value of possessions or money over the lives of other people. They may advance themselves through ruthless behavior to others. This extreme craving for power or rulership may well work against the native in the end.

The consequences of one's actions through careless behavior can be as a result of running unnecessary risks.

There is the possibility of separation, loss or death of a male member of the family. In a female's chart, this could indicate a possible abortion or miscarriage.

In either case, trouble through men who may try to exercise control over the native.

Sun opposition Pluto: At some time during this three year span in which Progressed Sun will oppose Natal or Progressed Pluto, a male individual will be opposed to the native's ideas with such vehemence as to force the native into striking back.

This is not the time to seek favors from influential individuals. There is a possibility of separation through a child who has moved to another city, or through breakup of relationship due to misunderstandings. Hinderance in vocation. Divorce or separation in marriage.

In the general sense, there is great difficulty in understanding the moods or emotions of another person. Lack of communication, secrecy, or a withdrawal from close contacts. There is a harboring of resentment towards the native who is unaware of the animosity of feelings directed at him, until the situation explodes out of control.

Prolonged opposition of forces can eat away at the nervous system, causing extremes of blood pressure.

Sun inconjunct Pluto: There is a strong, unyielding, determination to get even with someone, whom the native feels has undermined him. Whether this has actually occurred is of no consequence, in the person's mind, he feels justified in what he is doing, and the revenge that he is seeking.

Changes in his field of operation through new machinery, new methods or advance techniques may upset the native, who may not have the physical/mental capacity to cope with these new standards of operation. Or, the changes may involve the rotation of shifts where the native previously had always been on days.

112

MERCURY

Mercury acts principally on the intellectual faculties. Mercury aspects stimulate the desire for travel and promote an interest in furthering one's studies. Will reveal changes that may take place in the manner of speaking, thinking, writing and communicating. Mercury will introduce new and varied outlets of interests simultaneously. Dealings with books, papers, important documents and the use of good or bad judgment in the making of decisions.

Change of attitude toward one's brothers, sisters, neighbors, close relations and young people. The affairs of siblings and those in the immediate environment. Co-workers, employees, working conditions, domestic pets and the affairs of aunts and uncles also come under the direction of Mercury.

When concerned with health, Mercury governs the nervous system, ulcers, gastric upsets, lungs, breathing problems, shoulders and arms.

The Sun advances steadily through the Zodiac at the rate of 1° per year and never retrogrades. Mercury, on the other hand, is not as dependable in its mean motion as the Sun. Progressed Mercury can turn retrograde in motion through progression, revert back, and in due time conjoin its own natal position. Mercury is a personal planet and when it conjuncts its own Longitudinal position at birth, care should be noted when applying the major transits, Eclipse and other progressed aspects that may be in force at the same time.

Natal Mercury will eventually change signs through progressions. However, Mercury will rarely venture more than one or two houses away from its natal position in the progressed chart. It will always huddle rather closely to the Progressed Sun's position.

Mercury conjuncts Ascendant: A conjunction between Progressed Mercury and Natal Ascendant can only occur if Natal Mercury is positioned in the Natal Eleventh or Twelfth House. As Progressed Mercury advances through the Zodiac from this natal position, it will eventually reach the conjunction of the Natal Ascendant. Naturally, should Mercury turn retrograde in motion, this can retard the process.

Should Natal Mercury be positioned in the Natal First or Second House, the Progressed Ascendant will advance through the Zodiac and eventually

113

conjoin the Natal Mercury. The latter position is easier to access for the possible age of occurrence as Natal Mercury retains its Longitudinal birth position, and one merely advances the Ascendant to Mercury's degree.

The age factor plays an important role for Mercury's energy is applied mainly to thought and learning. For example, a native with 28° Sagittarius on the Natal Ascendant and Natal Mercury is positioned in the First House in 4° Capricorn, one can surmise that the child will be approximately 6 years of age at the time of the conjunction. This marks the time of his first experience with the educational system, teachers and schoolmates. Should Natal Mercury be further advanced from the Ascendant than our example, the child may change schools, enter high school or college or graduate. One young man was 21 years of age when his Natal Mercury conjoined his Progressed Ascendant, and he received further education in Radar Control in the U. S. Air Force. His Natal Mercury was positioned in Aquarius, the sign of electronics.

In the general sense, this aspect denotes a very busy time. Many diversified interests and activities, some involving journeys or changes of residence, or of employment. Important papers must be signed, much in the line of paperwork, correspondences or letter writing. The affairs of a sibling may play an important role in the life of the native.

Mercury conjunct Midheaven: A conjunction between Progressed Mercury and Natal M.C. can only occur if Natal Mercury is positioned in the Natal Ninth or Eighth House. As Progressed Mercury advances through the Zodiac from this Natal position, it will eventually reach the conjunction of the Natal M.C. Naturally, should Mercury turn retrograde in motion, this can retard the process.

Should Natal Mercury be positioned in the Natal Tenth or Eleventh House, the Progressed M.C. will advance through the Zodiac and eventually conjoin the Natal Mercury. The latter position is easier to access for the possible age of occurrence as Natal Mercury retains its Longitudinal birth position, and one merely advances the M.C. to Mercury's degree.

This aspect is often associated with the birth of a brother or sister. Note the condition of Progressed Third, planets therein, its ruler, and aspects to Natal Mercury for confirmation.

Mercury conjoined with the M.C. can stimulate additional studies that will enhance present career. There is much activity concerned with business, correspondences and possible travel. The native may be placed in the role of an instructor in his line of business. If not as a teacher in a public school system, then perhaps in teaching others how to operate a certain type of machinery, or handle a routine set of details. This is generally a period in which a more than the average amount of paper work is involved, or perhaps, the signing of documents or contracts. Others may enter into business with a sibling, or work for an aunt or uncle.

Mercury conjunct Descendant: A conjunction between Progressed Mercury and Natal Descendant can only occur if Natal Mercury is positioned in the Natal Sixth or Fifth (but close to the Sixth House Cusp). As Progressed Mercury advances through the Zodiac from this Natal position, it will eventually reach the conjunction of the Natal Descendant. Naturally, should Mercury turn retrograde in motion, this will retard the process, or even prevent the conjunction from occurring.

Should Natal Mercury be positioned in the Natal Seventh or Eighth House, the Progressed Descendant will advance through the Zodiac and eventually conjoin the Natal Mercury. The latter position is far easier to access for the possible age of occurrence. Natal Mercury retains its Longitudinal birth position, and one merely advances the Descendant to Mercury's degree.

The Seventh House Cusp as does the First governs a grandparent, and nieces and nephews. It is not uncommon for a grandparent to become a source for mental concern should the ruler of the Progressed Fourth or Tenth also receive afflicting aspects while Mercury conjoins the Descendant. Indicating that the native's parent (4th or 10th) is worried about their parent (1st or 7th).

Should a niece or nephew be the main concern, one will find afflicting aspects linking the ruler of the Third House with the Seventh House Cusp. Or, the ruler of the Third House Cusp, or planets therein, will receive afflicting aspects at the same time that Natal Mercury conjoins the Descendant. The Third House is your sibling, the Seventh is their Fifth House of children.

The native may be drawn into the role of counselor, teacher, or have frequent dealings with young people. This is also an aspect of contacts with educators. The age factor should determine what grade level is involved.

Marriage is possible, especially if the ruler of the Natal or Progressed Seventh House Cusp is activated by progressed aspects.

Mercury will describe the potential marriage partner. They may be of a Gemini or Virgo type, highly nervous, and diversified in many fields of interest.

Mercury conjunct I. C.: A conjunction between Progressed Mercury and Natal Fourth House Cusp can only occur if Natal Mercury is positioned in the Natal Third or Second (but close to the Third House Cusp). As Progressed Mercury advances through the Zodiac from this Natal position, it will eventually reach the conjunction of the Natal I. C. Naturally, should Mercury turn retrograde in motion, this will retard the process. Or, even prevent the conjunction from occurring in a natural life span.

Should Natal Mercury be positioned in the Natal Fourth or Fifth House, the Progressed I. C. will advance through the Zodiac and eventually conjoin the Natal Mercury. The latter position is far easier to access for the possible age of occurrence. Natal Mercury retains its Longitudinal birth position, and one merely advances the I. C. to Mercury's degree.

The conjunction of Mercury and the I. C. instigates an active period within the family affairs; possible change of residence, much in the way of coming and going, communications involving a parent, the home or property. A busy time with paper work which may be handled in the home, as with insurance agents or busy executives who take extra work home. An office may be established in the home. The native may temporarily conduct classes in his home. Driving to and fro, writing letters and many phone conversations may have to be made in settling the affairs of a parent.

Mercury sextile or trine Ascendant/Descendant: This is an excellent period for thoughts and ideas in connection with writing, lecturing, teaching, or expansion of business if one is in a Mercury field (as in printing, radio, TV delivery service and other forms of inner city travel of communication).

This aspect brings into the native's sphere, new acquaintances of active imagination and good salesmanship. Important documents, letters, books or printed material will aid the native in some beneficial manner.

The native is possessed of good sound judgment, and capable of making clear cut decisions.

Success can be attained through additional studies. Such a favorable aspect might bring the financial assistance from a corporation to aid in obtaining a Master's Degree, or other various level of achievements. Scholarship awards are possible.

There is great ease and rapport in the ability to talk and exchange ideas with others, and with less chance of being misunderstood or misquoted. A natural harmony with all individuals under Third House matters, as with brothers, sisters, neighbors and close relations.

One of the best aspects for mental alertness, and for those who must project themselves to the public (as with salesmen, lecturers, politicians and public relations, or receptionist).

Mercury square, semi-square or sesqui-quadrate Ascendant/Descendant: This aspect can result in an inner degree of high nervous tension. The native tends to fret and worry over every little thing. Very often these matters are insignificant, but expanded out of proportion through the mental faculties.

This aspect is considered far more serious should Mercury afflict the Ascendant sign of which it rules, or the sign on the Descendant. For example, the native has 3° of Virgo on the Progressed Ascendant, and Natal Mercury in 3° Sagittarius is now squaring its own sign. Or, Mercury in Pisces squaring the Gemini Ascendant.

Someone or something within the immediate environment is making the Native extremely upset. This could be the native's job, parent, sibling or a co-worker. There is disharmony or an unfriendly attitude towards others. The tendency to come to conclusions without looking into the entire situation, often judging others wrongly or accusing them of misconduct. The native is too quick to criticize others. Should avoid spreading gossip and rumors and belittling or degrading another, whom the native feels has done them an injustice.

There may be a breakup or separation from a family member or a sibling due to gross misunderstandings.

At some time during this two or three year time span (depending upon the speed of the Ascendant Sign), the native may become obsessed over some kind of printed material (a book, bible or a letter), to which he may unreasonably place the importance of this material thing over the value of a personal relationship.

When Mercury afflicts the Ascendant, the native can misplace an attachment to a material thing rather than a person.

Petty gossip may take up a good deal of the native's time and should be avoided. There is also trouble through carlessness in speech and details, and not making oneself clearly understood.

This aspect can work on the health through the nervous system, and the lung area. If the native smokes, one should try to give it up at this time, for there may be some danger signals. Any tightening in the chest area, pain when breathing, or heavy coughing should be checked immediately by a physician.

Should the sign Virgo or Gemini be on the Descendant, then the Seventh House partner may be a source for concern, and their health should be given a thorough check-up.

Mercury sextile or trine M.C./I. C.: A possible chance for advancement in one's career that deals with teaching, writing, lecturing and general communication. Depending upon the sign placement of Mercury, the native may open an auto repair shop, a book store, a moped/bicycle shop, or perhaps a computer/ video outlet. In Libra, perhaps a cosmetic or hair stylist shop, or a florist.

The native feels an urge to be busy, and doing something with his spare time. This is an aspect of holding down two jobs simultaneously. Or, attending college and having a part time job. Scholarship awards are possible.

Change of residence or the purchase of a second home, perhaps an income property.

Mercury square, semi-square, sesqui-quadrate the M.C./I. C.: The native must exercise caution what is said to those in authority or connected with one's vocation, for the native may be misquoted or misunderstood. The native may be fraught with heavy work loads involving much detailed work that is taxing to the mentality.

Errors may result in shipping orders, communications go awry, and all prove costly in the business world. The native may be blamed and lose his position. Petty quarrels and gossips surrounding the affairs of superiors should be avoided.

Quarrels or constant bickerings can ensue among family members. Possible loss or separation through a sibling or a Gemini/Virgo type of parent.

Mercury conjunct Mercury: It is possible for Progressed Mercury to conjoin its own natal position. Mercury can turn retrograde in motion sometime after birth and regress back in due time, to its own natal position. Perhaps Mercury was retrograding at birth. Note when it turns direct and how soon will it conjoin its own natal position, after going forward.

Mercury is a personal planet, and the houses that it rules (both in the Natal and Progressed Chart) will be of paramount importance. Should the two Mercuries (as they are conjunct) receive an afflicting aspect, it will double the strength and compound the problem.

Nervous tension, non-alertness, and lack of attention to details can open up the native to possible accidents. Trouble through slanderous attacks and petty gossip. Misjudgment in the signing of important papers due to unnecessary pressure from others.

Arguments or separation from siblings and close relatives.

The favorable aspects will enhance the mental awareness of new studies and obtaining of additional degrees. All matters connected with printing, automobiles, transportation, and communication are favored.

Mercury sextile Mercury: This may never occur in many of the natal charts due to the possibility of Mercury's retrograde motion. It is possible, however, and it generally occurs around the age of 60 to 70. This is an aspect of mental alertness and intellectual stimulation. The native may be considering making changes within his immediate surroundings, such as relocating or adding an office to the present home. New studies, new educational programs and new hobbies, that involve manual dexterity or mental application, are introduced. The native may join an organization in which many field trips are undertaken or bus tours.

Depending upon the house placement and sign position of both Mercuries, the native and a sibling may decide to live together.

Mercury semi-square or square Mercury: The semi-square is likely to occur between the ages of 40 to 50 years of age depending upon the mean motion of Progressed Mercury. The latter will not square itself until later in life, generally between 70 to 90 years of age. In some charts, this may never occur due to Mercury's retrograde motion shortly after birth.

The native begins to have problems remembering things. Mental confusion or forgetfulness is the rule of thumb. There is the tendency to be inconsistent, irritable, overly critical and faultfinding. The native may change his mind frequently, much to the despair of others. The native may become demanding and difficult to please. Quick to judge, and less likely to admit his errors. The imagination runs overtime, and may indulge in idle gossip causing dissension among family members and siblings.

The native is extremely nervous and worries over insignificant matters. He may expand every imaginary illness out of proportion. Ulcers and gastric stomach may upset the system. The native should avoid smoking, for the lungs are now at a vulnerable risk (with both rulers afflicting one another).

Mercury opposition Mercury: Not possible.

Mercury inconjunct Mercury: Not possible.

Mercury conjunct or parallel Venus: Stimulates the mentality into artistic endeavors in the study of music, art or dancing.

This aspect increases social contacts with the general public. The native is tactful, outgoing, and considerate in his manner of speech. An excellent period for lecturers, salespersons, and those requiring a pleasant, amicable personality.

Women are likely to play an important role during this period. Many invitations are likely to be received to attend parties or social functions.

Mercury is a neutral planet, and requires an aspect from another planet to give a female or male connotation. Progressed Mercury in conjunction with natal or progressed Venus can indicate a possible birth of a sister.

Should this conjunction receive afflicting aspects from a major transit, an Eclipse or another progressed planet, there may be serious concerns surrounding the health or affairs of a sister or an aunt.

Possible disputes with women and especially a close relative.

In health, this aspect can affect the kidneys through overindulgence of the wrong foods.

Mercury semi-sextile or sextile Venus: As Mercury is a neutral planet, a semi-sextile can aid in linking the two to indicate a possible birth of a sister.

This can be verified by other progressed aspects in force at the same time. Look for a Progressed planet in Leo to sextile or trine the Natal or Progressed M.C. (a child, Leo, born to a parent, 10th House Cusp). Or a progressed planet in Gemini favorably aspecting the M.C. The Progressed Third House, planets therein or its ruler should provide additional insight, if indeed, a sister is to be a new addition to the family.

In general terms, Progressed Mercury sextile Natal or Progressed Venus, generates a busy sociable time with parties, weddings and showers to attend.

The native takes an interest in the fine arts, music or dancing. May purchase a musical instrument. There is greater tact, diplomacy, and consideration towards others. Excellent for those employed in the advertising, lecturing or public relations field.

Improvement may be experienced in the affairs of a sister, an aunt or other close relatives. The native's personal health and hygiene undergoes new dietary habits for improvement of appearance.

Mercury square or semi-square Venus: This is a period of time in which the native will have to be careful when dealing with women, especially a sister or a co-worker.

Lack of tact and consideration for others, or indulging in idle gossip can result in disputes, misunderstandings, and possible separation through a female friend, co-worker or sibling.

Excessive socializing while working may create inefficiency or the neglect of work and responsibility. The native will have to use care and good judgment in social, romance and business communications.

Possible difficulty through the occupational environment is apt to involve the employer, co-worker or a superior.

Health can suffer from incorrect dietary habits, and not drinking adequate amounts of water to maintain balance within the system.

Mercury opposition Venus: Not possible.

Mercury inconjunct Venus: Not possible.

Mercury conjunct or parallel Mars: This is an aspect of mental stimulation, and one can be easily stirred into action. The mind is quick to grasp new ideas, and is just as quick with the speech. They will usually have the last word in any argument.

With favorable aspects to the conjunction of Progressed Mercury and Natal or Progressed Mars, the energy level is at its best. Excellent for those interested in body building, sports or gymnastics.

This is also an aspect of developing new skills in the mechanical, technical or engineering trade. The mentality is open to new ideas and experiences. Will forge ahead with more than the usual amount of enthusiasm and courage.

Unfavorable aspects to this conjunction may indicate trouble and disputes with siblings. Possible accidents due to impulsive or impetuous actions.

The native may have to take a forceful stand on certain issues involving important documents or written contracts. May have to do much driving about or communicating in an attempt to clear up an upsetting matter.

This may be a period of time in one's life in which frequent mechanical defects with automobiles, machinery or appliances require constant repairing.

Something will happen that will cause the native great mental and nervous stress. Many heated arguments will result, upsetting the native's stomach and nervous system. The Progressed House position of Progressed Mercury, its sign containment and the House position, and sign of Natal Mars should provide some clue as to the situation. The houses they rule, should reveal the consequences of this matter.

Mercury sextile or trine Mars: A very resourceful aspect with a strong desire to express oneself through instructing, lecturing, or writing. There is mental energy and considerable initiative in the handling of affairs.

In a young man's chart, there could be an interest in developing skills in mechanical matters. Depending upon the house and sign placement, some may join the military service, or study for the police and fire department examination.

In a general sense, this is a successful period for the attainment of one's goal through the spirit of energetic application towards new enterprise with the power of determination.

Some individuals seek to enhance their health, and increase their energy level through vigorous exercise and a sensible diet. Either an exercise routine is adopted or a health spa is joined.

Mercury square, semi-square or sesqui-quadrate Mars: The mentality of Progressed Mercury is stimulated in the wrong manner through the square aspect with Natal or Progressed Mars.

Impulsive and rash behavior can create accidents and quarrels. There is a tendency to exaggerate, or accept challenges beyond the native's capacity.

The native should guard extremes of independence and wilfulness, which defies the following of rules and regulations. Obstinacy toward certain ideas and issues can involve the native in serious controversies and disputes.

In some cases, there is the tendency to act upon a given situation without proper forethought. These premature actions can cause trouble with police or through lawsuits.

121

The health problem centers around an increase in reflex-action and nervous irritability. There may be lack of proper rest and over taxing of the mind. Instead of acquiring a state of relaxation when it is time to retire at night, the native lies in bed mulling over the days events. This lack of proper rest adds to the high state of nervous tension.

Mercury opposes Mars: The native should avoid any unnecessary confrontations with siblings, neighbors and co-workers. Should be on the alert against possible trouble or treachery through a relative.

This is not a good time for signing of contracts, and the native should not permit others to coercive them into signing any type of agreements. Conclusions are reached too quickly.

Should either Progressed Mercury or Natal Mars rule the Natal or Progressed 2nd or 8th, be positioned therein, or be in the sign of Taurus or Scorpio, the native should not sign major agreements for purchases on the spur of the moment, or permit themselves to be pressured into doing so. Such rash and impetuous behavior will prove costly later.

Extra care and precaution should be taken in the maintaining of the car to avoid the possibility of accidents. Fast driving and dangerous risks should be avoided.

New undertakings will not go as well as expected. The native may be angered by unnecessary paper work, or feel that someone in his immediate environment may be hindering his chances for opening a business. Argumentativeness and a sarcastic manner will alienate others.

In health, one should guard against accidents to the hands and shoulders. Use care with machinery, lawnmowers, or other equipment with sharp blades. Take time out for proper rest.

Mercury inconjunct Mars: This aspect mainly affects the health through mental tension and irritability, that results in nervous disorders, ulcers and gastric disturbances.

Possible trouble through job related situations. The native may feel he is entitled to a certain position granted to another and retaliates.

An accident prone aspect in a job related situation, as with machinery, hot material, or through foolish lack of proper safety precaution. The native would be wise to conform with safety shoes and safety glasses, if he works in a large manufacturing plant.

Mercury conjunct or parallel Jupiter: An excellent period in which writing, teaching, higher education, religion, traveling and the handling of legal affairs are all favored.

The native may deal with letters and communications from others in faraway places. A favorable period for negotiations, contracts, and successful business transactions. New acquaintances of professional backgrounds will prove advantageous to future growth.

Should major transits (an Eclipse or a progressed aspect) afflict this conjunction, the native can get involved in a legal dispute over written or verbal statements.

Avoid any possibility of plagiarism or use of other people's material without written consent.

Impatience leads to errors of judgment, so this is not the best time for signing of legal contracts or making serious commitments. The native is likely to scatter his forces, and promise more than he can possibly deliver.

Possible concern over the health or welfare of a brother or sister-in-law or a sibling, who resides at a distance.

Mercury sextile or trine Jupiter: Excellent for dealing with the public. A good instructor capable of putting people at their ease. Gives social and general popularity and respect of their peers. May feel an urge to write. If already an author, the published material will be successful. Whatever enterprise the native undertakes at this time should be rewarding and gainful.

A favorable indication of fortunate events, awards, scholastic achievements, financial or successful gains, and general good fortune. Possible benefit through travel, foreign affairs and influential persons.

An excellent aspect for the handling of legal matters, negotiations and signing of important contracts; for opening a book store, mail order enterprise, print shop and other fields of communications.

There is clarity of the mind with the ability for deep and serious subjects. Good judgment is gained through comparison and education.

Mercury square, semi-square or sesqui-quadrate Jupiter: The native should be careful of written and verbal statements. He should make it a point to save all important papers, whether they appear to be so or not. Legal disputes may rise, and could prove costly if such a document must be produced but cannot be located.

Possible failure in business through negligence, lack of foresight, or inability to keep promises due to misrepresentation.

Not a good period for writing, promoting of books, or seeking favors from publishers.

If the native owns a company, he should be careful of dishonesty or unreliability of hired help, especially through their bookkeeper or salesperson for a possible loss that could lead to bankruptcy.

New enterprises and business ventures should not be attempted at this time.

Although the mind may be alert, it shows a lack of good judgment towards unreliable ideas. Many obstacles and difficulties may arise to hinder such an accomplishment, perhaps due to the lack of an educational background necessary to operate a business.

Any kind of investment or speculation is not advisable at this time.

Mercury opposition Jupiter: This is not a favorable time to enter into a new business. There is the tendency to rely too much on hunches and luck. The native is certain his ventures will succeed, while others may view his ideas in the exaggerated form, and therefore, hesitate to provide the necessary financial backing.

Care should be taken in signing of documents. The judgment is poor. Legal disputes can arise from the situation.

Travel plans, education, or published material may undergo revision. In-laws or siblings who live at a distance may be a source for concern.

Mercury inconjunct Jupiter: There is the tendency to take on too many projects. This forces the native to slack down on some of his promises, or there is failure in fulfillment of obligations.

The native undermines his health through the scattering of forces and disorganization of time, which takes its toll on proper rest.

Mercury conjunct or parallel Saturn: The conjunction of Progressed Mercury with Natal and Progressed Saturn serves to steady the mind, and produces profound thought in an orderly manner. Yet, at the same time when afflicted by other planets, creates mental depression, apprehension and suspicion of others.

The most noticeable influence is the desire to achieve personal ambition. The emotions are no longer moved by sympathy. The native has outlined a definite goal and purpose for himself. However, there may be some hindrance in achieving this task. An older individual, possibly a parent (if Mercury or Saturn should rule the Natal or Progressed Fourth or Tenth House Cusp), may require extra care and attention. The native "feels" it is his duty, whether rightly so or not, to handle this responsibility himself.

This can be an aspect of self-imposed restriction, if one is not alert to the implications. The native lacks foresight in seeking an alternative solution to his restrictive problems. Misplaced responsibilities burden the native and result in a delay of one's ambition, or is a direct loss of important opportunities.

124

The native should avoid becoming a recluse. The desire for solitude will prevail. If isolation seems appropriate or necessary, then this period of self-imposed restriction should be spent productively, as in the writing of a profound text book or in doing deep and heavy research.

Mercury sextile or trine Saturn: A good time to develop your writing skills, or return to further your education in the scientific, medical or government field.

There may be important papers that require careful handling. Now is the ideal time to take care of them and bring these matters to fruition.

This aspect endows strength of will, tact, persistence and determination with sound judgment. Ideas that have been pending for some time can now be put into action with surprising success.

Many short travels or correspondences undertaken now will promote business trends. It is possible the native may consider a business venture with a sibling, an aunt, uncle or with a parent.

Someone older than the native or from the native's past, will play an important role in the possibility of promoting a steadfast business.

Mercury square, semi-square or sesqui-quadrate Saturn: The native may be required to sign contracts during this time. He should understand that they will be legal and binding and therefore given serious deliberation to avoid making a serious error.

In some cases there may be hinderances or delays in getting a book published, frustrations in reaching agreements with contracts.

Although the native may be careful and persevering in business, there are unlooked for obstacles, disappointments and delays.

Lack of opportunity or assistance and unfavorable circumstances at a time when the native is in critical need.

Possible gossip or slander attacks upon the native's reputation. Disapproval of an authoritative figure.

Mental depression and a sense of loneliness due to failure in one's career or inability to make headway in one's personal aim.

The native may go through a period of doubt, frustration, mistrust, or lack of faith in others. There is a sense of despondency and becoming somewhat selfish, and one feels that others are taking unfair advantage of him.

The native works hard. He receives little recognition for his efforts, while others seem to reap the benefits with far less effort, even with the use of unscrupulous tactics.

Temporary health setbacks through frequent colds and a tired, rundown feeling. Should strive to exercise to build up one's stamina.

Mercury opposition Saturn: An opposition produces opposing forces that require difficult decisions. Some will have an effect upon the career, reputation and public image.

If possible, one should try to maintain a low profile, and avoid initiating any major changes or make any important decisions. Avoid legal disputes at all costs, even if others are gossiping or making slanderous remarks against your reputation.

Put your mind to tasks that require depth of thought perseverance and personal isolation, as in research or writing of profound subjects. You will emerge triumphantly when this aspect has subsided, and be well rewarded for your past efforts and hard work.

Avoid confrontations with figures of authority, siblings or a parent. Separations are possible, if one does not compromise. You may be blamed for loss of important papers or contracts due to mismanagement or misunderstandings in communication.

Health problems can stem through mental anxiety and mental depression and overwork.

Mercury inconjunct Saturn: This is an aspect of adaption and of service to others.

The native may become depressed due to frequent delays and hinderances in career advancements.

The native may be placed in a position in which he may have to assume responsibility of an ill parent, which further restricts progress in life.

Ill health can result from a sense of weariness due to over work. Trying to care for another, while at the same time, holding down a full time job.

The native feels unloved, unwanted, rejected and lonely. In retaliation, he may deliberately isolate himself.

A difficult situation may arise, causing one to withdraw from close contacts with co-workers and siblings.

Mercury conjunct or parallel Uranus: New and unique ideas stimulate the mentality. The mind is original, creative and inventive, open to new and advance studies or methods. There is an interest in Astrology or the writing of occult books. The purchase of a computer and possibly enrolling in a study course, to gain additional insight in computers.

The native may undertake new studies with the idea that it will open new doors, in his present vocation; or totally change his present career into a new line of endeavor, something that he has never tried before.

Travel will be spontaneous and hold surprising and unexpected experiences.

There may be the joining of a club or organization that takes frequent bus tours.

126

Letters, documents and unexpected communications may play an important role during this phase.

Afflicting aspects to this conjunction can result in sudden disputes or separation from a sibling or co-worker. Possible accidents while traveling or many unexpected or electrical problems with the automobile.

The native is very high strung in temperament. The mind is overly active and seldom rests at bedtime, leaving the native weary and nervous.

Mercury sextile or trine Uranus: A revolutionary mind. An inventive thinker with a talent for lecturing, teaching or writing books on topics of Astrology, the occult, mathematics, electronics or the general science.

Unexpected news, communications or short trips will be beneficial to the native.

Friends or clubs and organizations may inspire the native into taking unexpected and enjoyable travel tours.

Trips may be undertaken with a group of people for additional educational and learning purposes, as in the attending of conventions or seminars.

An exciting and unexpected event is likely to happen to a brother or sister.

Unexpected awards or recognition through a club or organization.

On the whole, this is a busy, eventful and happy period with many new friends of different background, stimulating the native's social circle.

Mercury square, semi-square or sesqui-quadrate Uranus: This can prove to be a serious obstacle to success chiefly due to one's lack of tact, lack of discretion or a stubborn, unyielding adherence to certain issues.

There is the tendency to wastefully over-tax the energy through too many projects, resulting in nervous tension and confusion.

The mentality is active and ingenious, but hindered through peculiar or extreme ideas that draws public criticism.

The native appears nervous and restless with a constant desire for new fields or new modes of operation, but the daring and defiant attitude defeats any successful attempt.

One may have to keep their opinions to themselves, for they appear unpopular to others at this time.

Caution should be exercised while driving, traveling or working with electrical equipment. This can be a dangerous aspect if not heeded wisely. The car may undergo frequent breakdowns due to battery, starter or electrical trouble.

The native may quit his membership with a club or organization due to misunderstandings. Possible loss or separation through friends. Unexpected troubles arise through a sibling, an aunt, an uncle or a co-worker.

127

Unexpected difficulties arise in one's field of occupation, as with sudden change of shifts or of departments, requiring the native to adjust to new situations and new co-workers.

Health upsets through inability to concentrate and difficulty in falling asleep, as the mind is constantly going. Highly nervous, often feels shaky inside, sometimes for no apparent reason.

Mercury opposition Uranus: There are sudden and unexpected moves, changes, upheavals and removals. The nature is restless, discontented, defiant and dissatisfied. This aspect may begin a new direction in life. An erratic desire for complete independence, to be free from former restrictions, routine and regulations.

Friends and family members find the native difficult to understand, and a break-up in relationships may result due to his new and unconventional standard of living.

New friends may replace the old, but they may be unreliable, unstable or eccentric, and may draw the native into serious trouble.

Note the house position of Progressed Mercury in the Natal Chart in opposition to the house position of Natal Uranus, and seek the consequences through the houses they rule in the Natal Chart.

Now, look in the Progressed Chart, and again, note the house position of Progressed Mercury in opposition to Progressed Uranus. The sign position of Progressed Mercury will afford a clue along with the houses both Mercury and Uranus rule in the Progressed Chart for the consequences of the action.

One must understand that Progressed Uranus does not advance too far from its natal Zodiac degree. Although Progressed Uranus will be in a different house in the Progressed Chart, Progressed Mercury will still remain quite close to its own natal position. It is for this reason that the sign position of Progressed Mercury is important along with the houses they both govern.

Both Natal and Progressed Charts should compliment one another, providing additional insight as to whom the individual may be, the circumstances of the matter and the ultimate consequence.

Mercury inconjunct Uranus: This is a non-conformist aspect. Disliking of routine and responsibilities. Cannot tolerate having a foreman or boss huddle over their shoulders while working. The native may become bored with present job situation and try to instigate changes others find disturbing. For example, striving to get a union in the shop or company when the co-workers are clearly against the idea.

The self-employed native, should try to establish regular working hours. Disorderly hours and routine leave little time for proper rest and relaxation, giving way to irritation, restlessness and nervousness.

Mercury conjunct or parallel Neptune: A beneficial aspect for the imaginative faculty, music, art, creative projects, photography and the study of nursing or medicine. This is an aspect of psychic ability and intuitive insight. The native may have an inner sense or foreboding to do/or not to do a certain thing.

In some cases he may be able to sense the thoughts of others and know intuitively if they are deceiving him.

This conjunction can have its dangerous points through mental confusion, self-deception and lack of clarity. Some may apply the use of mind expanding drugs, while others seek to escape from reality through over-indulgence in heavy drinking. The average individual may use ''sleep'' as a diversion from everyday problems and burdens, or build a dream world of fantasy as to what they think their life could be.

Short trips with an air of secrecy surrounding them, may take place. Important letters, communications or correspondences may become lost or misplaced. One should make it a point to read the fine print before signing any kind of legal documents to avoid misunderstandings.

A sibling may be on drugs, drink heavily, or develop an illness that is difficult to detect.

The native may develop a sensitivity to certain medication or require the taking of certain drugs to control a health problem.

Mercury sextile or trine Neptune: This endows a powerful imagination. The native develops a kind of sympathetic attitude towards others. Is gifted with intuitive thinking and mental perception. Has the art of visualization, in which they can invision in their mind how a certain project should be done, and then proceed to do so with ease and confidence.

An excellent aspect for poetry, creative writing, detective stories, music and art.

Letters, documents or correspondences that the native has forgotten about, or may contain secretive information will come to the fore and be of great beneficial assistance to the native.

Trips may be undertaken for educational purposes that will enhance the intuitive ability, as in attending psychic seminars or conventions.

An illness that was formerly difficult to treat will react favorably to new medication.

Strange or disturbing situations surrounding the affair of a brother or sister may be resolved.

An excellent aspect for the study of criminology, psychology, nursing or other scientific fields.

Mercury square, semi-square or sesqui-quadrate Neptune: The native should be careful in the signing of documents which may contain hidden or confused clauses.

Important papers may be lost, altered, misplaced or stolen from the native's possession to create an air of confusion, deception or hidden intrigue.

The native would be wise to exercise caution in speech, and avoid revealing personal plans before they are ready to be put into action.

Events are tangled, confused, hurried and strained. Not the best atmosphere for making important decisions.

The general tone is much mental anxiety and anguish. May waste valuable time fussing over insignificant matters. Unreliability creates difficulties in private and business affairs. Schemes are impractical, and best left alone for the time being. Take the time to check and re-check important information received, which may prove to be incorrect.

Difficulties may arise while taking short trips due to day dreaming, confusion and detours in which one gets lost or involved in a serious accident. The native should avoid the use of drugs, medication and alcoholic beverages while driving.

A sibling or other close relative may enter the hospital.

The native should choose his friends wisely and avoid those who will use him as a "sounding board" for their own personal problems.

Health problems can stem from sensitivity to certain medication or drugs. Do not reach for medication while under a state of mental confusion, you may take the wrong one, or forgotten that you already have taken the required dosage.

Mercury opposition Neptune: Slanderous and damaging remarks may be made against one's reputation. The native is totally unaware of what is happening, until others bring it to his attention. This may cause the native to react through outburst of angry resentments when he discovers that no one is going to come forward in his behalf.

The native then retreats into a self-imposed isolation, determined not to assist anyone again for he feels betrayed by those whom he considered close friends.

An opposition is a confrontation with someone. A physician, who may have difficulty determining the native's illness, perhaps prescribed the wrong medication. It is for this reason that one should always seek a second opinion when concerned with health problems that appear illusive.

Possible deception through a sibling or co-worker, or perhaps concerns over their confused state of affairs.

Travels and communication may have hidden overtones that suggest something is going on that deviates from the norm.

Mercury inconjunct Neptune: One must guard against drug abuse, excessive drinking, or errors in prescriptive drugs, which can react upon the mental state.

The native is highly susceptible to his work environment. Co-workers that are emotionally unstable, and use the native as a sounding board or create confusion with work related duties, will upset the native's mental state.

Sometimes a boss may induce the native into handling a job, that is far too taxing for his mentality. Or, one that involves a great deal of detailed work, that utterly confuses him.

The native may continue to work with the job because he feels he owes it to the company even though it is making him extremely nervous and is emotionally upsetting to his health.

Mercury conjunct or parallel Pluto: A powerhouse aspect. The mind is centered towards one main objective. A fanatical pursuit of one's plans. The native may become deeply interested in the unknown, the mysterious, or life after death and the occult.

May have to deal with insurance companies, an attorney for the handling of wills or an inheritance, or the IRS.

Many short trips, frequent phone calls and correspondences may be required to resolve an issue involving Social Security or Disability payments, alimony, retirement funds or joint finances.

Afflicting aspects to this conjunction may create a stubborn adherence to one's belief, even to the point of imposing them onto others. The native may lose a sibling, or one of the brothers or sisters may have to undergo surgery.

Mercury sextile or trine Pluto: This aspect opens the door to a new line of specialized thought, ideas and studies, never before considered. A probing mind with good powers of observation that can grasp a situation quickly and come to an immediate and sound conclusion.

This aspect enables the native to speak before a group of people with complete intellectual domination over the masses. The power to influence the public through the art of persuasion.

Many short trips or correspondences may be necessary in the successful dealing or solution of problems stemming from insurance companies, inheritance, social security, retirement funds, alimony or the IRS.

This is an aspect of a birth of a brother or sister if the rest of the chart agrees, or the affairs of a sibling changes for the better.

Mercury square, semi-square or sesqui-quadrate Pluto: This stimulates a high degree of mental stress and anxiety.

The native is placed in a position in which he must cope with many diversified factors that taxes his mentality to the extreme.

Fanatical demands are made upon him by family members who make additional inroads on his time along with a full time job. The native finds himself under extreme pressure in the handling of so many various tasks. His stomach reacts through gastric upsets and there is an inner shaky feeling that belies his exterior appearance.

At some time during this three year span of time, the native will have to make many disturbing decisions in regards to a family member. Sometimes there are no easy solutions to his decisions. As a result, he may have to seek the aid of an organization that deals with social security and disability or insurance benefits. Making frequent short trips and many phone calls and correspondences. In the end, it seems that all these efforts were for nothing. Either the petition was denied; or the person, for whom the native was applying this aid for, passes away.

A brother or sister, through some kind of underhanded trickery and deceit, will cheat the native out of his rightful inheritance.

The health could pose a problem with a possible mental breakdown if there is too much stress or overwork.

Mercury opposition Pluto: An aspect of disagreements over joint finances, insurance settlements, alimony payments, taxes and inheritance.

Favorable aspects to this opposition can bring additional revenue through work related activities. Perhaps a bonus for introducing a new and better method of operation, that will save the company large sums of money. Or, an award for turning in a co-worker, who is smuggling goods out of the plant. In this case, the opposition poses a decision that the native must make against a co-worker.

In extreme cases, the native may be asked to spy upon a fellow worker or a foreman and be rewarded for information divulged.

Trips and communications concerning matters to do with death is possible. One may lose a brother, a sister, or be concerned of their health and welfare.

An opposition can become a compromise, if the native is willing to yield a bit of his stubborn resistance towards others.

Mercury inconjunct Pluto: An aspect of adaption to changes in one's work-a-day world. New procedures may be introduced that are contrary to what the native has formerly applied. New equipment or new machinery may be brought in, that may affect the use of the arm and shoulder muscles to the extreme. Causing aches and pain, requiring these unused muscles to be restrengthened.

Bosses and co-workers may be overly demanding and critical of the native's work, demanding perfection when it is not possible.

The death of a co-worker may leave an impression upon the native who had been working extremely hard and long hours.

The native may have to partake of workers' compensation due to a company accident or related illness.

VENUS

Venus stimulates the emotions of love, sexual attraction, love of beautiful things and adornments, social affairs and functions. The ability to get along well with family relations. The striving for peace and harmony with the general public through tact, diplomacy, propriety and convention.

Venus favors marriage, business partnerships and an attraction to the opposite sex. All occupations dealing with art, music, flower shops, beauticians, cosmetics, interior decorating, jewelry, candy making, court reporters, attorneys, law and marriage counseling. Can bring a gain or a loss in dealing with women in general, whether they be friends, family relations, the wife or co-workers.

In a male's chart, Venus represents the type of women he would be attracted to. For example, Venus in Cancer would not indicate an interest in older women, for Venus is a young person, but merely makes her a mother. Therefore, a male nativity with Natal or Progressed Venus positioned in the sign of Cancer may be attracted to a young female who already has a child, not necessarily as a result of marriage.

When concerned with health, Venus governs the throat, mouth, oral cavity, thyroid glands, kidney, blood clot, bladder, circulation, urinary tract and veins.

Venus, in similar fashion with Mercury, is not dependable in its mean motion and can vary in speed and turn retrograde in progression. Thereby, holding back some of the promises through the applying sextiles and trines being offered in the Natal Chart.

Venus is a personal planet. It is of extreme importance if she should rejoin her natal longitudinal position in her retrograde motion through progression. Both Natal and Progressed Venus will be in the same sign and degree and naturally the same house position. Favorable or unfavorable aspects from major transits, an Eclipse or other progressed planets will react through the consequences of the houses Venus rules in the Natal and Progressed Charts. Both houses must be given serious consideration to determine the individual or circumstances that will come to the native's attention.

Natal Venus will eventually change signs through progression. However, Venus will rarely venture more than one or two houses away from its natal position in the progressed chart. Venus will always huddle rather closely to the Progressed Sun's position.

Venus conjuncts Ascendant: A conjunction between Progressed Venus and Natal Ascendant can only occur if Natal Venus is positioned in the Natal Eleventh or Twelfth House. As Progressed Venus advances through the Zodiac from this natal position, it will eventually reach the conjunction of the Natal Ascendant. Naturally, should Venus turn retrograde in motion, this can retard the process.

Should Natal Venus be positioned in the Natal First or Second House, the Progressed Ascendant will advance through the Zodiac and eventually conjoin the Natal Venus. The latter position is easier to access for the possible age of occurrence as Natal Venus retains its longitudinal birth position, and one merely advances the Ascendant to Venus's degree. Do take into consideration whether the Ascendant is of Long or Short Ascension, for this can advance or hold back the event a little.

Much depends upon the age of the nativity in question. One cannot say that a six year old child will hear the beckoning of romance. The conjunction at that age is more likely to introduce new playmates, learning to get along with others. An exciting year of beginning school and purchase of new clothes.

This is a vulnerable age, and parents should closely guard the child's dietary habits. It is important to maintain adequate amounts of fluid intake to keep the child's system in balance. This will help to avoid bladder and kidney infections. Afflicting aspects to the conjunction of Progress Venus and the Ascendant can be dangerous.

In adults, this aspect stimulates new hair style, clothes and a new vibrant personality. Friends are pleased with the new "you."

This aspect can open the door for marriage opportunities, but is not sufficient by itself. Confirmation is necessary with the rulers of the Natal or Progressed Seventh House Cusp or planets therein.

In general, this is a pleasurable period for gaiety, invitations and social parties. Women will play an important role during this trend.

Venus conjuncts Midheaven: A conjunction between Progressed Venus and Natal M.C. can only occur if Natal Venus is positioned in the Natal Ninth or Eighth House. As Progressed Venus advances through the Zodiac from this Natal position, it will eventually reach the conjunction of the Natal M.C. Naturally, should Venus turn retrograde in motion, this will retard the process.

135

Should Natal Venus be positioned in the Natal Tenth or Eleventh House, the Progressed M.C. will advance through the Zodiac and eventually conjoin the Natal Venus. The latter position is easier to access for the possible age of occurrence as Natal Venus retains its longitudinal birth position, and one merely advances the M.C. to Venus's degree.

Venus conjunct the M.C. is another opportunity for marriage. As in all cases, confirmation through progressions should bear this out. Check the condition of the Natal and Progressed Seventh House Cusp, its rulers and planets therein. What about the major transits or the Eclipse during this time span? Do they hold the promise of marriage? If already married, this may be birth of a child. The family increase may come through birth of a sibling, should Venus rule the Natal or Progressed Third House.

This is an aspect of increase in social functions. Some may come through one's career. General popularity in the public's eye.

Should an Eclipse or a major transit conjunct Venus and the M.C. or otherwise afflict the conjunction, the house that Venus rules will bear watching. Should Venus rule the Natal or Progressed 7th, in either male or female's chart, the spouse may be a source for concern. Should Venus be position in Leo, perhaps the marriage partner may have to undergo surgery on the eyes, back or heart.

Venus conjunct Descendant: A conjunction between Progressed Venus and Natal Descendant can only occur if Natal Venus is positioned in the Natal Sixth or Fifth (but close to the Sixth House Cusp). As Progressed Venus advances through the Zodiac from this Natal position, it will eventually reach the conjunction of the Natal Descendant. Naturally, should Venus turn retrograde in motion, this will retard the process. Or, even prevent the conjunction from occurring.

Should Natal Venus be positioned in the Natal Seventh or Eighth House, the Progressed Descendant will advance through the Zodiac and eventually conjoin the Natal Venus. The latter position is far easier to access for the possible age of occurrence, as Natal Venus retains its longitudinal birth position, and one merely advances the Descendant to Venus's degree.

Social functions are highly stimulated during this time span. One may join an association such as ''Parents without Partners,'' and perhaps be placed on the entertainment committee. As with the other two angular conjunctions, this too can inspire the opportunity for marriage. In a male's chart, she may be very young and attractive. In a female's chart, he may have the coloring of a Taurus or Libra. That is, he may have Taurus or Libra Sun, Rising, or Moon in Taurus or Libra or Venus positioned in the Natal First House.

As Venus conjoins the Descendant, it also opposes the Ascendant. Any afflicting aspects from a major planet, an Eclipse or other progressed planets may bring disharmony with a female. The native may have to come to terms with a female who is in opposition with the native's views. A compromise is necessary, or a separation will be eminent. The native may not agree with what he hears and even argue that the issues are out of balance. He may still have to yield for the sake of peace and harmony.

Venus conjunct the I. C.: A conjunction between Progressed Venus and Natal Fourth House Cusp can only occur if Natal Venus is positioned in the Natal Third or Second (but close to the Third House Cusp). As Progressed Venus advances through the Zodiac from this Natal position, it will eventually reach the conjunction of the Natal I. C. Naturally, should Venus turn retrograde in motion, this will retard the process. Or, even prevent the conjunction from occurring in a natural life span.

Should Natal Venus be positioned in the Natal Fourth or Fifth House, the Progressed I. C. will advance through the Zodiac and eventually conjoin the Natal Venus. The latter position is far easier to determine for the possible age of occurrence. Natal Venus retains its longitudinal birth position, and one merely advances the I. C. to Venus's degree.

Venus in conjunction with any angular house cusp can signify marriage if the condition of the Natal or Progressed Seventh House, its rulers or planets therein agree.

The Fourth House is the finishing of an old matter. Should Venus be position in Pisces for example, this may be the end of a clandestine affair. Venus in Leo, may indicate the departure of a child relocating to another state, getting married or leaving for college.

Others are inspired to re-decorate the home. If Venus receives no afflicting aspects at the time of this conjunction, this could be the most opportune time for buying or selling of home or property.

Venus sextile or trine the Ascendant/Descendant: A busy period of social functions, weddings, engagements and birth invitations. If the native is single, an opportunity for marriage. Possible gain through associations with women.

Finances are on the upward trend. The native takes pride in personal appearance and begins to dress more stylish.

Venus square, semi-square or sesqui-quadrate Ascendant/Descendant: One of the most difficult aspects should Venus also rule the Ascendant sign. The sign position of Natal Venus in square aspect with Progressed Ascendant (for example, Natal Venus in Cancer square Progressed Ascendant in Libra), or Progressed Venus in square aspect with Natal Ascendant (example, Venus in Leo square Natal Taurus Ascendant), should indicate the health or personal affair causing a crisis.

The implication of one's ruling planet afflicting its own sign is far more serious then having it in afflicting aspects with other signs. Venus in Cancer, one should look for malfunctions in the breast or stomach area.

Venus in Cancer can denote possible cysts or tumors in the breast or stomach area. Venus in Leo, possible back or eye problems. The blood pressure and heart should also be watched. Venus in Scorpio, the reproductive organs of the body, rectum and colon area.

Venus governs close relationships and it is possible that a love relation can be broken, a divorce or separation in marriage. Misunderstandings and conflicts with women in general. A feeling generates that one is losing their self-esteem and is no longer attractive to others.

If one belongs to an organization that places the native on the entertainment committee, the planning of social affairs and functions may make heavy demands upon the native's time. Lack of cooperation from others may lead to resentment and a feeling that the native is doing it all without adequate assistance.

The main point to consider is, if Venus is the ruler of the Ascendant sign in question, take precautionary measures and get a complete physical.

Venus sextile or trine the M.C. or I. C.: Indicates a period in which there is a general increase in prosperity and finances. If the native is employed when he comes before the public, this aspect can enhance popularity and public recognition.

As with any favorable aspect with an angular house cusp, this one can hold the promise of an engagement or marriage. An increase in the family through birth of a child or sibling.

Venus square, semi-square or sesqui-quadrate the M.C./I. C.: The public's image of the native is diminished. Associations with women can be a source of friction. Not the best aspect for anyone seeking a position requiring tact, diplomacy and a balanced judgment.

In the past, the native may have enjoyed handling the social affairs of the company's various functions. This aspect of Venus in conflict with the M.C. can create a withdrawal from wanting to serve on the entertainment committee. The native may feel that he has been far too imposed upon.

Too much socializing after hours can take its toll on the home environment. The busy executive or sales agent spending more than the average amount of time entertaining so called clients can leave the marriage in a questionable state. The husband or wife, may resent this time spent away from home. Or may feel that they are doing more than just patronizing a client.

One should guard against extravagance and unnecessary spending for finances will not be gainful at this time.

This aspect generally denotes conflicts in the emotional expression with the opposite sex. Possible trouble through business or marriage partner. There is also the tendency to be drawn into relationships with others who are lacking in good manners and refinement. The native will need to exercise selectivity in the choice of friends and romantic partners.

Venus conjunct Venus: Not of any great importance by itself. The conjunction of Progressed Venus and Natal Venus (due to retrograde motion) requires additional aspects from a major transit, an Eclipse or other Progressed planets to give it force.

The favorable aspects will highlight birth and wedding announcements. A pleasurable period for social affairs. Partnerships and new love interests are favored. Possible financial gains or gifts from someone.

The afflicting aspects to this conjunction stimulates misunderstandings in the marriage state or with a business partner. Separation or disappointments in romance. Loss through financial expenditures.

Venus sextile Venus: This may occur around the age of 60. At a time when the affairs of the marriage partner takes a turn for the better through possible retirement.

Should the native be single (widowed or divorced), this aspect stimulates the opportunity for romance and possible remarriage. Look to the Natal and Progressed Seventh and Ninth for confirmation, and the condition of their rulers and planets therein.

A time for family increase through birth of grandchildren. A pleasurable period for social and family gatherings.

Venus semi-square or square Venus: The semi-square can occur between 40 and 50, depending upon the mean motion of Venus. The square can occur between 70 to 90 years of age.

Not the best aspect for anyone who makes public appearances. There is lack of tact, diplomacy with the tendency to say the wrong thiong at the wrong time. The public's opinion will not be in the native's favor.

In a male's chart, he may be concerned with his wife's health or a female relative on the wife's side of the family.

A difficult period for health problems with the throat, mouth, thyroid, kidneys, urinary tract, blood clots and the bladder.

Venus opposition Venus: Not possible.

Venus inconjunct Venus: Not possible.

Venus conjunct or parallel Mars: Favorable aspects to this conjunction from major transits, an Eclipse or other progressed planets, can stimulate new business ventures that could prove financially rewarding.

The native may seek new and challenging ventures in which to increase personal funds.

The native may meet a new individual who will play an important role in one's life. Should this conjunction receive afflicting aspects, this new person may create serious trouble. Therefore, one should choose their companions and business partners wisely before venturing into an enterprise.

The conjunction of Progressed Venus with Natal Mars can prove to be a dangerous period for jealous acts of violence, if the conjunction is heavily afflicted.

The emotions are easily aroused and impulsiveness may lead to difficulty in connection with the affections.

There may be lack of discretion in choice of love relationships. Impulsive love affairs. Strong sensual nature that needs controlling. Inclination to immoderation. Possible seduction or unwanted pregnancy.

In a male's chart, possible disputes with women or a rift in the marriage.

In a child's chart, if this conjunction receives difficult aspects, it may indicate the possibility of sexual assault and abuse.

Venus sextile or trine Mars: An increase in social, romantic and sexual activities.

The native displays a greater degree of personal magnetism and vitality.

New energy may be applied towards artistic and creative pursuits along new lines of endeavors. Creative ideas may enhance personal income. Partnerships, marriage, engagements or a new love interest are favored.

Venus square, semi-square or sesqui-quadrate Mars: Indiscretion likely in love affairs. The native should guard against sensual or dangerous impulses.

Carelessness over money, overindulgence in sex or pursuit of pleasures can create problems in close relationships. The native may become overly concerned with satisfying one's own desires and fail to maintain an awareness of the feelings and needs of others.

Possible misunderstandings in marriage or with a business partner. Domestic friction is impossible. Separation or disappointments in romance and social affairs are likely. A period of extravagance and financial loss.

In a male's chart, women may be a source of conflict and the cause of much anxiety. Watch the temper, Venus in dire aspect with Mars can lead to heated arguments with those one loves the most, whether they be brother or sister, a child or the marriage partner.

This is a health hazard aspect for possible throat, kidney or bladder infections and an above average number of headaches or sinus attacks. Much depends upon the sign position of Progressed Venus and Natal Mars.

Care must be taken in selection of friends. There may be a preference for associations with people who are lacking in good taste and refinement. Individuals who may lower the native's own standard of moral behavior.

Venus opposition Mars: Venus is the planet of peace and harmony and adaptation. An opposition to Mars is not necessarily evil but more of a requirement of compromise. Unless one does so, circumstances occurring during this time span may force separation and eventually lead to a divorce. For example, the native's husband is in the military service and is sent overseas. They will be apart for an extended period. The wife must accept this new situation and compromise.

Perhaps both husband and wife are separated literally due to both working different shifts. They rarely see one another except on weekends. They must either learn to adapt to this upsetting situation until a workable solution is reached, or this opposition will cause a rift in the marriage.

Afflicting aspects from a major transit, an Eclipse or another progressed planet to this opposition may indicate quarrels and difficulties in marriage or business relationships.

Jealousy and mistrust can spark up between husband and wife, giving way to possible separation or divorce.

Venus inconjunct Mars: The native should be careful not to permit personal relationships, that are emotionally upsetting, to react upon the health or cause difficulties at work.

The native may have some discrepancy with monies earned through work. He should keep a record of his own of the total number of hours worked due to possible errors in the paycheck.

Disputes and disagreements over money connected with insurance settlements, alimony, taxes and joint finances are possible.

Venus conjunct or parallel Jupiter: This aspect increases personal popularity. Material or financial benefits may come through travel, individuals of a foreign background, higher education or lawsuits.

Romance is possible for the single individual with someone of a different background or professional standing. A good period for planning an extended vacation, taking a trip to far away places or for pleasurable pursuits.

Afflicting aspects to this conjunction may bring concerns of a female in-law or a relative who resides at a distance.

141

Slanderous statements made by a female may result in a lawsuit. One must be careful of extravagance and unnecessary expenditures.

Venus sextile or trine Jupiter: An aspect of opportunity for marriage if the Natal or Progressed Seventh House holds further confirmation.

An aspect that endows one with a warm, charming and magnetic quality. A romantic period for the college student.

There is the possibility of good fortune through football pools, lottery, church raffles, bingo games and other financial benefits that depend upon sheer stroke of luck.

An increase in popularity and public image. Excellent for individuals striving for re-election of an office or a public servant.

Possible gains through the creative arts, travel, lawsuits and in-laws.

Venus square, semi-square or sesqui-quadrate Jupiter: Stimulates undesirable conditions that attract people into your social circle which you would normally avoid.

The native should be careful not to foolishly permit other people to make impositions that could prove costly.

This aspect stimulates instability of emotions and a tendency to exaggerate through affections and finances. Love affairs, too much socializing and financial indiscretion can keep one in a constant state of turmoil.

Travel and vacations during this period may cost more than first anticipated.

The romantic partner may be experiencing difficulties with his or her divorce or other legal battles.

In-laws or close family relations that live at a distance may be subjected to financial problems.

Venus opposition Jupiter: An opposition calls for collaboration with another individual. With favorable aspects to this opposition, the native may gain financially through creative ideas and suggestions offered by another person. This can be a rewarding period for the native as long as the relationship remains on even keel.

Afflicting aspects to the opposition of Progressed Venus and Natal Jupiter is a period of time in which one spends too much on social affairs, travel and luxury items. A new car, for example may be necessary, but one may unwisely purchase the larger, more expensive model. This can create difficulties when the payments come due.

This is also a decision making aspect in which one must take an alternate course of action. For example, a child previously has selected a local college to attend with the idea of cutting expenses by living at home. Suddenly, the child decides that the selected college is no longer adequate. A large college is selected, one that is out-of-town. Decisions now have to be made concerning food, dormitory living and travel expenses. Circumstances have created a situation that increases expenditures for a college education.

A confrontation with a close member of the family or an in-law is possible. Lawsuits are best avoided, if at all possible.

Venus inconjunct Jupiter: At some time during this influence, legal steps may be undertaken to collect money that is overdue for services rendered. In some cases, other people may demand more of your time and services with no extra monetary compensation.

If the native is self employed, he should have a contract drawn, specifying labor and material costs to avoid possible disputes and misunderstandings.

A health aspect that can interfere with work due to over-indulgence in food, social affairs or alcohol. Extremes in certain foods can cause a flare-up in health condition due to sensitivity.

Venus conjunct or parallel Saturn: This aspect may last longer than the three years while Progressed Venus is applying, exact and separating from the conjunction of Natal Saturn. Depending upon the age of the native, this aspect can extend itself up to five years or more. For soon after Progressed Venus has left the conjunction of Natal Saturn, it will soon apply to the conjunction of Progressed Saturn.

If the native is young, this aspect may bond a close relationship between the child and an older person. According to the house and sign position and planets therein, this could be a grandparent, parent or an aunt or uncle.

The child is likely to express difficulty in emotional expression. May even become a loner, preferring one or two close playmates and the company of older family members. Any serious affliction to this conjunction in a child's chart may indicate loss of a parent or a close family member.

In an adult male's chart, an attraction to an older woman or one of Capricorn coloring and maturity. However, these same afflictions may indicate a cooling off of the present romantic relationship. Concern and worry that he is losing his love relationship.

A sense of duty and responsibility prevails and the native may "feel" he must take care of someone. This could be the assuming of responsibilities of younger brothers and sisters while both parents work. In other cases, the duty and care of one's own ailing parent.

Duty or some form of limitation may stop or alter the full expression of love and desire. Marriage plans may have to be set aside or delayed. The native may feel as though his love relationship has become a noose around his neck, through smothering possessiveness and suspicion.

Extreme caution is advised in all business and financial matters, which have a way of turning on the native in the form of heavy burdens and monetary restrictions.

Venus sextile or trine Saturn: Does not deny marriage, but presents an opportunity for one with someone of a May/December type. Where there is a vast difference in age. The love affair will be morally correct, discreet and loyal. A steady, dependable and reliable love relation. A long lasting relationship is indicated. If the association is not of vast difference in age, then it shall be someone the native has known before. Someone from the past that he has met at one time or another.

An excellent time for constructive success in financial matters. Benefits can be had through sound business ventures. An older person, a parent or a figure of authority will be of beneficial gain or opportunity for the native.

This is a culminating aspect of long standing issues. Perhaps a long term love affair finally ends in marriage. The final payment on a long drawn out mortgage, car or business loan.

Venus square, semi-square or sesqui-quadrate Saturn: Smothering possessiveness and jealousy complicates close relationships. The native suffers emotional difficulties and the affections are thwarted or broken off.

Not a good time for one seeking re-election to a political position. The public's opinion of the native is one of cold, detached indifference.

This is a very heavy aspect in which the native feels a deep sense of abandonment and loneliness. Friends seem to have forgotten him. A self-imposed restriction from all social functions and close attachments may be the native's choice.

Separation or bereavement through close members of the family is possible.

There may be heavy responsibilities or restrictions through a love relationship. For example, the girlfriend has an accident which leaves her crippled. The native may feel compelled to remain true and loyal even though the relationship may never be consumated into marriage.

To state it frankly, Progressed Venus in an afflicting aspect with Natal and Progressed Saturn is one of the most serious and depressing of the progressed configurations. The house and sign position will disclose the misfortune through the consequences of the houses that Venus and Saturn rules.

This aspect brings a very difficult period of unpopularity, reversals, disapprovals, disappointments and possible separation through marriage or business partnerships.

The native may go through a period of self-torment, doubt, lack of self-confidence and emotional inhibition.

Health problems in the area of kidney stones, obstruction in the throat (as a goitre or pulmonary emphysema) and crippling arthritis.

Venus opposes Saturn: An aspect of restriction. The native may be confined to the home with small children to care for and feel overworked, unloved and heavily burdened. Depressed with a situation that has no apparent solution.

Or, the restriction may come through an older member of the family as with an ill or demanding parent. The native may break off the love relationship because of the unfair restriction that this responsibility imposes upon him.

Everyone and everything appears to work against the native's interest.

The native will have to yield and compromise with older individuals, a parent, or a figure of authority. Otherwise, loss of job or affection, separation or serious quarrels will result.

Venus inconjunct Saturn: An inconjunct is an aspect of adaption to circumstances due to the required services that one must perform for others.

Venus in an inconjunct aspect with Natal or Progressed Saturn may require one to set aside temporarily, one's social, romantic or professional interest due to the care or responsibility of an ill member of the family.

In other cases, the native may have to work long hours which make it difficult for the native to carry on a decent social program, let alone a romantic interest. Venus may increase the earnings, but Saturn restricts the native from enjoying the fruits of his labors because there is never the time to do so.

There may be an imbalance between pleasure and work responsibilities. The native cannot attend certain social functions (weddings and parties) because he is required to work weekends. Or, he is placed on the night shift while his girlfriend works days. Restricting the emotional and romantic relationship. The native begins to worry and show concern that he may lose his girlfriend, for he fears the restriction of his night shift is creating a rift between them.

If one is expecting refund checks, dividends, sick benefits or other monetary compensations, there may be some delay in receiving the benefits, or the sum will not be as much as the native anticipated.

Venus conjuncts or parallel Uranus: There is the making of new friends through unconventional and unexpected circumstances. These individuals will be of a totally different background than the native has ever experienced before.

One's social life may be enhanced through the joining of various clubs and organizations. A new, sudden romantic attachment is possible and will greatly affect or change the native's life. There may be something unconventional or out of the ordinary surrounding the romantic interest.

Money or gifts may come through unusual sources or through unexpected events.

Afflicting aspects to this conjunction may indicate a termination of existing romantic relationships or business partnerships.

Monetary expenses go haywire and bills come in at the most unexpected and inopportune time.

Possible loss or separation through a close relationship. The house and sign position of Progressed Venus and Natal or Progressed Uranus may indicate who the person is, a.._ _: houses they rule sets the circumstances of the parting.

Venus sextile or trine Uranus: A period of great personal popularity, new romances, love at first sight, new friends, the joining of clubs and group activities and unexpected good fortune and gain are possible.

An aspect that stimulates new love interests that are unique, interesting and magnetic. Not conducive to marriage however, unless the condition of the Natal or Progressed Seventh House and planets therein, not only confirm, but add a stabilizing affect to the Venus/Uranus aspect.

Women will play an important role in connection with group organizations and introduce new social interests. The native may join a club or organization that takes an active part in the study of computers or Astrology.

Many new friends will be made which will enhance the social whirl and group activities. Women may receive unexpected and beneficial gain through finances or the receiving of gifts.

Venus square, semi-square or sesqui-quadrate Uranus: This aspect stimulates emotional difficulties. A tension that keeps the native constantly on edge, unable to relax. As a result, he undergoes periodic emotional, nervous storms.

The usual length of influence is three years, however, like the Saturn aspect, Venus will soon extend the afflicting aspect from Natal Uranus to Progressed Uranus, which may be a few degrees in difference, equal to an additional year or two.

This aspect does not deny the forming of a new love relation and friends, but rather stimulates the opportunity of meeting the wrong kind. Close relationships formed under this aspect are apt to cause the native great deal of financial loss. This may be due to the fact that he may be paying more attention to pleasurable times than to responsibilities at work.

These new found friends and attachments are likely to be odd, strange, unpredictable, eccentric and may behave most erratically.

Separations and the break-up of love affairs or close relationships are possible due to changeable disposition or lack of tact and diplomacy in dealing with others.

Divorce is possible or unexpected separation of business partners. There may be sudden and unexpected losses in financial matters. The native should curb the tendency towards extravagance and unnecessary spending on social affairs and pleasures.

Venus opposition Uranus: During this time span, the native may go through a period in which friends will take unfair advantage of the native's generosity and good nature. New friends are met that will make inroads on the native's time and personal funds. For example, the native is required to use his car for transportation of friends to social functions or back and forth to work with no monetary compensation for his kind deed or gasoline expenditures.

Venus is a female individual and in opposition to Natal or Progressed Uranus, loss, sorrow and separation through one is possible. The house and sign position of Venus and Uranus should disclose the circumstances and the houses they rule the consequences of the matter. Whether they be the mother, a sister, sister-in-law, aunt or a child and a friend.

The emotions are highly erratic, somewhat similar to a roller-coaster ride. One minute the native is on an emotional high and shortly after, drop down to an emotional pit of despair. This can take its toll on the health and nervous system.

Venus inconjunct Uranus: Female co-workers may thrust certain jobs upon the native's shoulders that they don't wish to tackle themselves. They may be the source of unexpected and upsetting conditions prevailing at work. Such as a work stoppage by refusing to work on certain electrical machinery or with computers.

If the native is not careful of records there may be unexpected loss of funds through errors in company funds, home expenses, or in payroll.

Unexpected financial loss through insurance settlements, alimony, inheritance or joint finances.

Venus conjunct or parallel Neptune: An emotionally sensitive period in one's life. Especially if one has Taurus, Libra or Pisces Rising, natally or on the Progressed Ascendant. The native wants very much to be loved and accepted by others. Instead, one may find themselves used, abused and taken for granted. An easy victim or prey for a con artist, or anyone for that matter, who seeks to confuse, deceive or exploit the native.

A dreamer, who lives within himself. One who seeks beauty in everything around him, yet cries silently alone when he discovers that life is cruel and ugly, and people are unfaithful.

A period in which sorrow and loneliness may enter the life. Depending upon the age, the native's helth may become delicate or he may develop a sensitivity to foods or medication. It is possible a child may be institutionalized or frequently ill.

With adults, possible disappointments or deception, through love affairs or the marriage partner. Before anyone should jump to conclusion, the Natal and Progressed Chart will bear the confirmation.

For illness of the mate, check the native's 12th, for this is the 6th House health of the 7th House marriage partner. Use both Natal and Progressed Charts. The sign on the 12th, planets therein and the aspects thereto should reveal the source of the illness. The rulers of the Natal and Progressed 12th reveal the consequences of the illness.

Afflictions from major transits, an Eclipse or another progressed planet to this conjunction may indicate a lengthy stay for someone in a sanitarium, clinic or institution. This could be the mother, sibling, aunt or a child. Generally, the person should leave this sheltered confinement about the time that Venus leaves the separating aspect of Progressed Neptune.

A favorable aspect for those dealing with creative art, music, dancing and hair styling.

Any romance entered into during this three to five year span, will have a clandestine coloring. Either one of the two parties are married. Or, if both are single, one may be ill and on medication, and perhaps will not reveal this source of affliction. Or, the romantic lover may be an abuser of drugs and a heavy drinker.

Kidney problems and water retention are possible health problems.

Venus sextile or trine Neptune: This aspect stimulates an interest in art, music, dancing, and dreams of a cottage by the lake or a chance for seclusion in beautiful surroundings.

Money may be spent on water beds or an aquarium of tropical fish. This configuration may open the door for romantic opportunities, but not necessarily conducive for marriage. The native, looking through rose colored glasses, views the new found love relationship as the most idealistic imaginable that he has ever encountered. As idyllic or inspiring this relationship may seem to be, this will only last until Progressed Venus has passed from the separating aspect of this sextile or trine with Neptune. Then, little by little, the true nature and idiosyncrasies of the love relation becomes apparent. The native begins to wonder what it was, that so magnetically induced the affair.

Money or gifts are received through unusual events, or as a result of forgotten incidents. Hospital bills are paid when the native thought there was no coverage for his particular illness, as with plastic surgery or psychiatry.

In general, this is a highly creative, emotional and romantic period. Financial gain or assistance through hidden resources.

Venus square, semi-square or sesqui-quadrate Neptune: Individuals generally act foolish under such an aspect. Undesirable friends or hidden affairs could damage one's reputation. The native is likely to be susceptible to the influence of others.

Disappointments and disillusioning experiences in love affairs. The native may be attracted to someone already married, who keeps the status a secret, or a great lover, dancer and charmer, an ideal love relationship in every sense except through loyalty. They could profess that you are the one and only, while seeing others at the same time.

This aspect causes great emotional trauma through deception and deceit. The possible meeting of someone who is emotionally, mentally or physically handicapped. They may be unemployed; and in their dire situation, they can sense your giving sympathetic and vulnerable nature. Either sex of the nativity may be subjected to this abuse of their generosity and time. For example, they move in with you, borrow your car, use your gasoline and even borrow money without any real intent of repayment.

A female client with Progressed Venus in Cancer squaring her Natal Neptune in Libra was supporting her unemployed boyfriend, who also lived with her. A power failure occurred at the office and she arrived home earlier than usual to find him in "her" bed with another girl.

This gal had been cautioned earlier in the year in being too gullible and trusting with the opposite sex. There was no getting past the stars in her eyes. She was convinced she had found the ideal love relation. He was so sensitive to her needs, gentle, loving and affectionate. Yes, she had been supporting him for the past six months and yes, he was having trouble finding suitable employment. After the glow was over, her one main regret when the affair finished was in giving her boyfriend all the stocks and bonds her father had left her.

In a child's chart or with those who may not yield to a clandestine affair, there is the possibility of hospital and the confinement of someone in the immediate family. A relative may be suffering from an illness that is difficult to diagnose or requiring a lengthy recuperation.

The native must guard against fraudulent schemes and the temptation to make money the easy way. There may be some confusion or hidden factors concerning personal finances. For example, the native pays off a debt, but the store claims they never received payment. Frequent communications and trips were necessary to clear up the matter only to discover that the store had placed the payment on another account with a similar name or number.

Should Venus or Neptune be in Scorpio, in the 8th House or ruler thereof, the native should check the insurance policy for adequate protection against theft, loss and damage.

A client with Progressed Venus in Scorpio square Natal Neptune in Leo, had a child who accidently set the house on fire. Unfortunately, the client did not read the fine print of her home insurance policy and later discovered that her beautiful and expensive furniture was not covered in the policy.

In health, one must drink plenty of water to maintain balance in the system and keep the kidneys flushed.

Venus opposes Neptune: This aspect stimulates confusion, deception, loss or separation through business, financial and love relationships.

The native is far too trusting and easily led and influenced. False rumors and scandalous statements against the native's reputation may bewilder him. Especially when the native feels they are unjustified, and he has done nothing against his open enemy to perpetrate such actions.

The native however, must carefully monitor his own actions. Any form of indiscretion against another at this time will surely reflect back at the native at a time when he least expects it.

This is a "Do unto others, as you would have them do unto you," type of aspect.

During this period of time, the native will discover undermining tactics going on about him. Perhaps someone is after his position and tries to discredit the native's ability.

The male nativity may feel that he has found the girl of his dreams, only to be disappointed through hidden and deceitful action on her part. For example, he calls her for a date, she accepts, and then she doesn't show up.

Emotional trauma and a tendency to withdraw from close relationships due to hurt feelings often accompany this aspect.

Venus inconjunct Neptune: A period of time in which the native wants to be well liked and appreciated by his superiors and co-workers. He may permit himself to be exploited by others in doing undesired tasks or working with equipment that the native does not like. Should this trend of self-sacrifice continue, the native will soon find he has undermined his health and has become emotionally unbalanced.

The native finds it difficult to say "no," when someone makes a plea to his sympathetic nature. Then, the native becomes angry with himself for not standing up for his own principles. He realizes after a time that others have coerced him into commitments that he totally dislikes. After the aspect of Progressed Venus separates from Natal or Progressed Neptune, the native will stand up for his own rights and demand to be taken off that job or machine that he has previously been forced into.

The native may come in contact with co-workers who are highly emotional and unstable or going through a confused state of affairs. It would be wise to avoid these type of individuals who may try to use the native as a "sounding board."

Venus conjunct or parallel Pluto: This is an aspect of a major turning point in one's life. Affections are likely to undergo upheavals and changes in connection with one's marriage partner and attitude towards love relationships.

This aspect stimulates certain secret passional and emotional desires. Accentuates attraction to the opposite sex and an inner compulsion to seek new and different romantic companionships.

An aspect of jealousy and possessiveness, with the tendency to go to the extremes. This is no middle of the road emotion, it is either hot or cold, love or hate. The intensity is so strong that if someone does not return your love you will dislike them completely and may even seek revenge.

The native develops an aura of mystery and magnetic attraction.

Favorable aspects to the conjunction of Progressed Venus and Pluto may indicate an inheritance or some kind of financial gain. Possible through an insurance settlement, alimony or other joint financial situations.

Venus sextile or trine Pluto: Stimulates a positive turning point with close associates, the marriage partner and through love affairs.

Endows the native with an exceptional magnetic attractiveness.

Monetary gain or inheritance from a close female associate. An aspect of creativity and artistic talents.

There is the possibility of sexual changes in which the female native no longer desires further birth of children and undergoes sterilization. Or, one will undergo surgery to increase the possibility of having a child. When volunteer sterilization is undertaken, it is for sexual freedom from worry of unwanted pregnancy and enhancement of sexual awareness and enjoyment.

Venus square, semi-square or sesqui-quadrate Pluto: The feelings become intensified, leaving little room for "middle of the road" emotions. The native is inclined to go all out in regards to matters and individuals that touch or otherwise affect his life.

Disturbing changes involving a love relationship is likely to produce deep emotional conflicts. Trouble, reversals and unpleasantness in the emotions. Intrigues and faithlessness may result in divorce or separation.

Obstructions create disturbing conditions with financial situations. Loan payments become overdue, or an application for a loan or a second mortgage may be denied.

Conflicts may arise over income tax, alimony, insurance settlements and other joint financial interests.

In health, a female family member may have trouble with the ovaries, an infection or undergo surgical repair. Should there be confirmation with the Fifth House, possible miscarriage or a hysterectomy.

Venus opposes Pluto: Changes in close relationships in which the native feels his marriage partner or love relationship is becoming increasingly difficult to understand. The marriage partner or love relation may become overly jealous or possessive and make excessive demands upon you and your time.

This aspect does not necessarily have to lead to a divorce or separation, if the native seeks a compromising solution to this dictatorial attitude of the mate.

A female may harbor jealous tendencies and try to undermine your professional career or standing in the community.

Contracts should be signed with the utmost care to avoid any possibility of a financial loss or burdens through heavy commitments.

Venus inconjunct Pluto: An emotional suffering through the illness of or departure of a close member of the family or a love relationship.

Possible sexual harassment through superiors or co-workers. Monetary loss through sex discrimination, in which, someone of the opposite sex is given an advancement or a pay raise that you feel should be yours.

This aspect can create an obsession that someone has a personal possession of yours or something belonging to the deceased. This idea may drive a wedge between you and this person as you are obstinate in your belief that they are holding or keeping this item from you, which you feel is rightfully yours.

In health, possible infection or damage to the generative organs, which may require surgical repair.

MARS

Mars is the principle planet of energy in the chart. The provider of strength and endurance in the accomplishment of arduous tasks. How one channels this energy and the usage in which it will be applied is determined by the Natal House placement, its sign position and aspects thereto.

Young people have the greatest difficulty in the proper channeling of Mar's energy. They often misdirect this energy through impulsive, impetuous and impatient behavior, giving way to flare-ups of temper and a quarrelsome nature. Sometimes there is an overly aggressive or arrogant manner that resents any hint of control of their freedom and independence. Defiant attitudes towards a figure of authority whom they feel is trying to boss or restrict them.

As these young people get older, they begin to realize that this type of behavior and attitude is not conducive to success. The Progressed Chart reveals the manner in which the native changes, and applies the positive uses of Mars' energy.

Mars is the stimulator of new ventures and undertakings with the capacity to get them off the ground floor. The determination of Mars is formidable, remaining strong, only as long as the project continues to be of a challenge.

It is unfortunate that this exciting and adventurous planet is also an indicator of danger. When afflicted, accidents, cuts and bruises, fires, murders, shootings and robbery, rape, quarrels and contention are just a few of the difficulties associated with Mars.

Mars governs young men as a rule, the Armed Forces, police and fire department, the butcher and barber and anyone else who uses sharp instruments in his line of work: iron workers, machinist and engineers, fighters and bullies.

When concerned with health, if afflicted, Mars can induce high fevers, inflammations, burns, cuts, headaches and sinus conditions. It is associated with surgical operations. If Mars is in Aries, surgery on the head or face; Taurus, the throat; Gemini, the hands and shoulders or lungs; Cancer, chest and stomach; Leo, the eyes, back or heart surgery; Virgo, ulcers and intestines; Libra, kidney and blood clots; Scorpio, the sexual organs and rectum; Sagittarius, the hips, liver or sciatic nerve; Capricorn, the knees, pins in the bony joints and trouble through teeth extraction; Aquarius, abortion, ankles, and muscles; Pisces, the feet, toes, bunions and related problems.

Mars is the last of the personal planets. In similar fashion with Venus and Mercury, is not dependable in its mean motion and can vary in speed and turn retrograde in progression. Thereby, holding back some of the promises through the applying sextiles and trines being offered in the Natal Chart.

It is possible for Mars to rejoin itself through retrograde or direct motion, returning back to the same longitudinal position that it held at birth. In itself, this position is not important. However, favorable or unfavorable aspects to both Natal and Progressed Mars in the same degree, can initiate immediate reaction. The house and sign position of Natal and Progressed Mars will indicate the matter and the house position of Aries will reveal the consequences of the event.

Natal Mars will eventually change signs, unless under heavy retrograde motion. It may not venture far from its own Natal position due to its faster rate of motion. As the degrees on the houses advances every year, so does the planet Mars.

Mars conjuncts Ascendant: A conjunction between Progressed Mars and Natal Ascendant can only occur if Natal Mars is positioned in the Natal Eleventh or Twelfth House. As Progressed Mars advances through the Zodiac from this natal position, it will eventually reach the conjunction of the Natal Ascendant. Naturally, should Mars turn retrograde in motion, this can retard the process.

Should Natal Mars be positioned in the Natal First or Second House, the Progressed Ascendant will advance through the Zodiac and eventually conjoin the Natal Mars. The latter position is easier to access for the possible age of occurrence as Natal Mars retains its longitudinal birth position, and one merely advances the Ascendant to Mars' degree. Do take into consideration whether the Ascendant is one of Long or Short Ascension, for this can advance or hold back the event.

This aspect stimulates new enterprise, self-assertiveness and personal action. The physical energy level is high, therefore, new projects requiring physical exertion can be tackled at this time.

The personality becomes somewhat aggressive and forceful, a fighting, competitive spirit. There is the urge to accomplish something and may plunge boldly into situations without considering the consequences. There is a desire to lead, but other people may resent what they consider, the native's forceful action and bossiness. The end result is friction and confrontations. Tact and diplomacy will be required in the handling of this aspect.

Afflictions to this conjunction of Mars and Ascendant may instigate danger of injuries to the head or parts of the body governed by the sign position of Mars.

In a child's chart, this aspect may induce serious illness as scarlet fever, measles, smallpox and sudden high fevers.

154

Mars conjunct Midheaven: A conjunction between Progressed Mars and Natal. M.C. can only occur if Natal Mars is positioned in the Natal Ninth or Eighth House. As Progressed Mars advances through the Zodiac from this Natal position, it will eventually reach the conjunction of the Natal M.C. Naturally, should Mars turn retrograde in motion, this will retard the process.

Should Natal Mars be positioned in the Natal Tenth or Eleventh House, the Progressed M.C. will advance through the Zodiac and eventually conjoin the Natal Mars. The latter position is easier to access for the possible age of occurrence as Natal Mars retains its longitudinal birth position and one merely advances the M.C. to Mars' degree.

This aspect can offer a new and challenging experience and changes through bosses and close associates, some of which may be the source of great aggravation and strife.

This aspect stimulates a vigorous pursuit of one's personal aims and objectives. Yet, at the same time, one may be forced to adjust to new circumstances and conditions.

A good period in which to pursue commensurations and negotiations in connection with corporations and business affairs.

Afflictions to this conjunction of Mars and the M.C. can manifest through difficult and upsetting situations concerned with one's profession.

A young man, whose description should fit the sign position of Progressed Mars, may be the source of conflict with one's professional career.

A boss or parent may have to undergo a surgical operation.

The native may decide on plastic surgery or other corrective surgery to improve the facial appearance. This may be desirable for those who appear before the camera, as a model, a TV personality or a movie star.

An excellent aspect for anyone wishing to join the military service, the fire department or the police force.

Mars conjunct Descendant: A conjunction between Progressed Mars and Natal Descendant can only occur if Natal Mars is positioned in the Natal Sixth or Fifth (but close to the Sixth House Cusp). As Progressed Mars advances through the Zodiac from this Natal position, it will eventually reach the conjunction of the Natal Descendant. Naturally, should Mars turn retrograde in motion, this will retard the process. Or, even prevent the conjunction from occurring.

Should Natal Mars be positioned in the Natal Seventh or Eighth House, the Progressed Descendant will advance through the Zodiac and eventually conjoin the Natal Mars. The latter position is far easier to access for the possible age of occurrence, as Natal Mars retains its longitudinal birth position and one merely advances the Descendant to Mars' degree.

This aspect may interest the native into forming a partnership with an exceptionally energetic individual. However, quarrels are likely to occur and should be controlled.

This may stimulate an opportunity for marriage in a female's chart. She is likely to meet an industrious, active man, who seeks to extend personal initiative and authority. One who will not tolerate being bossed. He may have a scar or mole on his head or face or on the part of the body indicated by the sign position of Progressed Mars. He could be a type of person who may ignore the feelings of others in pursuit of his own desires.

Afflictions to this conjunction of Mars and Descendant, may indicate many quarrels and strife after marriage.

If already married, the marriage partner experiences an increase in energy and ambition, to succeed in professional or business affairs. They may display rash and impulsive behavior. Carelessness on their part may lead to an accident or injury. They may arouse opposition and resentment because of a tendency to disregard the personal independence of the native.

This position of Progressed Mars may indicate difficulty in social, romantic marriage and business relationships.

Unfavorable aspects may bring about possible violence, quarrels and strained relationships with men in general.

A tendency to suffer accidents, injury, abuse and theft through another person.

Mars conjunct the I. C.: A conjunction between Progressed Mars and Natal Fourth House Cusp can only occur if Natal Mars is positioned in the Natal Third or Second. As Progressed Mars advances through the Zodiac from this Natal position, it will eventually reach the conjunction of the Natal I. C. Naturally, should Mars turn retrograde in motion, this will retard the process, or even prevent the conjunction from occurring in a natural life span.

Should Natal Mars be positioned in the Natal Fourth or Fifth House, the Progressed I. C. will advance through the Zodiac and eventually conjoin the Natal Mars. The latter position is far easier to determine for the possible age of occurrence. Natal Mars retains its longitudinal birth position and one merely advances the I. C. to Mars' degree.

This aspect stimulates activities within the family circle. Favorable aspects to this conjunction will initiate improvements in the home. Success in personal handling of real estate and domestic responsibilities. A good time to purchase or sell property.

Afflictions to this conjunction may induce possible death of a parent by accident, a serious illness or a surgical operation. This aspect will not manifest such violent reactions by itself but requires additional feedback through other progressed aspects in force by the same time.

Quarrels and dissension in the domestic sphere or with a parent.

Possible fire or serious damage to home and property.

The native becomes easily agitated by petty, daily annoyances of household members and family affairs.

In the nativity of a young person, this aspect may stimulate emotional confrontations with a parent and a desire to run away or leave home.

One should guard against the possibility of fires, theft and other serious occurrences involving home and possessions.

Mars sextile or trine the Ascendant/Descendant: Stimulates an active spirit of new enterprise, ambition and the realization of personal plans. Favorable for initiating action that inspires cooperation through marriage and business partnerships.

The native develops a frank and direct manner in self-expression and in dealings with others. There is the desire to take the lead in new enterprises and ventures. A very active period in one's life in which there are quick responses to their accomplishments.

This aspect increases invitations to social gatherings and parties through the power of personal attraction.

In a female's chart, this configuration holds great promise of marriage to a man of positive Arian qualities. He may have Aries Rising, Sun or Moon in Aries or Mars natally in the First House. If already married, there is the possibility of birth of a male child.

Men may play an important role in helping one to achieve a personal goal or objective.

The health and vitality is excellent with super abundant energy. An excellent time to attack projects requiring personal attention, decisive action and physical endurance.

Mars square, semi-square or sesqui-quadrate the Ascendant/Descendant: Can be a dangerous period, giving way to accidents and arguments, due to carelessness or rash behavior, not a favorable aspect for marriage.

There is misuse and wasted energy and an inclination to become violent physically.

Unwise premature action can result in separation through a business partner and suffer a professional loss.

Men in general will not be conducive to your well being. May bring about serious conflicts that can lead to loss of temper and physical blows exchanged.

The native or the marriage partner may require a surgical operation. Check the condition of the 1st House and the 6th, planets therein and their ruler for the circumstances surrounding the illness of the native. If free from affliction, then check the 7th and 12th Houses, planets therein, aspects thereto and the rulers for the consequences of the partner's illness. If no confirmation concerning the 7th House, then check the major transits and Eclipse that may afflict the rulers of either the 1st or the 7th House during the three year span that Progressed Mars afflicts the Asc./Dec.

Domestic affairs and family relations may become unsettled, create arguments or become troublesome.

Over activity, tension and extreme excitement can induce sudden attacks or migraine headaches. Sinus conditions and inflammation or fevers tend to aggravage the health.

Mars sextile or trine M.C./I. C.: Stimulates the attainment of success and recognition. The ability to grasp an opportunity quickly, and to act upon it. May advance to a position of authority due to sound judgment in career matters.

The native develops a dynamic energy level, with a tireless effort towards a certain goal or achievement.

Aggressive action in the positive sense in an attempt to achieve personal success.

There is an increase in activity in the domestic sphere. Possible birth of a male child. Marriage takes place among one of the family members residing in the home base.

May put forth its energy in home improvement and decorating. An excellent time to purchase or sell real estate and property.

A man will play an important role in helping the native achieve worldly success.

Positive changes in the home that includes a male individual entering into the family circle.

Mars square, semi-square or sesqui-quadrate M.C./I. C.: A very frustrating, aggravating time for work and business and with bosses or a parent.

The native may feel that the employer or a figure of authority, is imposing heavy work loads of responsibility.

Caution and care must be exercised to avoid accidents and injuries with the use of power tools and machinery that have sharp, cutting edges.

Possible suspension of work and difficulty or obstacles in obtaining new employment. May have to accept hard, manual labor for the time being.

There is a struggle between domestic duties and personal interests. Disharmony between a parent, partner, husband, father, boyfriend or a male companion.

Possible illness or death of a male member of the family.

Stirs up the emotions which may lead to excesses in food or drink. Petty arguments may lead to domestic brawls and possible violence, trouble and dissension with family members, and arguments over property rights or boundary lines.

Health problems through obstruction of vitality, weakness and inactivity. Possible teeth or skin eruptions or infections.

Mars conjuncts Mars: This is the last of the personal planets. Progressed Mars as with Venus and Mercury can advance in the Zodiac, and through retrograde motion, revert back to its natal longitudinal position. Should Mars be retrograde at birth, check in the Ephemeris for the year of birth to determine if Progressed Mars will go direct, and try to determine when it may return to conjunct its own Natal position.

By itself, this is not considered a dangerous configuration. One should, however, keep a watchful eye on the major transits, an Eclipse or other progressed planets that may afflict the conjunction of both Natal and Progressed Mars.

Unfavorable aspects can induce accidents, serious arguments and confrontations with others. Much depends upon the two houses that Mars rules in the Natal and Progressed Chart.

Favorable aspects to this conjunction may instigate extraordinary energy towards some new, personal and progressive enterprise.

Mars sextile Mars: Mars is likely to occur around the age of 60 to 65 in which the native makes new changes in his life through possible retirement.

The general health and vitality is good. If this takes place in a female's chart, and she is single, there is the opportunity for marriage or re-marriage.

This is also an aspect of an increase in the family with a possible birth of a grandchild, generally a male or a very independent female child.

ALL OTHER ASPECTS BETWEEN NATAL AND PROGRESSED MARS ARE NOT POSSIBLE.

Mars conjunct or parallel Jupiter: An aspect of great mental and physical exertion directed toward successful business and professional advancement.

Stimulates an active interest in sports, travel, religion and higher education. A good aspect for handling mechanical work that requires technical skill and know-how.

Men of a professional background and wealth or with a foreign accent will play a dominant role in the native's life during this span of time. An aspect of increase through birth or marriage.

Unfavorable aspects to this conjunction may result in legal disputes. Seeking of legal counsel because a manufacturing company fails to correct a mechanical defect in their product.

Possible concern or danger of accidents in regards to a brother-in-law or a close relative residing at a distance.

This is not the best time for travel or exertions with sports and heavy exercise equipment.

Mars sextile or trine Jupiter: Favorable for expansion and promotional interest of professional, legal, religious or education affairs.

Possible gain through travel, a new enterprise and publications. Personal action and quick decision bring about positive transactions through a stroke of luck.

Intuitive insight and hunches will play an important role by drawing the native into an advantageous situation at a propitious time.

Possible gifts or a successful settlement of legal action in the native's behalf.

A favorable outlook for love, marriage and getting engaged or births in the family.

Foreigners, people of a different color or background, successful and wealthy individuals and highly educated people will be fortunate for the native through some lucky course of action.

Mars square, semi-square, sesqui-quadrate Jupiter: A tendency to be overly confident and possibly over extend oneself in career or business.

Danger of a financial loss or one's professional reputation. On occasion, the native may act impulsively and aggressively, creating conflicts with employers, police, or other authoritative figures.

The native must cultivate an attitude of tact and diplomacy and moderation. Avoid arguments and physical confrontations.

Not favorable for long journeys, lawsuits or expressing one's personal opinion publicly or through written material and articles. The latter will be done in haste without proper forethought and later, suffer repercussions.

Injury and accidents are possible. Some may involve large equipment, semi-trucks, vans or motor homes.

Serious conflicts through foreigners, persons of a different race or color, learned and educated people, publishers and people of prominence.

Extravagance and squandering should be kept to a minimum.

A brother-in-law, or someone close to the native who may live in a distant city, may require a surgical operation.

One must bear in mind, that shortly after Mars afflicts Natal Jupiter, it will eventually approach the same afflicting aspect with Progressed Jupiter. Depending upon the age of the native, this can be a continuous 3 to 5 years of effectiveness. Or, if the native is older and Jupiter is more than a few degrees away from its Natal position, there may be several years of relief before the second afflicting aspect begins. Major transits are one of the clues as to whom the situation might involve. A major transit occurring at the first afflicting aspect of Mars and Jupiter may be different than those a few years later when this afflicting aspect is repeated.

The effects on the health are likely to be through over-exertion through work and play, and improper rest, blood and liver disorders from lack of moderation and danger through fires and accidents.

Mars opposition Jupiter: An inclination to rebel against rules and regulations and with those who represent a figure of authority.

Possible loss through divorce, separation, disagreements, litigation, theft or over-extension of credit.

Journeys may involve accidents or danger. Trips or vacations may prove more costly than first anticipated.

Trouble through in-laws, foreigners and individuals of a different background or social level.

The native should exercise caution with written and spoken statements that could be libelous. Impulsive and premature actions can be the native's downfall.

May go to the extreme and suffer losses resulting from over-optimism or gambling.

Mars inconjunct Jupiter: Liability may go to the extremes and act on impulse creating difficulties through work, resulting in recklessness and irresponsible actions that can cause accidents.

Quarrels with co-workers or supervisors make for strained relationships. The native should avoid the temptation to boss others.

Inability to settle down and finish tasks can hold back progress at work.

Over excitement can react on the health. Possible accidents, injury to the part of the body governed by the sign position of Mars.

Mars conjunct or parallel Saturn: Personal energy is applied towards the achievement of one's desire, ambition and career advancement.

There is the ability to work hard and in an isolated condition, if necessary, to complete a task. The native may come in contact with heavy or large machinery, metal products, hydraulics, the military or government projects during this period.

Should this conjunction receive unfavorable aspects, separation and grief is possible through an older member of the family, generally a male parent.

Progressed Mars conjoined with Natal or Progressed Saturn is a powerful configuration, and in some cases, can be dangerous.

An influential man can play a destructive role in the native's affairs.

This combination can induce heavy responsibilities, physical suffering, restrictions and delays in achieving personal aims. Severe despondency due to lack of advancement in career and many setbacks.

Personal activities directed towards a certain goal appears to be restricted and hindered by circumstances during this period of time. It may be necessary to try and work around these difficulties and try to persevere in overcoming them.

Any advancement during this time is accompanied by great stress and hard work.

Health setback through chronic conditions. An accident includes broken bones and bruises through falls.

In extreme cases, danger through fires, sunburn, stabbing, cuts and blows. Severe skin problems may also present itself.

Mars sextile or trine Saturn: An opportunity for new enterprise and career changes through the assistance of a powerful and important man. The native wants to establish a firm foundation with lasting benefits.

There are indications that this project has been in the back of the native's mind for some time. This favorable configuration, set off by Progressed Mars, gave it the necessary force to put it into action.

The native appears to others to become more organized. There is self-discipline in handling of tasks connected with work and business.

A good aspect for a new enterprise that requires long hours and hard work to get it off the ground floor. The native now has the physical endurance to tackle arduous jobs that would not seem possible before.

The degree of success will be determined by the native's own personal application of energy and enthusiasm.

In a female's chart, an opportunity for marriage of the May/December type. He may be a hard worker, dependable, but not fond of open display of affection, possibly a widower.

Mars square, semi-square, sesqui-quadrate Saturn: An extremely difficult period of time with frustrations and set-backs in the native's line of work or business, possible loss of job, bad credit rating or bankruptcy.

If not self-employed, heavy responsibilities are imposed upon by the employer. Refused an advancement of position or raise in pay, the native is likely to feel bitter and resentful towards the boss or another authoritative figure.

162

There can be difficulties through mechanical equipment or heavy machinery. Possible accidents with the company truck, fork-lift or other moving vehicle.

Strained, nervous tension may react through an explosive temper.

In a female's chart, possible violent separation or hostility, suspicion or mistrust through the husband or men in general.

Possible death, surgical operations or concerns over the ill health of a male parent.

In the native's health, one should guard against possible accidents to the knees or lower limbs. Frigidity and impotence is often associated with this aspect.

Mars opposition Saturn: A strenuous period in life in which others will place roadblocks in the native's path for personal success.

A parent may place heavy burdens of responsibilities upon the native's shoulders that restrict him from performing adequately in his career or profession.

Not a favorable time for dealing with older people, supervisors and figures of authority.

This is a "blow hot, blow cold" type of aspect. The native desires one thing and later decides against it. Personal recognition is met by frustration and setbacks. He may go to extremes of temperament, calm one day and a flare-up temper the next day.

There is danger of accidents to the bony structure of the body through machinery and automobiles. Skin and teeth may pose a problem.

Mars inconjunct Saturn: Although the native has the capacity to work hard, this aspect may induce a rigid attitude in the handling of work related duties. A non-yielding aspect that creates tension and friction with co-workers.

This configuration may introduce new machinery or equipment that is foreign to the native who has an established routine. The native becomes irritated and frustrated when forced to learn new methods.

Services and care may have to be provided for an ill male parent.

Caution should be exercised in lifting heavy equipment. Chronic health problems may stem through work related conditions, such as sensitivity to fumes, asbestos or odors that may affect the lungs.

Mars conjunct or parallel Uranus: This aspect intensifies the desire for personal freedom and independence. The native may try to achieve it through an abrupt and forceful manner.

This combination can introduce new and different methods and approach to certain situations that the native has not tackled before.

163

There is a high degree of inner tension in the nervous system that can cause irritability, shortness of temper and impatience. The native will need to exercise control to avoid explosive and temperamental outbursts.

Afflictions to this conjunction can result in separation from friends or associations.

Many unexpected events will occur during this span of time. Some will produce upsetting and disturbing changes.

The native may sever their membership with clubs and organizations or group participated activities.

Accidents are likely to occur. One must be cautious when working with live-wire equipment, electrical outlets and machinery.

Control the impulse to act without forethought and proper regard for safety.

The favorable aspects to the conjunction of Mars and Uranus are conducive to the military service, the study of Radar-Control, electrical technology, computer programming and Astrology.

Mars sextile or trine Uranus: Stimulates the utilization of new and unique working methods or the introduction of advanced technical equipment.

This aspect creates sudden and unexpected turn of events, that requires an adjustment to new conditions or situations.

Sudden surprises through advancements or a change in career is possible. Although there is still the strong desire for personal freedom and independence, the native is less abrupt in his manner of achieving it.

The native may feel a surge of extraordinary energy that can be applied with positive results.

There may be the development of an interest in electronics, mechanical engineering, aeronautics, computers or Astrology, possible appearances on TV or radio.

New, dynamic and unusual friends are likely to enter the native's social circle. The native may join a club or organization or other forms of group activities.

In a female's chart, the possibility of a new romance with a magnetic and exciting person who enters the person's life through an unexpected circumstance.

Pressing problems with health maybe resolved through new and advanced treatments.

Mars square, semi-square or sesqui-quadrate Uranus: Stimulates a high degree of nervous irritability and argumentativeness, the time is not favorable for dealing with men, or friends of unconventional standards.

One must use caution in driving to avoid accidents and possible arrest. The native should not expose himself to situations that can lead to potential violence and danger. Resist the temptation to mingle with associates that are erratic and disreputable with intent on over-throwing existing conditions or corporations. Such as the case with unauthorized strikers, and those who push for boycotts and shut-downs.

There may be the sudden death or separation of a family member or through a close friend. Women may have trouble with the marriage partner or a love relationship.

Difficulties in health from over-exertion, infection and inflammation of various types. Erratic habits, a violent temper can cause nervous stress and strain. One should use caution in the handling of fireworks, firearms, sharp tools, machinery and explosives.

Mars opposition Uranus: The native may feel short tempered, disagreeable or antagonistic at various times during this period.

There is the element of unexpected events that the native may find upsetting and disturbing to his daily routine. Electrical parts break down with the car. Electrical appliances or equipment require constant repair. Conflicts with these repairmen are likely.

Stress and strain with close friends and associates are possible. Under pressure or impulsive actions, the native may suddenly quit his membership with a club or organization, or make other rash and unsavory decisions that he will later regret.

Physical danger may occur through an act of violence imposed by another. Natives involved with dangerous activities or equipment in connection with their job should use extreme caution during this period.

Women will experience conflicts, separation and disagreements through men and companions. A divorce is possible, but one must seek confirmation through the condition of the First and Seventh Houses.

Mars inconjunct Uranus: This aspect is liable to create sudden, drastic and upsetting changes in work related situations. The native may feel new hours, change of shifts or routines are restricting his personal freedom of action. New machinery that may require the native to remain in one position, can prove to be of boring repetitious handling of duties, causing the native to rebel.

Unless the native controls his restless energy, a belligerent attitude may cause trouble with co-workers and possible loss of a job. This aspect requires patience and diligence to get through it without serious repercussion.

Mars conjunct or parallel Neptune: Favorable aspects to this conjunction stimulates the creative and intuitive faculties. Endows the native with the uncanny ability for visualization. He may be able to detect the breakdown of a machinery for example, just by visualizing it in his mind, and then go right to the source of trouble and correct it. Favorable for energetic, physical action and resourceful ingenuity if applied with common sense and caution.

An afflicting aspect to the conjunction of Progressed Mars and Natal or Progressed Neptune may induce lack of energy and motivation. There may be unrealistic attempts at get rich schemes. Searching for ways to earn a living that requires less effort on his part. A desire for a more complacent living with less hard work involved.

Many personal disappointments through the unwise trust of dubious characters may have instigated this desire for personal escapism from the harshness and reality of life.

A male member of the family or a close associate is likely to enter the hospital.

Ridicule, deceit and behind the scenes activities through enemies may create an inferiority complex or lack of self-worth.

There is danger through the acceptance of stolen goods, psychic obsessions, fraud, illusions, abuse of drugs or alcohol and sexual perversity. In a female's chart, this aspect can induce sexual assault or abuse through perverts.

The men she meets during this trend are likely to be deceptive, emotionally, physically or mentally handicapped or a heavy drinker.

The best way to handle this aspect is through spiritual involvement.

Mars sextile or trine Neptune: This aspect stimulates a high degree of personal attraction and popularity. Strong, sensitive emotions, but with the ability to keep them under control.

Creative possibilities of the imaginative and intuitive faculties and inner vision. Favorable for art, music, dancing, photography, fishing, boating and conditions related with water.

Success and assistance through a sympathetic and understanding individual. The native is receptive towards the wants and needs of others. Success in business dealings as a result of positive hunches and intuitive insight.

In a female's chart, there are opportunities for romance or marriage, with a very sensitive, affectionate and caring person. A religious individual, a former alcoholic, or someone with a slight handicap or one that requires medication for control of an illness.

A constructive aspect for hospital and institutional work or volunteer work.

In health, a new drug or medication may prove effective in correcting existing conditions. Unusual surgical techniques or a newly developed mechanical device may correct a physical handicap.

Mars square, semi-square or sesqui-quadrate Neptune: A period of time in which the native can become involved in dubious situations and with questionable characters. Patience and discretion is a must to avoid forcing certain issues. Whatever is attempted during this period is likely to be based upon impulses that are misleading.

Lack of energy and vitality may lessen the native's efforts in satisfactory, productive work. Possible loss of employment from refusal to work overtime or taking too many days off.

Emotions can get out of hand and attract peculiar situations. The native may feel uncertain of the intentions of another person. A sense of foreboding that one is being deceived or tricked into a commitment that may be questionable, illegal or unscrupulous.

In general terms, this aspect can induce victimization through men. Women will have to use discretion in their choice of male companions, who may be deceptive, married, heavy drinkers or of weak characters.

The native will have contacts with someone who will be hospitalized or confined in an institution or prison.

In health, a tendency for impulsive and erratic behavior that may lead to danger of overindulgence in alcohol or drugs, susceptibility to infections, swollen ankles due to retention of fluid (watch salt intake), possible foot surgery, hidden health problems and medication errors. Use caution in the handling of inflammable fluids, gas, oil and chemical products.

Mars opposition Neptune: There may be possible fraud, deception and trickery through men. Secret enemies will enter the native's life and cause bewildering situations.

This is an aspect of confrontations with police or law enforcement agencies, possible confinement in jail or prison.

The native should stay clear of what he suspects may be stolen property and avoid dealing with drugs in sales or purchase.

Illness may be misinterpreted and the wrong medication administered. The native should seek a second opinion to determine the true cause. It is possible that complications may result through anesthetics while undergoing surgery.

Mars inconjunct Neptune: The native's goals and ambitions are hard to define. His future plans are unrealistic. Wasted energy, lack of self-discipline and perseverance will reflect upon the native's work performance. Lack of motion induces loss of advancements.

The native applies for a position, knowing full well what the job entails. Then, after he is hired, becomes dissatisfied and starts complaining.

167

A health aspect in which one must use care in the taking of medication and avoid abuse of drugs or sedatives. Use care in the handling of bottled gas, inflammable fluids, turpentine, paints and harmful chemicals.

Mars conjunct Pluto: A painful crises that is likely to bring an end to one situation and force the native into a new beginning.

This aspect is favorable for starting a new business for there is the capacity to work hard and the ability to put in long hours necessary to get it off the ground floor.

Adverse aspects to this conjunction of Progressed Mars and Natal Pluto, can result in over-taxing ones strength and endurance. One should not expose themselves to situations that can bring about physical danger or exhaustion.

There may be possible contacts with ruthless individuals of brutal instincts, who can perpetrate violent acts.

A possible loss of someone close to the native or a family member.

Disagreements and arguments over insurance settlements, alimony, inheritance and other related joint finances.

Mars sextile or trine Pluto: Positive changes ahead in some new field of endeavor. The house and sign position of Progressed Mars and Pluto in the Progressed Chart should reveal the circumstances and the houses they rule reveal the consequences of the matter.

There is ability to achieve success through extraordinary energy and endurance. A good time to correct and eliminate bad habits and improve one's appearance.

Improvement of monetary situation through inheritance, insurance, dividends, lottery and other forms of joint finances.

Mars square, semi-square or sesqui-quadrate Pluto: Stimulates serious trouble in regards to financial affairs, inheritance or property of the dead.

Danger of theft, fire or damage to the home, car or possessions, requiring one to make a claim with their insurance company.

The female native should be careful in her choice of male companions. There is possible danger through rape, stabbing and serious injury.

Death of someone close to the native, a friend, or family member.

The native may undergo maltreatment through another person and become obsessed with revenge. An aspect of underground activity or involvement with gangs, criminals and murders.

In health, prostate gland surgery, hysterectomy, hemorrhoids, venereal disease, infections of the sexual organs and possible abortions or miscarriage.

Mars opposition Pluto: During this trend, it is possible that the native may get involved in a serious dispute with another individual over services rendered, money owed or through disagreeable views and opinions.

An opposition is an aspect of confrontations. This one between Mars and Pluto can be dangerous, resulting in serious arguments over money and financial settlements. Also, danger through men involved with the underworld.

The native should make it a point to have auto insurance under such an aspect as this. Car accidents can be costly and result in temporary loss of driving privileges, especially in states where laws require auto insurance coverage or proof of financial responsibility.

Mars inconjunct Pluto: This aspect induces serious arguments over money or goods belonging to the dead through someone who has an obsession concerned with these matters.

Disputes are possible over payments the native feels are justly his, through Workers' Compensation, sick benefits or unemployment.

Money can be gained through the use of underhanded tactics; as in collecting a percentage reward for turning in an income tax evader, or being rewarded by the company for turning in a fellow employee for theft of company property.

Overwork and stress may hinder the native from proper elimination of the bowels resulting in hemorrhoids.

JUPITER

Jupiter is the planet of luck and protection from want. A forgotten dividend check arrives, just in time to pay an overdue bill. Jupiter instills a desire for material wealth and personal comfort and the knowledge in which to obtain it. In the higher form of consciousness, Jupiter represents justice and fair-play, moral and religious endeavors, optimism, generosity and compassion. The planet of opportunity and expansion. The house and sign position of Jupiter indicates the individuals or circumstances most fortunate for you. The aspects reveal the manner in which you apply the energy of Jupiter through the consequences of the house that Jupiter rules.

As we grow and mature, new opportunities for gain and knowledge will enter our life. This is shown by the new house position of Progressed Jupiter in the Progressed Chart.

Jupiter governs conditions to do with travel, higher education, religion, courts of law and lawsuits, published material and public opinion, and widespread communications such as newspapers, long distance phone calls, telegrams, radio, TV and C.B.'s.

Individuals who will enter your life through the influence of Jupiter are likely to be foreigners, people of different color or religion, in-laws, religious leaders, publishers, educated people and persons of wealth, law enforcers and contacts with those residing in distant cities.

Unlike the faster moving planets (i.e. Sun, Venus, Mercury and Mars) Jupiter does not advance too far from its natal longitudinal sign and degree. However, it can advance through as many as four houses in one lifetime.

Every year through progressions, each house cusp advances approximately one degree. Jupiter does not advance in degrees that fast, therefore, Jupiter is drawn closer and closer to the house cusp of its natal position, until it finally leaves to enter the next adjoining house. It is for this reason, that the natal house position of Jupiter and the three houses to the left will be of great importance. Jupiter's energy will color these houses at various stages through progressions.

Always remember, that planets are stronger in the house in which they are positioned rather than the one they rule. This holds true for Progressed Charts as well.

Due to the slow mean motion of Jupiter, it is less apt to change signs during the course of one's life. It can change, however, if the position is in a high degree and advances into the next sign. Or, it can be in a very low degree and through retrograde motion, return to the former sign. For example, Natal Jupiter in 27° Libra and through progression, enters into 0° Scorpio. New experiences will affect the native's life, for the energy of Jupiter is now motivated through the progressed sign position of Scorpio.

In the Natal Chart, a major transit or an Eclipse aspecting Natal Jupiter in 27° Libra will activate matters concerned with business and marriage partners.

In the Progressed Chart, a major transit or an Eclipse aspecting Progressed Jupiter in 0° Scorpio will activate matters concerned with insurance, alimony and joint finances. As one can see, a new element and outlet for opportunity and gain has been introduced into the native's life.

Jupiter is not considered a personal planet and therefore, one does not take into consideration the possibility that it may rejoin its own natal longitudinal position due to retrograde motion.

One does however, take into consideration, the difference in degrees that Natal and Progressed Jupiter are apart from one another. This knowledge will enable the astrologer to determine the length of time that a personal progressed planet or a major transit will remain in force. The following example should give a clear picture of length of effectiveness.

Nativity	Natal Jupiter	Progressed Jupiter
19 yrs. old	24° Libra	26° Libra

Suppose our client has Progressed Venus in 23° Gemini. We note that she is applying in a trine aspect with Natal Jupiter in 24° Libra. One year later, Venus will be exact in 24° Gemini, and separating in 25° Gemini. A total of three years in effect. As we glance into the Progressed Chart and notice that Progressed Jupiter is in 26° Libra, Progressed Venus in 25° Gemini is now applying to the trine aspect with Progressed Jupiter. We permit one more year for exact and the following year in which Venus will be in 27° Gemini and separating from Progressed Jupiter in 26° Libra. A grand total of five years from the time that Progressed Venus applied to Natal Jupiter until she has left the separating orb of Progressed Jupiter.

In older individuals, where Jupiter is a few more degrees higher, there is a quiet period of perhaps a year or two, between the two aspects. Until such a time that Venus advances in degrees and applies to the beneficial aspect with Progressed Jupiter.

Jupiter conjunct Ascendant: Jupiter pushes back the limitations and opens the door for expansion. Stimulates the opportunity for marriage or increase in family through birth of children.

General prosperity and good fortune is possible through lottery winning, football pools or other games of chance.

Excellent for job promotion and assistance through influential people. Travel, lawsuits and higher education can be to one's advantage.

Unfavorable aspects to the conjunction of Jupiter and the Ascendant may endow an overly optimistic attitude. One may see more in an opportunity than is actually there, because they tend to see what "they" want it to hold for "them."

An over-confident attitude may prevent one from taking the immediate advantage offered by an opportunity.

This aspect stimulates the tendency to promise more than what the native can actually deliver. It also gives the effect that one has more time than there actually is. Invariably, this makes one late for appointments or careless with service.

Health problems stem from weight gain that often accompanies the aspect due to a general feeling of optimism.

Jupiter conjunct Midheaven: Increases chances of promotion, job opportunities and assistance through influential people.

Gain through public office or affiliation with a religious order. Travel or relocation may be necessary in connection with one's job.

This is another favorable aspect for marriage or an increase in the family through the birth of children. In a child's chart, this aspect is more likely to affect the parents and their good fortune.

Unfavorable aspects may require one to relocate to an area not well liked but accepted in order to keep one's position.

A parent, parent-in-law or a boss may be a source of serious concern.

This is not the time to get involved in legal disputes or with individuals that have a questionable background. One may have disturbing contacts with law enforcement agencies or the police department.

Jupiter conjunct Descendant: An opportunity for marriage if single. If married, the partner obtains an advancement in career which produces profitable results. Partners and associates appear to have less concern for mutual endeavors, especially for your part in any undertaking. (A compromise may have to be reached to avoid misunderstandings.)

Someone of a different background, color, race or religion will enter your life and make a marked impression on you.

Afflictions to this conjunction may delay travel plans due to the interference of another person. Pressing for personal freedom and independence in a forceful manner can generate separation through personal relationships.

Favorable aspects can be beneficial through influential and powerful individuals.

Jupiter conjunct I. C.: Any planet that conjuncts the Fourth House Cusp, is an indication of changes within the home environment.

This implies that the energy of that planet is getting ready to leave the influence of the Fourth House, thereby altering the condition of the matter connected with the house.

If an in-law was residing in the home, Jupiter conjunct the I. C., may signify the departure of that relative. Perhaps a child leaves the home base to accept a position in another city, or may leave for college or gets married.

If a legal matter has been pending concerning property or real estate, a major transit or an Eclipse to the conjunction will indicate a favorable or unfavorable conclusion of this issue.

The Fourth House governs an end to long standing matters, with new beginnings ahead. Jupiter can be beneficial in the conclusion of these conditions.

This is an aspect of marriage, increase in family through birth of children, moving, selling, expansion of the present home or relocation to a new city. Gain through parents or property.

Unfavorable aspects to Jupiter conjoined with the I. C. may result in property loss, divorce, bankruptcy or liens.

Jupiter sextile or trine Ascendant/Descendant: A fortunate aspect for marriage and parnership and dealing with the general public. Publishers, influential people, persons of wealth, different color or race and those residing in distant cities will play an important role in the native's life.

If transiting Jupiter is favorably aspecting a Natal or Progressed planet at the same time, this can be a most propitious period.

A lucky streak prevails through sound hunches and intuitive ability. This enables the native to win "big" through the lottery, football pool, raffles, bingo or other games of chance.

One of the best aspects, bringing increased opportunities and chances for betterment in occupation or social affairs.

Practical advancement of one's ambition in some new enterprise. Public recognition and success through being in the right place at the right time.

An overly optimistic attitude calls for a realistic approach necessary in the handling of personal affairs. There is the disadvantage of centering one's attention on what one wants to see. The individual may pay less attention to the real problem at hand, placing more optimism on new opportunities than the circumstances actually warrant. Determine whether this new venture is as promising as it appears otherwise you may be spending valuable time on undertakings that prove to be of little value and time consuming.

Jupiter square, semi-square or sesqui-quadrate Ascendant/Descendant: This is not the time to get involved in legal entanglements. Attainment of success may undergo temporary setbacks or brief periods of discouragement.

The native tends to promise more than they can actually deliver, because, this aspect gives one the effect that they have more time than is actually there.

The native should be careful not expand opportunities out of proportion. One tends to see only what one wants it to hold for them.

May be overly confident and push their luck too far. They could neglect to take immediate advantage of opportunities.

Sometimes, premature actions may spring from taking for granted something that an excessive sense of urging has induced one to neglect or examine thoroughly.

An aspect in which one should try to avoid excesses and extravagance.

The urge for personal freedom of action and expression which may induce the desire for extra-marital affairs or result in divorce.

Jupiter sextile or trine the M.C./I. C.: This aspect clears the way for successful accomplishment of business and enterprise. Matters run smoothly, without delays and hinderances. Whatever one undertakes at this time is likely to succeed.

Powerful and influential people will assist in furthering the native's career. Legal matters are resolved in the native's behalf.

Fortunate means for travel are possible, as with a paid expense account through the company funds or winning of a trip for being the best salesman of the year.

This is one of the most prosperous periods in which there is the attainment of one's goal and ambitions.

Favorable for dealing with domestic affairs and purchase or sales of property. Increases in family through marriage or birth.

Jupiter square, semi-square or sesqui-quadrate the M.C./I. C.: Not the time for entering into new enterprise or for expecting increases either through business or finance. Possible legal entanglements through job or property.

Poor judgment in business or handling of property matters. One should avoid extravagance in money matters which may cause setbacks in business or loss of property.

Difficulties through one's occupation may result in litigations, as in sex or racial discrimination.

The native should use extreme caution in signing of legal contracts or documents which may commit them to more than what they can actually handle.

Jupiter conjunct or parallel Saturn: Saturn and Jupiter relate to two opposite principles which act so closely, the one with the other, that neither is understandable without the other.

Saturn is the principle of limitation and constitutes a challenge to the liberating effect of growth. The challenge, being constructive because Jupiter may urge you at times to overdo physically, emotionally or financially.

This aspect can bring to fruitation a long standing issue. Favorable for far-reaching goals and objective through perseverance and fortitude.

Creates an atmosphere for solitude that permits the writing of profound subjects and lengthy articles. Whatever the native ventures into at this time, will be well planned, organized and thoroughly examined.

The native may realize that education is important for the betterment of financial security and return to college or higher education classes.

Favorable aspects to this conjunction can induce successful and constructive changes in one's occupation with long lasting benefits.

Afflicting aspects from a major transit or an Eclipse to this conjunction may result in the death of a parent-in-law, grandparent, an old friend or an older relative that lives in a distant city.

Jupiter sextile or trine Saturn: Good common sense in business dealings and general activities, luck in practical matters, favorable for honors and recognition and possible attainment of a promotion or an advancement in one's career. Whatever one undertakes at this time is likely to produce long range success.

Influential friends formed now may be productive of beneficial results later.

Beneficial help or assistance possible, from a parent, a matured individual, a parent-in-law or through people with influence.

Benefits are generally a result of past efforts, hard work or old projects that are finally beginning to pay off.

Should either Jupiter or Saturn rule the Natal or Progressed Seventh House Cusp, romance or marriage is possible and likely to prove fortunate, steady and reliable. They may be of a ''May/December'' type, previously married or a widow and of serious disposition.

Jupiter square, semi-square or sesqui-quadrate Saturn: A frustrating period in which ambitions are thwarted. Efforts for expansion are delayed through various setbacks.

Not the best time for dealing with people of prestige, wealth or power. An enemy can easily be made with someone affiliated with politics or of influential background.

Be careful of making false or libelous statements, as it could lead to possible litigation. You may have to yield to an authoritative figure even though you know the standards or methods of what they are doing are wrong or in complete error.

This aspect gives a general feeling that one must put up with certain forms of limitations and delays even though everything else apparently looks great.

A parent-in-law, an old friend or a parent that lives at a distance may be a source for concern in connection with their health. This is an aspect of separation or death through a parent or an older member of the family. However, there must be other confirmations to this effect, either through another progressed planet, a major afflicting transiting or an Eclipse.

Jupiter opposition Saturn: Ambitions are thwarted through the opposition of powerful and influential peopie. Not the time for speaking out of turn and making public statements that can harm your career.

Involvements with litigations hit a snag. Court trials are delayed and drawn out. Possible loss through legal affairs.

Plans for expansion seem to be in a state of limbo. The native places one foot forward, only to place two back. Obstruction, disappointments and difficulties go hand in hand with this configuration.

One is constantly beset by delays and hinderances in business dealings. Orders are miscalculated. Shipments are lost or held up. Truckers go on strike.

The native must use caution in dealing with individuals who may be dishonest or misrepresent their claims.

This is an aspect of success that can only be achieved through the application of hard, grueling work and long hours. Perseverance and elimination of pessimism.

Jupiter inconjunct Saturn: Care, service and responsibility may have to be rendered to a senior member of the family, a grandparent, parent or aunt or uncle.

The native may be forced to take additional training or further his education to achieve security in his position.

An aspect of possible racial discrimination in which government officials may be called in to intervene.

The native should be careful around large machinery, lift-trucks, farming implements and construction sites.

Jupiter conjunct or parallel Uranus: The conjunction of Progressed Jupiter with Natal or Progressed Uranus can remain in effect for a number of years. It would take a progressed aspect from a personal planet, a major transit or an Eclipse to add the necessary force to push this conjunction into action.

Favorable aspects produce beneficial results through travel, invention, publication, radio, TV and the occult subjects.

176

Gain through friends of all walks of life and associations with clubs and organizations.

An exciting period in which unexpected circumstances take the native into new realms of experience through sheer stroke of luck.

The native may travel for the purpose of gaining knowledge, as in the attending of seminars or an astrological convention. He may travel with a group of people or with a tour.

With unfavorable aspects, there is an inclination for independence in certain beliefs where the native goes overboard in his one-sided view.

Unexpected loss of a close friend through an accident.

Death or unexpected separation through an in-law or some close member of the family who lives at a distance.

Jupiter sextile or trine Uranus: New and original ideas can be combined effectively in new enterprise or group associations.

A good time to become concerned with the social welfare of others. Unexpected good fortune is possible through unusual circumstances, speculation, invention or publication and success in fund raising for charitable organizations.

There is the forming of new friends through group activities or the joining of clubs and organizations. Unexpected opportunities for higher education and travel or pursuits of humanitarian endeavors prove beneficial. Personal aims can be achieved along the lines of science, computers, engineering, aeronautics, radio, TV and Astrology.

Unexpected winnings and financial gains through lottery, football pool and raffle tickets, or contests.

Jupiter square, semi-square, or sesqui-quadrate Uranus: Not the time to get involved with new, fanatical or bigoted reform groups. Possible loss of good opportunities through bad judgment in business.

A time to lay low and be moderate in ideas and actions. Avoid the attraction to unconventional situations and Bohemian type of new acquaintances that may enter your life during this trend.

Possible conflicts with those in authority due to a headstrong temperament. Be wary of a stubborn adherence to misguided opinions in regards group activities. A rebellious attitude makes for difficult relationships with others.

Unexpected losses are possible due to travel, litigation or ties with clubs and organizations.

Sudden separation and grief through loss of friends, an in-law, or a close member of the family, that lives at a distance.

An individual of foreign background or of a different race or color, that you have befriended may suddenly turn against you.

Avoid involvements with persons of erratic, eccentric and unconventional behavior with a reputation for getting in trouble with the police.

Jupiter opposition Uranus: Stimulates an attraction to unusual and unconventional groups with a questionable background.

The native should not get involved with new organizations until they have had the chance to investigate their aims and policies.

Sudden change of plans in travel matters. One may suddenly change his major in college. Lawsuits undergo constant upsetting and unexpected delays.

A situation may arise in which the native may have to take decisive actions as to whether or not he will file a lawsuit against his friend.

This is an accident prone aspect and one should carefully watch the major transits or an Eclipse that may force it into action.

Jupiter inconjunct Uranus: The native has to be careful of voicing one's opinions or participating in group activities that are not conducive to his job. The native wants to make changes in his place of employment which he feels will benefit the workers. However, starting a union, for example, in a company shop may seem like a good idea but not if the co-workers refuse to back you up.

Unexpected changes in work concerning hours of a shift may interfere with the native's higher education classes.

Jupiter conjunct or parallel Neptune: Beneficial gains through unforeseen circumstances. Unusual protection through hospitalization insurance coverage of an accident or surgery. Gain through a lawsuit involving a hospital or a pharmaceutical product.

Intuitive hindsight urges one to purchase a church raffle ticket or join a contest and you win.

The conjunction of Progressed Jupiter with Natal or Progressed Neptune can remain in effect for a number of years. It would take a progressed aspect from a personal planet, a major transit or an Eclipse to add the necessary force to push this conjunction into action.

The favorable aspects will enhance the psychic and intuitive ability. The native may return to higher education for art, music, photography, the study of psychology or law enforcement.

Unfavorable aspects to this conjunction may instill a temptation to accept merchandise that you suspect may be stolen, thus involve you in illegal intanglements.

Being too trusting of others may find you bilked of personal funds or personal possessions. Best not to commit oneself to anything that is not clearly stated in written form.

Jupiter sextile or trine Neptune: This aspect stimulates the creative faculties. Inspires an interest in music, art, the metaphysical, spiritual or religious studies.

The compassionate nature is enhanced, and the native may go out of his way to do things for those less fortunate or handicapped.

Long journeys and trips may be undertaken to attend psychic seminars or the attending of spiritual retreats.

Psychic or intuitive experiences, the meeting of people who deal with the occult or psychics will have a strong influence upon the native's life.

Possible beneficial or financial gain through hidden matters. You may be rewarded for a kind deed or a favor shown someone in the past.

Jupiter square, semi-square or sesqui-quadrate Neptune: Too much emotionalism makes it difficult for the native to see what is actually happening to him until it is too late. There is instability in the selection of so-called friends or lovers.

Irresponsibility, complicates the matters of the house ruled by Jupiter and Neptune so that these affairs become terribly mixed-up.

The native suffers through poor judgment of others resulting in fraudulent or deceitful actions. Legal matters are tinged with underhanded tactics. Individuals of foreign descent or of a different background may take advantage of your good nature through over abuse until you realize you've been had.

Not the time for signing important documents without proper assistance through an attorney.

A relative may have difficulty coping with a drug habit or alcoholism or may be suffering from severe mental problems.

An in-law may have an illness that is difficult to define. May require special treatment at a large clinic, VA hospital or a medical university in a distant city.

Jupiter opposition Neptune: Hidden and unforeseen situations can draw the native into a complicated legal battle.

Through a strange twist of fate, one may have to sue an in-law or the native becomes mixed up in a tangled web surrounding the legal affairs of an in-law.

This is an aspect of wool gathering, the real versus the unreal. A tendency to escape from reality through daydreaming, sleeping more than usual or abuse of drugs and alcoholic beverages.

Jupiter inconjunct Neptune: This is an aspect of dissipation of energy. Tackling too many projects at one time because of making unrealistic promises.

The native has to be careful while traveling and at work. He tends to daydream rather than keep his mind on what is at hand.

Legal aid may have to be obtained to straighten out mixed-up conditions concerned with hospital payments or sick benefits.

Jupiter conjunct Pluto: A powerful aspect, can enhance religious beliefs or strengthen one's desire to return to their religion from which they formerly broke away.

An indication of a new beginning in life. A new job, marriage, relocation or advancement in present position.

There is the desire for power, leadership and personal achievement. Favorable gain through inheritance or insurance and assistance through the in-laws or individuals of influence.

Unfavorable aspects to this conjunction can still promise gain through inheritance, but unfortunately it may come as a direct loss of some close member of the family or an in-law.

Honesty must be adhered to where one is placed in control of other peoples' money. Extravagance must be curbed, to avoid possible credit loss.

Jupiter sextile or trine Pluto: Stimulates luck through the use of extraordinary powers of concentration and mental application. Possible gain through legal pursuits involving insurance companies, Workers' Compensation, alimony or sick benefits.

Should an Eclipse or a major transit favorably aspect this configuration, the native can amass a large sum of money through a lottery winning, a raffle ticket or through a contest.

This is an aspect of major changes in which the native may benefit through relocation, publication, or higher education.

Financial gain through an in-law or someone of prominence.

Jupiter square, semi-square or sesqui-quadrate Pluto: This is not favorable for speculation or gambling. The native must be wary of involvements with underground characters or those with a questionable background.

There may be a possible loss of social standing and reputation. One should be extremely careful in the handling of joint finances and conditions involving alimony, inheritance, insurance settlements, income tax and charge accounts.

May become involved in a lawsuit with an insurance company. May be swindled out of an inheritance through an in-law or other unscrupulous people.

This is not the time to overextend oneself. A time for common sense with charge accounts to avoid extravagance and loss of a credit rating.

There can be a possible loss through death of an in-law a close friend or family member that lives at a distance.

An opportunity may come your way to make money through illegal or underhanded methods. If you do decide to become a "bookie," and take gambling bets, handle the money carefully and keep good records. This can be a dangerous period for anyone who tries to withhold money that belongs to others, especially from individuals with questionable backgrounds.

Jupiter opposition Pluto: This is an aspect of possible income tax evasion or income tax auditing.

The native may be drawn into court for back alimony, bankruptcy, or illegal acceptance of money as through a bribe or pay-off.

Be careful of acceptance of illegal money or goods that may impose a heavy fine later. For example, working and accepting a paycheck while, at the same time, collecting unemployment benefits, or fraudulent income tax in which one withholds certain large gifts or winnings.

There can be a possible financial loss through poor judgment in purchases or investments, not the time for relying on the advice of others when it comes to investing large sums of money. Travel, for the sake of winning it "big," as to Las Vegas or Atlantic City, may result in a considerable financial loss.

Travel plans may have to be altered or are interrupted due to the death of a family member.

Jupiter inconjunct Pluto: A co-worker can be the source of great agitation when he tries to dictate and manipulate certain work related duties. A self appointed record keeper of every one's hours to make sure no one is getting more hours and making more money than he.

There can be a possible lawsuit through sexual harassment or racial discrimination.

SATURN

Saturn chiefly governs the latter part of life. It appears that one must reach maturity to fully appreciate the value of perseverance, patience and economy and the willingness to accept responsibility, hinderances and delays.

Saturn enables one to see clearly and logically what is before him with no illusion of false optimism or self-deception, which may be the case with Jupiter and Neptune. Saturn is cautious, for he must ponder and assimilate the facts before him through the necessity of prudence. Saturn is the principle of self-preservation, that motivates the ambitions, forever onward, steadily and relentlessly towards a desired goal. The laborious efforts put forth in achieving one's ambition is determined by Saturn's Natal House and Sign position. The consequences are shown through the house that Saturn rules.

Our goals and ambitions change as we learn the acceptance of responsibility and gain the respect of our peers. Past experiences have laid the foundation for future growth, revealed by the present House position of Saturn in the Progressed Chart.

Saturn governs conditions concerned with old matters, past and stagnant conditions, and the value of hard work, patience and endurance. The need to organize one's time constructively and economically. Thrift through proper handling and distribution of material. He inhibits, restricts and delays to keep man from acting foolishly and impulsively. He strengthens character, sets up obstacles and teaches acceptance of responsibilities. He is the teacher who helps us learn from past experience.

Saturn governs agriculture products, mining, land, real estate, construction, political parties, heavy duty equipment and matters affiliated with government affairs.

Individuals who will enter one's life through the influence of Saturn are likely to be older, serious, responsible citizens and matured individuals. People who appear to be rather aloof, reserved or inhibited, until they are certain of your intentions. They can be one's parents, grandparents, older members of the family, the boss and those in authority over the native, government officials, old friends and those from the past.

Unlike the faster moving planets (i.e. Sun, Venus, Mercury and Mars), Saturn does not advance too far from its natal longitudinal sign and degree. However, it can advance through as many as four houses in one lifetime.

Every year through progressions, each house cusp advances approximately one degree. Saturn does not advance in degrees that fast. Therefore, Saturn is drawn closer and closer to the house cusp of its natal position, until it finally leaves to enter the next adjoining house. It is for this reason, that the natal house position of Saturn and the three houses to the left will be of great importance. Saturn's energy will color these houses at various stages through progressions.

Always remember, that planets are stronger in the house in which they are positioned rather than the ones they rule. This holds true for progressed charts as well.

Due to the slow mean motion of Saturn, it is less apt to change signs during the course of one's life. It can however, if positioned in a high degree and will advance into the next sign. Or, it can be in a very low degree and through retrograde motion, reverses to the former sign. For example, Natal Saturn in 29° Virgo and through progression, enters into 0° Libra. New experiences will affect the native's life, for the energy of Saturn is now motivated by the new sign position of Libra.

In the Natal Chart, a major transit or an Eclipse aspecting Natal Saturn in 29° Virgo will activate matters concerned with vocation, health and co-workers.

In the Progressed Chart, a major transit or an Eclipse aspecting Progressed Saturn in 0° Libra will activate matters concerned with the affairs of one's marriage or business partner. A new motivating outlet for one's ambitions and career interests have been introduced into the native's life.

Saturn is not considered a personal planet. Therefore, one does not take into consideration the possibility that it may rejoin its own natal longitudinal position due to retrograde motion, or from retrograde to direct.

Saturn is slower than Jupiter in its mean motion. A progressed personal planet, a major transit or an Eclipse in aspect with Natal Saturn will merely extend the period of time, until it has passed the orb of influence with Progressed Saturn.

Saturn conjunct or parallel Ascendant: In a child's chart, this can be a dangerous period. Complications through childhood diseases are likely to take its toll. Measles, chickenpox, rheumatic fever, and other serious illnesses should not be taken lightly. Parents with children, who have Saturn near the Ascendant should be on the alert. Determine the difference in degrees between Natal Saturn and the Natal Ascendant. This is the approximate age of the impending danger. For example, a child has 5° Scorpio Rising and natal Saturn is in 12° Scorpio. The difference between the two in degrees should equal to 7 years of age.

The child may be forced to mature in a hurry due to responsibilities of younger brothers and sisters, as in the case of both parents working.

There can be a possible separation through/or loss of a parent, grandparent, or other close member of the family.

This is an aspect in which the native feels a sense of isolation, loneliness and rejection. The condition may create an inferiority-complex and lack of self-worth. The child may withdraw within himself and become a loner. Only love, patience and understanding will see this child through these terrible three years.

The matured adult has been seasoned by rejection and restriction, this aspect may induce a slowing down period in his personal affairs. One may possibly be burdened with the responsibility of an ill parent. Delays in job advancement or other important matters in his life.

A very dismal time in which one feels mentally, and emotionally drained and depressed.

The favorable aspects may induce a lasting relationship with the possibility of marriage. A May/December type of relationship.

Saturn conjunct Midheaven: This conjunction would have to be well aspected by a personal progressed planet, an Eclipse or a major transit to gain through the affairs ruled by Saturn and the Tenth House. For Saturn is in conjunction with the very house it normally rules in the Zodiac denoting a double connotation.

Excellent for anyone running for office that is elected through votes: the mayor, a union president or an important post with a large association.

A responsible position working for the city may be gained through the influence of a politician.

Public recognition through merit of past efforts and hard work.

The afflicting aspects to this conjunction can be devastating: loss of a position, reputation or public esteem, bankruptcy, bad credit, possible loss of a parent or other older member of the family.

A time in which one must not attempt anything that might discredit their reliability.

Saturn conjunct Descendant: A partnership may be formed, but new enterprises are not spectacular. In fact, they are somewhat held back, delayed or hindered.

Some of the causes may be due to the heavy burdens or responsibilities of another person such as a parent or an ill marriage partner.

Personal plans undergo a delay or a setback due to the unfavorable reactions of another. A general feeling of depression prevails as progress slows down.

Sometimes one feels like withdrawing from the world and that there is no use in trying for any personal achievements.

This is the most likely time to spend on projects that need finishing. There is a clearing up of old matters. Accept the added burdens of a parent, relative or marriage partner even though you must put personal interests aside for the time being. When the burdens have eased, you'll not be plagued with self-guilt complexes. You will have done your duty.

Spend the year that Saturn opposes your Ascendant as a time to stop and reflect about your future. Take up new studies, engulf yourself in learning about things you've not had the time to do before. Write a book, create a flower arrangement or take up pottery making. But, do keep yourself busy to avoid mental depression. Your energy span will be low so start an exercise program or begin a walking routine.

This is a year of challenging tests. It is less easy to express oneself in large circles of people. May draw away from social involvements, desiring a more retiring pursuit or "intimate gathering" of just a few close friends.

Individuals may enter your life during this span of time who will try to dominate or irritate you almost beyond endurance.

Saturn conjunct I. C.: The Fourth House governs the final ending of a long standing affair. This may be the departure of a chronically ill parent or grandparent.

Someone leaves the home base that placed a heavy restrictive influence or burden upon the family. Perhaps they moved to the home of another family member.

It will be a year or two, until Saturn leaves the orb of influence, before one feels an uplifting of spirits in the home environment. A desire to perk up the home surroundings and to entertain again.

The favorable aspects to the conjunction of Saturn and the I. C., may be the realization of the final mortgage payment. Possible gain of property or real estate through a parent or grandparent.

Unfavorable aspects to the conjunction, may require a second mortgage due to heavy repairs on the home. Delays in sales or purchases of property, or having to take less than the asking price.

There are heavy burdens of a family member or loss of parent.

Saturn sextile or trine Ascendant/Descendant: Stimulates the ambition and the self-control or self-discipline to achieve.

Gains the respect of another through hard work, reliability and perseverance. Older or influential people will be of benefit to the native.

This does not in itself indicate an opportunity for marriage, but rather stabilizes the present married state. Especially if the marriage was formerly on shaky ground. Will re-kindle faithfulness.

Social contacts can be productive of new and lasting associations of prominence, excellent for business partnerships, consolidating and reaching settlements, successful signing of contracts and the conclusion of old matters.

Possible inheritance or beneficial assistance through parents.

Saturn square, semi-square or sesqui-quadrate Ascendant/Descendant: Denotes a heavy, sad, depressing and restrictive period in which personal affairs are held in check.

Plans have to be set aside due to pressing responsibilities. Disappointments in love affairs, social functions, marriage and business partnerships. This is a slowing down period of general activities.

Difficulties with/or through a parent or parent-in-law and those in authority over the native.

The native seems to lack in his ability to relate to others in a warm and friendly manner. One appears standoffish, cold and indifferent to other peoples' feelings.

Possible health problems relating to the teeth, skin, knees and the bony structure of the body.

Saturn sextile or trine the M.C./I. C.: Stimulates the ambitions and leadership abilities. Advancement is possible into a position of trust with the power to control or supervise other people.

Progress in career matters appear slow, but the advancements will be of long lasting and continual improvement.

Good sound investments in real estate may yield generous results, success in sales or purchase of property, gain through parents or other figures of authority.

Excellent for matters of importance that require working in seclusion. Good for contacts with influential and authoritative figures who may assist in the obtaining of contracts and business connections.

Good for negotiations with city officials or for government contracts.

Saturn square, semi-square or sesqui-quadrate the M.C./I. C.: May suffer a reversal in occupational affairs. A downward trend in business and finance.

The native is beset by obstacles, delays, disappointments and restrictions.

If involved in politics, may lose the election or present position may lead to notoriety.

Can be a loss of the credit rating and possible bankruptcy.

Not the time for branching out into new enterprise which will add to present responsibilities. Possible loss of property or heavy burdens in maintenance of same.

Emotional concerns of/or loss through a parent, grandparent or another older member of the family.

Restrictions in the home due to heavy responsibilities of an ill family member.

Saturn conjunct or parallel Uranus: A slow progressed aspect remaining in force for a number of years requiring a personal progressed planet, a major transit or an Eclipse to probe it into action.

The favorable aspects to this conjunction, may stimulate a desire to break away from old established routines. A period of time in which the native changes his beliefs, habits and ideas that were traditionally a part of the family upbringing. May move suddenly out of the home or relocate.

The native may discover new and unique devices to aid him in his field of occupation. At first he finds them upsetting to his old, established ways of performing tasks, until the realization of their sound and practical usage sets in. For example, learning to operate a computer can be a tedious task, but once the learning process has been accomplished, the native realizes what a time saver they really are.

Old friends may suddenly come back into the social circle. If new friends are made, they are generally older, or vastly younger.

Afflictions to the conjunction may result in an abrupt loss of position, unexpected loss of/or separation through old friends, unexpected death of a parent, grandparent, or other older family members.

Saturn sextile or trine Uranus: A Progressed aspect that remains in effect for a number of years. When stimulated into action, can induce sudden advance in occupation, through the intervention of an old friend.

Much depends upon the house and sign position and the houses both Saturn and Uranus governs in the Natal and Progressed, to determine the potential. However, it is possible one may be elected to a prestigious position of an important organization.

Should either planet rule the Natal or Progressed Seventh House, a sudden attraction can lead to a lasting relationship and possibly marriage.

Long lasting benefits through clubs and organizations and close associations.

New and advanced methods of operation will be introduced in one's line of work, as with the use of computers or robots.

This is an aspect in which one combines practicality of thought with originality, leading to possible gains through sound, creative inventions.

Saturn square, semi-square or sesqui-quadrate Uranus: A progressed aspect that remains in force for a number of years, but when stimulated into action can induce a sudden and unexpected loss of a job. The company may move, merge or go out of business.

A very unsettling period of life in which many unexpected and upsetting events create setbacks in personal or business affairs.

There may be difficulties through friendships and close associations. The native may display a sloppy, disorganized or haphazard approach to his job, resulting in loss of an advancement or a pay raise.

Possible, sudden, loss of a parent, or another authoritative figure. The native may be upset with the introduction of new and different methods or machinery that disturbs his established routine.

There can be trouble with health, poor circulation or spasmodic conditions of the calf muscles — "Charley Horse."

Saturn opposition Uranus: A progressed aspect that remains in force for a number of years. But when stimulated into action can induce the break up of an old relationship. A disagreement with friends over an established code of ethics. One feels they have been betrayed through false and unreliable friends.

The native is at a turning point in life. Having to choose between an established order of existance and the urge for personal freedom and the attraction to the unconventional.

He may suddenly rebel against the establishment, seeking personal freedom and independence without regard for responsibility of family members.

Saturn inconjunct Uranus: A slow progressed aspect that remains in force for a number of years, but when stimulated into action can induce restriction of one's freedom and independence due to the responsibility of a chronically ill member of the family.

There can be sudden and unexpected changes in the occupational field such as being forced to work nights or alternative shifts which is upsetting to the native's established routine of living habits or being suddenly switched to another department, so that the native does not know from one day to the next where he will be working. Sometimes, there are spasmatic hours that break up the day, resulting in great stress and strain in the nervous system. Rebelling against a figure of authority because they may be much younger than oneself.

Saturn conjunct or parallel Neptune: A slow progressed aspect remaining in force for a number of years. When stimulated into action, it can induce uncanny intuitive ability that enables one to make correct and practical judgments connected with business matters. The foresight to correctly forge ahead or hold back on expansion and improvements.

Excellent for anyone in the medical field where sympathy can be expressed without the emotional involvement.

Afflicting aspects to this conjunction may require one to assume the care and responsibility of a chronically ill parent or someone who is emotionally, physically or mentally handicapped.

Powerful secret enemies may try to damage one's reputation. Be careful of your actions concerning the affairs of others. This is an aspect in which the past comes back to haunt you. You may get your just dues, for harm or defamation of character you may have imposed upon others.

Saturn sextile or trine Neptune: Stimulates a subtle change in one's business — a merger, an addition of a new and unusual product, the changing of the company's name or one may adopt a "nom de plume."

May induce one to become interested in the medical field, nursing, dental technician, psychiatry or other related fields. If, already employed in the medical branch, may change jobs, bosses or departments.

Very good for inspirational ideas in the practical arts and science.

Intuitive insight and ideas coupled with sound judgment can bring beneficial results in some new field of endeavor. Beneficial and hidden gains through an older person or through someone you have done a kind deed for without expecting any reward.

A good aspect for working or seeking employment with an institution that cares for the elderly or a senior citizens group. Or, obtaining a police security job in a hospital or other places of confinement.

Saturn square, semi-square or sesqui-quadrate Neptune: A very confusing and grim period. May get involved with morally corrupt individuals. Possible losses through deception and treachery.

Deception through bosses or other authoritative figures in which the native is unjustly blamed, for various mixed-up situations.

Confusing elements, false impressions, misunderstandings and complicated situations will surround the native's position or career. Someone may try to discredit or undermine one's reputation.

Should the native be involved in politics, he must be careful of nebulous conditions surrounding him, and refuse to become a part of it.

Grief, sorrow or heavy responsibilities of a seriously ill individual plays an important role in the native's life or a parent, an old friend, or a long standing clandestine love relationship.

Health problems may develop through incorrect fitting shoes leading to trouble with the feet, bunions, corns and spurs.

Saturn opposes Neptune: The native is subjected to constant torments of deception and insincerity through others. Rejection, ridicule and emotional hurts, leads to the mistrust of others and shunning of close relationships.

Chaos and nebulous events surround business dealings. Hidden elements should be investigated surrounding the affairs of one's marriage or business partner and other close associations.

Saturn inconjunct Neptune: Possible care or service may have to be administered to an older, chronically ill person.

Confusing elements at work, creates chaos through co-workers who may try to blame you for errors in production or the shipping of products.

A boss or supervisor may coerce the native into accepting a certain job that he strongly dislikes, but will accept because they "feel" it is owed to the boss for past favors.

A hidden health problem may lead to a chronic condition. Be sure to wear safety shoes and protect your feet against industrial accidents.

Saturn conjunct or parallel Pluto: A progressed aspect remaining in force for a number of years. When stimulated into action, it can produce professional changes in one's career often taking him into a new and completely different line of work. If the native is of retirement age, he may think seriously of doing so.

An aspect in which old relationships have fulfilled their usefulness and thus are eliminated to make way for the new.

A possible sexual attraction to an individual of the May/December type. He may be 10 to 15 yers younger than she or vice versa. This aspect is also associated with the finishing or ending of a long standing clandestine relationship.

Afflicting aspects to this conjunction may indicate the death of an old friend, an authoritative figure, a parent or grandparent.

Saturn sextile or trine Pluto: Long range success through participation in mass efforts for the striving of recognition.

This aspect is generally accompanied with extraordinary energy and a fanatical desire to work hard in the pursuit of a personal goal. And, the will to assert oneself if necessary to achieve it.

Important changes and advancements take place in one's career. The blessed ending, through death, of a long chronic, suffering illness endured by a parent, an older family member or close associate.

The native may have foresight in making major moves or changes that will have long lasting beneficial results. For example, applying for early retirement because one's inner feelings sense that an upcoming union contract will not be as lucrative as the present one.

Saturn square, semi-square or sesqui-quadrate Pluto: Possible financial loss through poor judgment and bad investments.

The native may fail to achieve success or advancement in career, in spite of hard and laborious efforts, because someone else gets the credit for it.

Monetary funds through Workers' Compensation, Unemployment Benefits, sick benefits, social security, insurance settlements or retirement are delayed and hindered, through misinformation, lost papers and other countless detours. It appears as though it is taking forever to settle a claim.

There may be a death of an older member of the family, a parent or a close associate.

In general, this is an aspect of reversals in business, loss of one's public image and bad credit ratings. If one is running for public office, chances are, he'll lose the election.

Saturn opposes Pluto: This aspect tends to delay or restrict any claim the native may have concerning an inheritance, alimony, an insurance settlement or other joint monetary resources.

Major changes are apt to occur, requiring important decisions involving concerns of money matters. The native may have to alter existing conditions and take on additional responsibilities through a second job, if necessary, to augment the income and ease the financial burden.

An aspect of confrontation with another individual who may try to dictate or force their views and will upon you.

Saturn inconjunct Pluto: Don't take advantage of company's time, merchandise, equipment or duplicating machine to use on your personal projects. Chances are, you'll get caught.

Possible changes in job schedules may require one to work the night shift. Patience is a must, for instances may arise where you are low-man on the totem pole and everybody wants to boss you, even your co-workers.

Changes may take place concerning dental and health or hospitalization plans, where formerly the coverage was fully paid, the company may now require you to pay half, or some of these benefits may be dropped completely.

191

URANUS

In similar fashion as Saturn, the energy of Uranus is not fully appreciated or understood until the individual has reached maturity. At which time rebellion against rules and regulations and authoritative figures broadens out towards humanitarian endeavors. The selfish demands for personal freedom and independence, undergoes a change towards understanding and compassion for humanity.

Uranus is the original mind, the inventor, always alert for the new, the different and the unconventional. Where Saturn's nature is to solidify and assimilate, Uranus breaks up and separates man from its stagnant existence.

Changes are a necessary part of growth and future development. The manner in which we adjust and accept the element of the unexpected is expressed by the new House position of Uranus in the Progressed Chart.

Uranus governs conditions to do with aeronautics, air travel, clubs and organizations, friends, CB, TV and radio, inventions, the unexpected and the unconventional. ''Acts of God'' concerned with lightning storms, tornadoes, hurricanes, earthquakes and volcanoes.

Individuals who will enter your life through the influence of Uranus are likely to be astrologers, advisors, electronic technicians, friends, inventors, hypnotists, peculiar and bohemian type of people.

Unlike the faster moving planets (i.e. Sun, Venus, Mercury and Mars) Uranus does not advance too far from its natal longitudinal sign and degrees. However, it can advance through as many as four houses in one lifetime.

Every year through progressions, each house cusp advances approximately one degree. Uranus does not advance in degrees that fast, therefore, Uranus is drawn closer and closer to the house cusp of its natal position, until it finally leaves to enter the next adjoining house. It is for this reason, that the natal house position of Uranus and the three houses to the left of it will be of great importance. The energy of Uranus will color these houses at various stages through progressions.

As with Jupiter and Saturn, the mean motion of Uranus in progression is slow. It is unlikely that Uranus will change signs, unless in 29° of a sign and advancing forward in the Zodiac or 0° of a sign and retrograding back into the Zodiac.

One does not take into consideration Progressed Uranus in close proximity with its own natal position. The one or two degrees that Uranus progresses or retrogrades will merely extend the influence when aspected by a personal progressed planet, a major transit or an Eclipse.

Uranus conjunct Ascendant: This is a progressed aspect that remains in force for some time, but when provoked into action may stimulate the native into seeking his independence and personal freedom at all costs.

Is likely to make rash decisions without proper forethought. One is rebellious against those that try to restrain him. May be unconventional in actions and thinking.

If single, he may suddenly decide to get married. If married, may feel restricted and press for separation.

Nervous tension and intensity is ever present, making the individual difficult to live with. He may over-react, quickly and forcibly.

The sign should provide a clue as to the motivating effect of this conjunction. In Aries, the native is his own worse enemy, due to an abrupt manner and a flare-up temper; in Taurus, unsettling financial conditions, an obstinate nature; in Gemini, mental stimulation, sometimes a serious mishap concerning a brother or sister; in Cancer, emotional outbursts and crisis in the domestic circle; in Leo, obstinate pride and problems with children and so on.

Many unexpected incidents, change of residence or position. A very unsettling and disquieting period in life. Strange and unusual or unconventional people enter your life.

Uranus conjunct Midheaven: Can induce radical changes in the native's profession. The action is abrupt, unexpected and disturbing. Very often a complete reversal of one's career.

The native feels a rebellious attitude against those he thinks are trying to impose their will upon him.

If the aspects to this conjunction are favorable, the native may suddenly find himself before the public's eye, on radio or TV.

The general trend produces sudden and unexpected changes in the personnel department. One day, you have a male supervisor, for example, and the next day, you find he has unexpectedly been replaced by a female who is determined to "shake the basket," with her new and unique approaches to the handling of present business affairs. Consequently, she may cut your working hours, change your shift or place you in a different department that you may not like.

Uranus conjunct Descendant: Uranus can create eventful social activities, even when none were planned. Expect the unexpected for it can disrupt even the most carefully laid plans.

Social functions and affairs may take a surprising twist of events through unexpected and unusual circumstances.

Upheavals and disruption of life through the action of others are possible.

Surprising changes in personal and partnership affairs. Unconventional and unusual changing behavior patterns in the marriage or business partner may make them less likely to cooperate or listen to reason. This can have a devastating effect on the relationship and possibly lead to divorce or separation.

Should this conjunction receive afflicting aspects from a major transit or an Eclipse, the native's partner may develop a health problem that will be difficult to cure and perhaps require radium or X-ray treatments. They should exercise caution and guard against possible accidents.

The energy of Natal or Progressed Uranus on the Descendant and in opposition to the Ascendant, can take you into the opposite direction of which you intended to go. An unsettling and upsetting and uncertain period of time in which one just can't seem to count on anything.

Close friends and relationships will gradually, and some, even suddenly, drift away to venture on their own.

Sometimes this is the Uranian way of permanently severing a relationship that has outgrown its usefulness, only to pave the way for new ones after the opposition has ceased to be effective.

Fixed signs are more apt to be drastically affected, for they tend to cling to old, established patterns. Best to place less reliance on stability, and try to become more flexible to alterations. Open oneself to new and progressive undertakings and attempt the things one never had the courage to do before.

Uranus conjunct I. C.: Sudden and unexpected gain or loss through property or real estate. Family ties and home conditions are apt to undergo sharp new arrangements that, at first will seem upsetting but later will be seen as a change for the better.

Unsettling home conditions: upheaval or sudden change of residence is possible, separation from a family member, not necessarily through death but rather through their possible moving to a distant city or through abrupt misunderstandings.

Should this conjunction of Uranus and the Fourth House Cusp receive afflicting aspects, it can be a dangerous period for wind and electrical storm damage, or destruction through hail and tornadoes.

Uranus sextile or trine Ascendant/Descendant: A new sense of freedom and action is pronounced, colored with a magnetic quality that makes one stand out in a crowd. Many expected opportunities and changes ahead. Beneficial contacts through friends. Exciting new enterprises, ventures and undertakings.

New friendships are made. Creative or humanitarian endeavors, are possible on a group level, through the joining of clubs and organizations.

The possibility of an unexpected romantic attachment. This can stimulate an opportunity for marriage to someone that is original in thought, brilliant, interesting and unique.

Many unexpected invitations to weddings and parties. The meeting of unusual and unconventional people is likely to be interesting.

Uranus square, semi-square or sesqui-quadrate Ascendant/Descendant: Reputation may be affected through unwise choice of friends. Erratic behavior coupled with an abrupt nature makes the native hard to understand and to get along with.

Heavy stress results in close relationships often resulting in divorce due to the native's unyielding desire for personal freedom.

Unexpected accidents are possible. Sometimes unconventional relationships are formed opening the door to homosexual or perverted activities.

Many up and downs are experienced during this three year period. The changes are sudden and drastic. The unexpected events not only affect the native but those around him through illness, surgery or accidents according to the house position of Progressed Uranus and the house it rules in the Progressed Chart.

One may break up with a romance or business partner to pursue matters yielding greater personal freedom.

Uranus sextile or trine M.C./I. C.: Unexpected gain and good fortune through advancement in personal affairs.

The native has a magnetic quality that draws others to him, thereby assisting in the advancement of his career and profession.

Influential friends and clubs or associations of prestigeous background can enhance the native's reputation.

One may rise to a position of influence over a large group of people. A good time to invest in new and advanced methods of operation in one's field of occupation. Contacts with computers, electronic equipment, radio and TV will play a major role in the native's life during this span of time.

Unexpected sale or purchase of home and property. The home may serve as a meeting place for group activities that endeavor to support humanitarian efforts.

Uranus square, semi-square or sesqui-quadrate M.C./I. C.: Major upsets and sudden loss or reversal in occupational interests.

The severing of ties, or loss of a parent through death. Rebelling against the establishment may acquire you a reputation as a troublemaker or a radical. Check the aims and policies of the club and organization that you intend to join, or you may find more than you bargained for.

In a young child's chart, this may instill a desire to run away from home, due to what they think is heavy parental restriction of their independence.

Unexpected events of a devastating nature may occur surrounding home and property. Unexpected and upsetting events concerning affairs of family members.

Uranus conjunct or parallel Neptune: A progressed aspect of long duration. When stimulated into action can indicate the joining of secret societies or organizations.

The introduction of new friends who are either very creative and musically inclined or deceptive, unreliable and troublesome.

Serious afflictions to this conjunction can turn friends into enemies. Possible confinement of friends in a hospital or an institution due to drug addiction.

New, different, unique and unusual outlets for creative expression; as with the purchase of an electronic organ, or learning the art of belly dancing. Excellent for the occult, mystical experiences and the study of Astrology.

Uranus sextile or trine Neptune: Gives accurate psychic and intuitive feelings. Interested in attending psychic centers or astrological seminars and conventions.

Anything that is mysterious, secretive or unusual will hold an attraction for the native.

A romantic, yet unconventional, clandestine affair. There is a strong emotional attraction towards the opposite sex. But, for one reason or another, the affair must be kept a secret.

A unique aspect in unconventional and creative outlets. New, different and unusual inventions can prove to be very profitable.

Friends or clubs and organizations can be supportive in humanitarian endeavors and working with the handicapped.

Uranus square, semi-square or sesqui-quadrate Neptune: The reputation may be affected by a sudden reversal, especially through unwise choice of friends or associations.

A very upsetting time in the native's life in which faith in his fellow man is shattered. Friends prove to be treacherous and may implicate the native in a scandal. The native must be careful of joining questionable clubs and organizations or cults that are under investigation.

Friends made during this period are likely to be unstable, drug addicts, heavy drinkers, deceptive, thieves or possibly have a police record.

Heavy afflictions from a major transit or an Eclipse may pose a danger through unusual accidents, threatening enemies who may endanger the native's life, an abduction, or kidnaping.

Uranus opposition Neptune: Friends are inclined to turn against the native at a time when he needs them the most.

The native, in his humanitarian efforts may take the defense for someone, only to be left holding the bag by himself. Others disappear when it comes time to acquire support from them.

This is a time to question the true meaning of friendship, who are, and who are not your friends.

Rebellious conditions come to light through the most unexpected set of circumstances.

Acts of indiscretion and unwise choice of friends can bring you notoriety with perhaps your photo in the newspaper.

Uranus inconjunct Neptune: Loss of personal freedom due to the constant care required of an ill family member.

Disturbing events of an unexpected nature through unreliable friends create chaos and deceptive situations.

Poor choice of friends who deal in narcotics may get one in trouble with the law.

Co-workers who supposedly are your friends come to you with their personal problems and complaints. In your attempt to counsel them, the situation becomes confused and you find yourself being labeled as a trouble-maker, by your supervisors. You are dejected when you discover the co-workers have disappeared rather than coming to your assistance.

Uranus conjunct or parallel Pluto: Stimulates desire for freedom. Ability for deep research coupled with scientific investigation may produce profitable inventions.

Progressed Uranus conjunct Natal or Progressed Pluto is an aspect of long duration. When stimulated into action by other transits or an Eclipse is an indication of a turning point in one's life.

One is apt to feel courageous, yet foolhardy with a great surge for independence and freedom.

Unexpected situations arise involving mortgage payments, alimony, insurance, income tax or one's checking account is suddenly overdrawn.

Heavy afflictions to this conjunction may result in sudden break up of an old relationship to make it possible for another to enter the picture.

Possible unexpected catastrophes, resulting in a rebuilding or a renewal of that which was destroyed.

Uranus sextile or trine Pluto: The study of metaphysics, Astrology and the occult subjects are favored.

Sudden and unexpected financial gain through joint finances. A great, unexpected and beneficial turning point in one's life through the most unusual circumstances is possible.

The native may be placed in charge of a large organization or a group of people for the purpose of changing, revitalizing or reversing certain situations.

Uranus square, semi-square or sesqui-quadrate Pluto: A highly charged emotional involvement or experience can take the native close to the brink of a nervous breakdown.

Sudden and unexpected events bring disaster where one must rebuild a home or business and start anew. Perhaps through an "Act of God" or the devastating effects of a tornado or heavy windstorm damage.

Unexpected trouble through income tax auditing, alimony, inheritance or mortgage payments.

There may be the sudden death of a parent or close associate.

Uranus opposes Pluto: One of the most drastic and upsetting aspects. Unreliable friends can be the source of financial drain.

Possible danger through unwise choice of business associates who may be unscrupulous or have dealings with the underground.

The native may desire to sever a relationship, but finds it difficult to do so. The other person will not yield or compromise and remains obstinate in wanting to continue the relationship.

Uranus inconjunct Pluto: May stimulate a desire for a position as a healer or increase deep rooted healing powers and instincts.

An obsession to learn all things that are beneath the surface. The native may acquire terrific powers of observation, or begin study or research that requires painstaking efforts.

An urge predominates one to change a certain aspect of their job or enter into a new and completely different field, where they will have more control over their own duties.

NEPTUNE

Neptune is the planet of spirituality and psychic developments; the unfoldment of beauty, expressed through artistic creations, music, singing and dancing or photography and movie films. If one permits the pure energy of Neptune to enter the heart, Neptune can be sympathetic, compassionate and caring for the downtrodden, the handicapped and the ill or mentally disturbed.

Neptune in its purest sense sees beauty in all things. He can be blinded by the good that he wants to see and the people he wants to believe in.

Youth visualizes Neptune as a means of escaping from reality, sometimes through the abuse of narcotics, alcohol, the so-called thrill of stolen goods or sexual intrigues.

Maturity heralds the realization of Neptune's healing powers through nursing, physician, chemistry and psychiatry.

The Natal House and sign position indicate how one uses or abuses the energy of Neptune. The new house position of Progressed Neptune in the Progressed Chart reveals its influence upon us at various stages through progressions.

Neptune governs conditions concerned with drugs, alcohol and sensitivity to certain types of medication. Situations that are surrounded with deception, chaos and confusion, clandestine affairs, hidden secrets and fears, behind the scene activities, and being influenced by one's environment, permitting oneself to be exploited by others.

Individuals who will enter one's life through the influence of Neptune are likely to be: psychics, artists, musicians, beauticians, one's secret enemy, deceitful people; emotionally, mentally or physically handicapped persons, alcoholics, detectives or those connected with the medical field.

As with Jupiter, Saturn and Uranus, the mean motion of Neptune in progression is very slow. It is unlikely that Neptune will change signs unless in 29° of a sign and advancing forward in the Zodiac, or 0° of a sign and retrograding back into the former sign.

The one or two degrees that Neptune progresses or retrogrades will merely extend the influence when aspected by a personal progressed planet, a major transit or an Eclipse.

However, Neptune will progress through as many as four houses in the Progressed Chart in an average life span. These four houses will play an important role in the native's life as the energy of Neptune influences each house at various stages in progressions.

One does not take into consideration Progressed Neptune in close proximity with its own natal position.

Neptune conjunct Ascendant: Possible failure of personal plans through lack of perseverance or practical ability. The native appears to be surrounded by confused or mixed-up conditions. The tendency to be exploited by others for their own selfish purposes.

Can be intuitive, inspirational and creative. Very impressionable to surrounding conditions. May desire to own a water bed, a cottage by the lake, or develop an interest in tropical fish and purchase an aquarium.

Possible psychic, supernatural or mystical experiences.

Afflicting aspects to this conjunction from a major transit or an Eclipse may induce hidden, unusual or hard to detect illnesses. Possible severe reaction from drugs or medication.

The native may try to escape from reality through abuse of drugs, alcohol or sleeping more than is normal. One should seek an outlet through some form of creative activity, perhaps in the line of music lessons or dancing.

Neptune conjunct Midheaven: Confusion, deception and chaotic conditions surround one's professional career.

Others may try to undermine your reputation. Business associates and those you deal with, in public affairs, will take advantage of your generous nature.

Someone will steal something from you that is connected with your line of work. Be alert and guard against such possibilities happening.

Without any advance notice, you may discover your photo in the newspaper, on a convention flyer or in a magazine.

Afflicting aspects to the conjunction of Neptune and the M.C. may pose a serious illness and much hospitalization for a parent.

Neptune conjunct Descendant: Individuals that you formerly relied upon will seem less dependable than you would expect during these few years ahead, that Neptune will conjunct your Seventh House Cusp.

Don't be too trusting, it is possible that someone may agree to perform certain services on your behalf and then mislead you.

Double check all legal and binding contracts before you sign anything. Other individuals who enter your life during this trend may not appear to be on the level and could prove disappointing. Take constructive measures to avert them.

If the marriage partner is a former alcoholic, it may be possible that they will begin drinking again.

Heavy afflictions from major transits or an Eclipse may induce a serious illness affecting the marriage or business partner. One that will be difficult to define or cure, but, perhaps controllable through medication.

Use precautionary methods in the care and improvement of your own health. Avoid overindulgence in alcoholic beverages. Use only medication that is prescribed by your physician.

Neptune conjunct the I. C.: If there has been a seriously ill person in the home, progressed Neptune will soon be leaving the influence of your Fourth House, resolving the problem with this chronically ill family member. The ill person in your home will no longer require your specialized care. Either they have passed away, entered a nursing home or another family member has taken over the care of this patient in their home.

Ghosts or spirits that have invaded your premise may nct be seen as often as in the past.

In the present home, water damage, sewer or plumbing problems will be a thing of the past.

As Neptune is also opposing your 10th House Cusp, take the time to examine your career goals, for possible loopholes in the achieving of your aims. Guard against confusing elements through those in authority connected with your job.

A possible change of residence, perhaps from the acquisition or disposal of property. Domestic tranquility may be under subtle attack, guard against possible theft in the home.

If purchasing a home during this trend, be sure the papers you sign have been inspected by an attorney to avoid possible loss through deception or liens. Take the time to check the basement walls for damage. If newly painted, it could be a hidden factor. Check the bathroom floors for loose tile. If covered with a throw rug, pull up and inspect for pop-up tiles. Check plumbing leakage and above all, the bedroom ceilings for a leaky roof.

Neptune sextile or trine Ascendant/Descendant: The native develops an inner understanding of other people and becomes more sensitive and compassionate. A magnetic personality with the ability to gain through others.

An intuitive insight and knowledge of what others are going to say before they say it. Psychic awareness and dealings with people in the field of mysticism.

There is the uncanny sense that guides the native into the right place at the right time resulting in gain through unusual circumstances. For example, a chance meeting with an old friend who tells you about a job opening, the native applies for it and is hired.

An interest in music lessons on the guitar or an organ, or perhaps a purchase of a water bed, an outdoor pool, or an aquarium. Some take belly dancing, others go camping or purchase a boat or secluded cabin by a lake.

One's photo may appear in the local paper. If you lecture, the organization may feature your photo in their flyer and advertisement material.

Illnesses are detected before they get too far out of hand. You "feel" something is wrong and may correctly point out the problem to your physician.

Neptune square, semi-square or sesqui-quadrate Ascendant/Descendant: This is an aspect of disillusionments and disappointments in personal affairs and goals. There is much mental confusion with the inability to rationalize. Anger and hurt through deception of those you trusted the most.

It is like a fog, creeping up on you and one is not aware of these nebulous influences until the devastating damage is done.

Hidden illness or sensitivity to certain medications. Someone may enter the hospital for a mental, emotional or physical problem. The services of a psychiatrist may be required, if not for yourself, then for some close member of the family.

Should a major transit or an Eclipse provide additional afflicting aspects to this configuration, some may become so distraught that suicide may be contemplated. Every issue is expanded out of proportion. Some seek escapism through abnormal sexual experiences or sexual relationships only to discover that they have become caught in a web from which the other party will not release them.

The native is easily influenced and swayed by others. The harshness and reality of life is difficult to accept. As a means of escapism, some individuals may seek the intangible in the way of daydreaming, sleeping more than is normal, drugs, alcohol or clandestine affairs.

This aspect is sometimes associated with a desire for the strange and unnatural in appetite and tastes.

The main influence stems from not facing reality and seeing matters as they really are. This can open the door to disturbing emotional relationships in marriage and business partnerships. There can be abuse or betrayal of confidence one has placed in another.

Neptune sextile or trine M.C./I. C.: Intuition is sound and dreams can become reality. A most favorable aspect for psychic and mystical investigations. For seeking employment in a hospital, medical center, working with the police, or the handicapped. Your compassionate nature is boundless and you have great sensitivity.

Others notice the unusual change in your personality and thus become drawn to you like a magnet. They may ask many favors of you, just be sure you know when to draw the line. Learn the art of saying "no." New creative outlets may interest you. It is possible to instill them in your line of work. For example, teaching a combined routine of dancing and exercise for betterment of health.

An excellent time to look for your ideal home. Especially if you want to acquire additional space for a work shop or a teaching center in one part of the house.

Some may enlarge or remodel their present home. Perhaps, building or adding on a little niche for yourself. A place that other members of the family will not intrude upon and respect your desire for solitude and meditation.

Neptune square, semi-square or sesqui-quadrate M.C./I. C.: Deception, confusion and hidden intrigues surround professional and family affairs.

Best not to reveal personal aims and plans until you are ready to set them into action. There may be a conspiracy working against you, ready to betray your confidence.

Secret enemies may be jealous of your success and try to undermine your reputation and public image. Possible negative dealings with the police department. A family member or close associate may be hospitalized.

The native must always use caution in signing papers and reaching agreements in matters of property and one's career. You may see only what you want to see, and not what is really there.

Do not close your eyes to what is happening within the family circle, especially with young people still residing in the home. Secret intrigues and unusual circumstances surrounding their affairs may come to light in the most devastating manner.

Neptune conjunct Pluto: A progressed aspect that is impossible to achieve in anyone's lifetime. Neptune and Pluto have been maintaining an approximate distance of 30° to 60° apart from one another since the early 1920's.

Everyone will have this type of close approximation in their Natal Chart. The mean motion of these planets in progression is likely to be around 1° to 3° at the very most in one life span. It is easy to see that it would be impossible for Progressed Neptune to ever conjoin Natal or Progressed Pluto.

Neptune sextile Pluto: (Trines are not possible in progressions between these two planets.) This is a slow progressed aspect that will remain in force for a number of years. It will take a personal progressed planet, a major transit or an Eclipse to stimulate this configuration into action.

The psychic intuitive ability is enhanced and uncanny. A strong interest develops in the occult, the mystical and a life after death.

The native may enter a totally new field of occupation. Dealing with chemistry, dark room developing, graphic arts and other specialized fields. There is an urge to enter one's own business, to be in control of one's own time and actions.

This is a milestone aspect in which a turning point develops in one's professional or personal affairs. A new vocation, relocation or going into business for oneself.

Periodically, money through unusual ways and circumstances will fall into the native's lap, very often with little effort on his part. In other instances, a creative outlet that has been dormant, comes to light and is a tremendous financial success.

The native should tap his inner resources for any possibility that can help him attain his goal and aim in life.

A large sum of money can be won, through the use of the mental intuitive capacity. Permitting the psychic nature to select the raffle ticket, pick the lottery numbers or by joining unusual contests that one would not dream one would win.

There is the power of visualization and the uncanny ability to put it into constructive use. The ability to cope with great stress and unusual problems.

Inner vision, inspiration and imagination produces positive results with far-reaching goals in dealing with the masses.

Neptune opposes Pluto: As with the conjunction, this is an impossible progressed aspect to achieve in one's normal life span.

Neptune inconjunct Pluto: As with the conjunction, this is an impossible progressed aspect to achieve in one's normal life span.

PLUTO

Pluto is the planet of elimination. He purges and removes that which no longer serves a useful purpose, to make room for the new. The planet of rebirth and regeneration. Only through the painful process of death, can one be reborn again to begin life anew.

Pluto is the penetrating mind, with strong opinions which can be expressed in a forceful manner. There is the will to dominate, to control and influence others. The emotions are deep, intense and kept fully under control at all times. There is an intensity of sexual feelings, yet often kept in control through strong religious beliefs. Loyalty above all towards those he loves. Unrelentless revenge for his enemies.

Pluto governs conditions concerned with group cooperation, death, changes, elimination, ESP, nightmares, psychic dreams, compelling forces and inversions. Money belonging to others, alimony, Social Security, Workers' Compensation, mortgage payments, income tax, insurance, property tax, sexuality and surgery.

Individuals who will enter one's life through the influence of Pluto are likely to be gamblers, criminals, racketeers, mortgage or bank managers, funeral directors, insurance adjusters, income tax agents, leaders of large organizations, physicians, policemen or psychic healers.

As with Jupiter, Saturn, Uranus and Neptune, the mean motion of Pluto in progression is very slow. It is unlikely that Pluto will change signs unless in 29° of a sign and advancing forward in the Zodiac, or 0° of a sign and retrograding back into the former sign.

The one or two degrees that Pluto progresses or retrogrades, will merely extend the influence when aspected by a personal progressed planet, a major transit or an Eclipse.

However, Pluto will progress through as many as four houses in the Progressed Chart in an average life span. These four houses will play an important role in the native's life as the energy of Pluto's influence touches each house at various ages in progressions.

One does not take into consideration Progressed Pluto in close proximity with its own natal position.

Pluto conjunct Ascendant: The native tries to redo, or control certain situations in which they find themselves. They exert a subtle influence upon the circumstances, so that they may change it for their concern or personal or financial betterment.

A milestone aspect in one's life with revolutionizing tendencies. A complete change in developments, style of dress, hair or mannerism.

A turning point and a new beginning of a new phase in life. One senses that changes lie ahead and this intensifies the feelings and emotions. Gives great physical powers of endurance to help achieve important accomplishments.

Afflicting aspects to this conjunction may induce a preoccupation with death or sexual promiscuity. Danger of permitting the emotional intensity to get out of control and cause the blood pressure to rise, considerably affecting the health. Possible danger of accidents, possible death of a family member, a grandparent or close associate. There is a desire for the new, yet at the same time, hesitation to let go of the old.

An interest in the metaphysical sciences but should avoid the practice of black magic.

This aspect induces struggles and parting of the ways. The deepest urges are mastered. Disturbing events and a loss occurs that touches you deeply. This touch with death may change your attitude concerning life and the manner in which you are living it.

Pluto conjunct Midheaven: Change of vocation or new direction in career. A tenacious striving towards power and independence. Professional and occupational matters are full of struggles, taking unusual courses, hindered by crises and situational changes.

Dissatisfaction with your goal in life as it now appears to you. The urge to get into the public's eye and the business world, may get out of hand and create animosity with close associates.

There can be a death of a parent or close family member.

Favorable aspects to this conjunction can induce honors and advancements, fortunate success and power. Victory comes after a bitter struggle and much self-sacrifice.

Pluto conjunct Descendant: A radical change through one's marriage or business partnership. The native should guard against using forceful tactics with those they love, to obtain one's goal.

The native may be viewed as being anti-social due to his aggressive and domineering tendencies. The desire to bring other people under the rule of one's own will. A separative aspect and possible divorce. A crises period, which can lead to various litigations, many powerful and secret enemies.

206

Nervous tension, self-imposed restrictions or disciplinary trends. Inability to express emotional feelings to the opposite sex or towards those you love. The native may feel as though their mate is becoming too dictatorial, possessive, jealous, and defiant. May try to control the native, and if not handled properly, may lead to the parting of the ways.

If the individual is not married and has no business partner, the conjunction of Pluto on the Descendant, can react on the native's own personal health.

The native is envied for his knowledge and skill. May come before the public and attain public acclaim for a specialized field of endeavor.

Pluto conjunct I. C.: Major changes in the domestic sphere. Pluto is getting ready to leave its presence in the Fourth House. It will take aong with it, the removal of an individual who resides in the home, and has tried to dictate or control every activity of each family member. This may be a grandparent, brother or sister or a child. The removal is not necessarily through death, but rather, due to forced circumstances resulting through constant pressures and family disputes.

Children leave home to enter the service, college or get married. In some cases, the native may be forced to leave home due to pregnancy or rebellion against parental authority.

Death of a family member. Possible damage to home and property due to a major catastrophe and requiring complete rebuilding and renewal. Such may be the case through earthquakes, tornadoes or heavy wind storms.

Pluto sextile or trine Ascendant/Descendant: New phases enter the native's life in which change is easier to accept. There is the forming of new partnerships and making many new contracts, requiring a readjustment of situations or circumstances.

New paths, changes and a new way of life with new experiences, sometimes the changing of one's appearance. The ending of one era and the beginning of a new one. The urge is to renew or rejuvenate the image you project to others. May unconsciously try to change your personality.

Pluto, the planet of will power and striving for personal ambition, can initiate the individual to make necessary changes to their best advantage. An enormous power in overcoming trials and tribulations.

This aspect can indicate a complete change, the awakening of latent powers and the beginning of an absorbing new phase in one's destiny.

The native may involve himself in deep research or investigation of the use of mind control, magical forces and psychic powers.

Marriage potential that may completely change one's life style. Success through unusual and powerful contacts or associations. The ability to sway the masses through a fascinating power of influence upon others.

Pluto square, semi-square or sesqui-quadrate Ascendant/Descendant: A powerhouse configuration in which there is a battle of the wills between the native and those in his immediate environment, resulting in an anti-social reputation.

The native becomes obstinate in his will to control certain factors involving personal or business affairs. There is a strong desire to change or redo the image of the marriage, or business partner and close associates because, the native feels these changes are necessary. Those who resent the dictatorial attitude of the native soon become enemies.

Changes in life are difficult and disturbing with the removal of family members through death, an emotionally trying time.

Difficulties through inheritance, insurance or property of the dead. Sometimes there is a preoccupation or obsession with matters surrounding death.

Surgery is possible in the native's life. Women often have hysterectomies or other such forms of removal. Men undergo a surgical operation for possible prostate gland trouble or hemorrhoids.

Pluto sextile or trine M.C./I. C.: A major turning point in one's life through advancements in career and personal affairs. The native tends to persevere in the seeking of increased power and ambition. Will have necessary concentration and self-discipline to handle and complete difficult tasks that one would have thought impossible before, great powers of endurance, strength and courage.

Gaining of advancements that were long overdue, or through direct result of carefully laid plans and deliberate actions.

Gain in dealing with real estate or land development, possible gain of inheritance through a parent, and change of residence.

An excellent time for updating one's will and reviewing present insurance policy for adequate coverage. You see new ways for monetary gains.

Pluto square, semi-square or sesqui-quadrate M.C./I. C.: Radical changes in the professional career. Possible loss of position or a new, demanding type of boss that one finds difficult to understand or communicate with.

A very upsetting phase in one's life, possible loss of property through a foreclosure.

The native tends to be overly aggressive in personal behavior. Anti-social tendencies with those in authority and towards family members. This creates resentment and lack of harmony with others through constant battling of the wills.

The native should protect himself against possible burglary attempts, sexual assaults and other terrifying experiences.

Should avoid over-exertion of oneself that can be a detriment to one's health.

Death of family member or close associate.

THE MOON'S NODES

It has been this writer's experience through many years of teaching, counseling and research, that the North and South Nodes represent involvement with others.

Conditions and circumstances that bond the native in a close tie with another individual.

The Nodes obtain much of their influence through the ruler of their sign containment. Which will in turn, reveal the consequences of the matter. For example, Progressed Venus in 24° Virgo exactly squares the North Node in Gemini and the South Node in Sagittarius.

Venus in its square aspect indicates a possible illness (Virgo) of a female family member (Nodes in Gemini and Sagittarius).

Check the condition of Natal and Progressed Mercury to determine if it is a close relative of the native. Check the condition of Natal and Progressed Jupiter to determine if the relative is an in-law or one that resides at a distance.

Whichever planet Mercury or Jupiter that is presently activated by other progressed planets, a major transit or an Eclipse should offer the clue as to whom Venus represents.

ASPECTS

Conjunctions with the North Node are considered favorable and in the quality of Jupiter.

Conjunctions with the South Node are considered unfavorable and in the restrictive sense of Saturn.

Sextiles or Trines to the North Node will naturally have a favorable influence on the South Node.

Squares to the North Node results in a square to the South Node.

Progressed Sun conjunct, sextile or trine Natal or Progressed North Node: Promotes associations and a shared experience with a male person: the boss, the husband, a male child or a friend. Advance in career.

Progressed Sun conjunct South Node or square North Node. A dealing with a male person of low character. Possible separation or termination of a male association.

Progressed Moon conjunct, sextile or trine Natal or Progressed North Node: A close emotional bond and relationship through women. Harmony in the domestic sphere, marriage and gain or assistance through women in general.

Progressed Moon conjunct South Node or square North Node: Trouble through women. Lack of emotional response through women. Possible breaking off of a relationship with a woman, or separation.

Progressed Mercury conjunct, sextile or trine Natal or Progressed North Node: Business contacts and many simulating interest with young people. Social contacts with brothers and sisters. Many short trips.

Progressed Mercury conjunct South Node or square North Node: Unsocial attitude causes disturbances in relationships. Accident prone. Separation through brothers or sisters. Difficulty in collaborating with others in one's profession.

Progressed Venus conjunct, sextile or trine Natal or Progressed North Node. New advantageous acquaintances. Romances, engagements, gifts and active social affairs. Gain or assistance through female contacts.

Progressed Venus conjunct South Node or square North Node: Breakup of a romance. Disagreeable and lack of harmony with others. Trouble through women. Possible divorce.

Progressed Mars conjunct, sextile or trine Natal or Progressed North Node: Positive use of energy with new enterprise involving a male. Marriage. Birth. Sexual relationships.

Progressed Mars conjunct South Node or square North Node: Disputes lead to separation. Danger through accidents involving another. Quarrels with loved ones. Trouble through sexual relationships.

Progressed Jupiter conjunct, sextile or trine Natal or Progressed North Node: A period of good luck and good fortune through the resources of another. Family increase through marriage or birth. Associations prove advantageous. A joyful reunion with family or friends.

Progressed Jupiter conjunct South Node or square North Node: Conflicts with in-laws. Loss of business contacts through antisocial behavior. Legal disputes through misjudgment of others.

Progressed Saturn conjunct, sextile or trine Natal or Progressed North Node: A May/December love relationship. Favorable contacts through older or influential people. Close bond with parents.

Progressed Saturn conjunct South Node or square North Node: Difficulties and heavy responsibilities through relationships. Death of a close family member. A feeling of rejection and lack of cooperation through others. Separation through family due to professional responsibilities.

Progressed Uranus conjunct, sextile or trine Natal or Progressed North Node: New friends and acquaintances. Gain through group activities. Exciting and unexpected circumstances and events involving another.

Progressed Uranus conjunct South Node or square North Node: Conflicts through friends and close associations. Separation through/or death of a close friend. Accidents and unexpected catastrophes.

Progressed Neptune conjunct, sextile or trine Natal or Progressed North Node: A clandestine affair. Contacts with unusual people, artists, musicians and psychics. Gain or assistance through a secret alliance. Psychic experiences.

Progressed Neptune conjunct South Node or square North Node: Unreliable associations. Contacts with persons with mental or emotional problems. Drug addicts, alcoholics and criminals. Being exploited or at the mercy of others. Deceptive people.

Progressed Pluto conjunct, sextile or trine Natal or Progressed North Node: A new association marks the turning point in one's life. Control over large groups. Contacts with healers, psychics and mystics.

Progressed Pluto conjunct South Node or square North Node: Heavy burdens through the association of another. Exercising the power of one's will against another. Death of/or separation through close associates or a family member.

Progressed Asc/Dec conjunct, sextile or trine Natal or Progressed North Node: The development of a new personal relationship. A favorable turn of events through another. A favorable change of environment through another.

Progressed Asc/Dec conjunct South Node or square North Node: Difficulties with close ties. Separation, grief or loss of a close family member or an associate. Disputes with marriage or business partners.

Progressed MC/IC conjunct, sextile or trine Natal or Progressed North Node: Advances through favorable business contacts and associations. Coming before the public. Working together with someone towards a common bond.

Progressed MC/IC conjunct South Node or square North Node: Difficulties through professional and business relationships. Loss of reputation and public image. Poor credit rating through the extravagant tastes of another.

RETROGRADE AND
DIRECT MOTION OF PLANETS

Retrograde motion gives the impression of moving backward in the Zodiac. This illusion is created by the Earth's motion, the Sun's position and the motion of the planet itself. The Natal House and sign position of the Retrograde planet is of the utmost importance in determining how the retrograde factor will affect one's life. The new progressed house position of the Retrograde planet, indicates the change of circumstances at various stages of life.

A Retrograde planet can be pictured in the same fashion as a faucet that is barely turned on and going drip, drip, drip. When the faucet is fully turned on, as with a Direct Planet, the energy begins to flow, without hindrances, restrictions or delays.

Mercury Direct at birth and later Retrograde marks a turning point in one's life concerning affairs of siblings, moving to new location and change of mental attitude. A determination to learn some new phase or mental pursuit in which the native quietly sets his mind to assimilating facts, that will reveal itself at a time when least expected. The year that Mercury turns Direct in motion begins the time when the native decides to put into action what he has been assimilating in the past. Also denotes another possible change of residence.

Venus Direct at birth and late Retrograde affects social contacts and love relationships. Friends of questionable reputation come into the native's life. He goes through a period of feeling unloved and unwanted. No matter how much affection one gives this person, it just never seems to be enough. They end up selecting a marriage partner that is beneath their social status, or of a different religion. One the family generally disapproves of, or the partner of choice may have a serious mental, emotional or physical health problem. In other cases, the partner was previously married and burdened with the responsibility and support of children.

Venus turning Direct after birth marks the time of life in which the native begins to feel better about themselves. This inner compulsion for desiring someone to constantly shower them with love and affection has mellowed. They can have, and enjoy the company of the opposite sex without trying to turn every relationship into a romantic love affair. They show more style in manner of dress and appearance. They feel better about themselves, physically and emotionally.

Mars Direct at birth and late Retrograde affects the energy span. The native seems less interested in trying to achieve a personal goal, or they find it is too much effort and not worth the time and energy they have to put forth. Men often experience problems with sexuality or ability to perform. Surgery or accidents are always noted the year that Mars goes Retrograde through Progression. Women, with Retrograde Mars may be an easy prey for the affection of the opposite sex. If permitted, men will take unfair, sexual advantage of the woman with a Retrograde Mars. They generally experience an emotional upheaval, sometimes more than once, before they have learned a lesson.

Mars turning Direct after birth will suddenly spur the native's energy into some new enterprise. They feel a compulsion to conquer something that has a hint of challenge to the project. Men become active in sports, football or bowling. Women change their attitude about the men in their past. No longer do they feel an intensity to fill an empty void, or so they thought it was during the Retrograde Mars motion. It is uncanny how these individuals soon become obsessed with some personal achievement, that held no interest in the past.

Jupiter Direct at birth and later turns Retrograde marks the year in which an in-law may pass away or perhaps a relative who resides in a distant city. Legal disputes arise and while they can be in the native's favor, the settlement is somewhat less than expected. Possible relocation, birth or marriage, in the family circle. Overestimating one's resources will have to be guarded. The native may develop trouble with credit rating.

Jupiter Retrograde at birth and later turns Direct opens the door for possible travel, higher education and expansion in business or a larger home. This also favors marriage or birth of children. The native is more optimistic, generous and often concerned with the social welfare of others.

Saturn Direct at birth and later turns Retrograde marks the year in which heavy responsibilities in personal or business affairs take hold. The native may feel as though his business or enterprise is not advancing as quickly as he hoped. Others appear to receive recognition for far less effort on their part. While the native must put in more time and effort and laborious energy, and still not achieve the same quality. The year that Saturn turns Retrograde may indicate a serious illness of a parent or loss of same.

Saturn Retrograde at birth and later turns Direct is the person with a built-in inferiority complex. There is the general feeling of a lack of self-worth. Life has posed many hardships since birth. Perhaps an early loss of a parent, separation from same, or lack of compassion and affection from the parent. They no doubt were hard working individuals, but had trouble expressing love and devotion to this native. This is an aspect of an ambitious person who wants desperately to rise above his early environment, to gain success and recognition, thereby achieving self esteem.

215

Uranus Direct at birth and later turns Retrograde is the year in which major changes take place. The native graduates from high school or college. There is a major change of position or relocation. There is an inner subconscious feeling that the native must relent some of his personal independence and freedom, if he is to fit in the role that is presently opened to him. Many unconventional people and crazy situations will affect his life. The native will have to learn to control the urge to take part in these erratic behaviors. Many unsettling events lie ahead and many unstable people will affect the native's life. An interest in Astrology, but hindered by family or job.

Uranus Retrograde at birth and later turns Direct marks the year in which the native senses an uplifting of restraints on one's personal freedom. This also marks an important year in which a major change transpires. New friends and acquaintances. The possibility of joining group activities or clubs and organizations. An interest in Astrology, and the time to take up the study without too much interference through family ties or career.

Neptune Direct at birth and later turns Retrograde marks the year in which the native may have much to do with hospitals or other places of confinement. Contacts with emotionally, mentally or physically handicapped individuals are possible. The native in his desire to be appreciated may permit himself to be exploited by others. To be used, abused and taken advantage of through unscupulous people. Chaos, confusion and deception surround certain situations in his life. Negative police activity is possible.

Neptune Retrograde at birth and later turns Direct is a turning point in which the native decides he will no longer permit others to take unfair advantage of him. This begins a phase in which a substitute being comes into play. Stepparent, stepbrothers or sisters, stepchildren and stepgrandchildren (children of your son or daughter's first marriage partner). There is the possibility of a clandestine relationship. Some hidden intrigue may play an important role in the native's life.

Pluto Direct at birth and later turns Retrograde brought the native in touch with death through a close member of the family. This seems to unleash the realization that death was final in the elimination of someone. In a few of the cases with whom I have studied, this contact with death changed their attitude about the way they were living at the present time. Many made a complete turnabout in their life. A change of job that provided more leisure time with the family, or one that exerted less pressure upon the nervous system.

A few of the women spoke of sexual assaults through the father or stepfather. One incident began around the age of 11 in a female's chart at the time of Pluto's Retrograde motion. In the three cases noted, Retrograde Pluto was position in Leo in the Natal Fourth, in square aspect with Natal Sun in Scorpio. One female had Sun in Leo in the First House square Natal Neptune in

Scorpio (Pluto ruled) in the 4th House. She was assaulted by her stepfather. The third had Pluto in Leo in the First House squared by Natal Sun in Taurus in the 10th House. Other confirmations in their charts came from the 8th and 12th Houses. Confirming hidden secrets and fears in regards sex and a family member.

The few experiences with Pluto Retrograde at birth and later turning Direct in motion, brought about a complete change of life style, vocation and in some cases, relocation. It appeared to create a milestone in one's life.

BRIEF SUMMARY

1. One or two progressed aspects will not promote a major event by itself. They will, however, add a new dimensional coloring to the native's personality. In every major event, there has always been numerous aspects providing a link between the natal and progressed charts.

2. Make it a point to apply the usage of what I have termed ''Astro-Graphics.'' Draw on a separate paper, the natal and progressed aspects, with the planets in their sign position. Attach this sheet to your Progressed Chart. This graphic illustration will enable one to keep a weather eye on the Solar and Lunar Eclipse and major transits that are likely to set off these sensitive points. Examples of ''Astro-Graphics,'' begin with Chart #13.

3. The easiest method in working with ''Astro-Graphics,'' is to list all the aspects between natal and progressed charts in singular fashion. Then, link the aspects together, to form a graph. What is the purpose of using graphics? To enable the astrologer to recognize the seriousness of the event. To pinpoint the area of life that is presently undergoing heavy activity. It has been this writer's experience, that inconjuncts produce major events in progressions, if, one (or both) of the planets at either end, receive favorable or unfavorable aspects to reinforce the transpiring event.

4. In seeking the possible time of event (although this would really require another textbook on the subject), one must look for the same type of planetary energy that is being activated through the natal and progressed charts. For example, several progressed aspects to Natal or Progressed Saturn and Uranus, would require a close watch on transiting Saturn and Uranus. What aspects are they making to your progressed or natal planets? What about the houses they rule? Are they activated by a major transit or a previous Eclipse? All these things should be taken into consideration. Progressions do not indicate an event, but rather, time an event. When a progressed aspect occurs and has a profound affect on the individual, one will always find, that an Eclipse and a major transit, has transpired during that period of time.

5. To protect the privacy of the clients and students who so graciously granted permission in using their charts, their names, and birth data have been purposely omitted, to avoid any possible link as to their identity.
6. For those interested in the ''2 Charts in 1,'' illustrated in the latter part of this text, they can be ordered through the AFA catalog, #2455-06 Form 12-Sophia Mason.

Chart #1
(#9 — Important Features in a Progressed Chart)

At approximately age six, Progressed Saturn will progress into this native's First House. If you were to subtract the 9° Libra on the 2nd House Cusp from the Longitude position of Saturn in 15° Libra, the difference would be six degrees, equal to six years of life. At which time Natal Saturn entered the angular First House in this native's Chart.

Natal Neptune position in 17° Leo in the 11th House will enter the Progressed 10th at approximately 30 years of age. Subtract 17° Cancer from 30° Cancer to find the remainder of degrees of Cancer in that house.

$$\begin{array}{r} 30° \text{ Cancer} \\ - \ 17° \text{ Cancer} \\ \hline 13° \text{ Cancer} \end{array}$$

Add the 17° of Neptune's position in Leo to the 13° remaining in Cancer and the age factor will be 30 at which time Neptune would approximately enter the Progressed 10th House. This individual became an office nurse for a gynecologist who specialized in the delivery of babies (Leo).

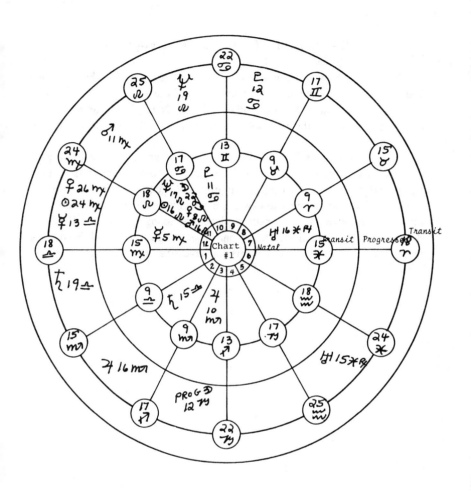

2 CHARTS IN 1
NATAL AND TRANSITS
PROGRESSED AND TRANSITS

Chart #2
(#15 — Important Features in a Progressed Chart)

Notice, how two major transits are affecting this individuals Second House of Money. Transiting Pluto in 2° Scorpio in the Natal Second. This person had an accident, transiting Pluto rules the Natal Third, she is having a terrible time settling the insurance claim with the other driver's insurance company.

Transiting Uranus in Sagittarius is in the Progressed Second House of Money. This native's daughter, suddenly (Uranus rules her Progressed 5th of children) decided to quit her job and return to college (Uranus in Sagittarius).

She is now financially assisting her daughter with college tuition. This individual has two major transiting planets affecting her Second House of Money. One in her Natal Second and one in her Progressed Second. Both major transits are creating different incidents that have a direct bearing on her personal finances.

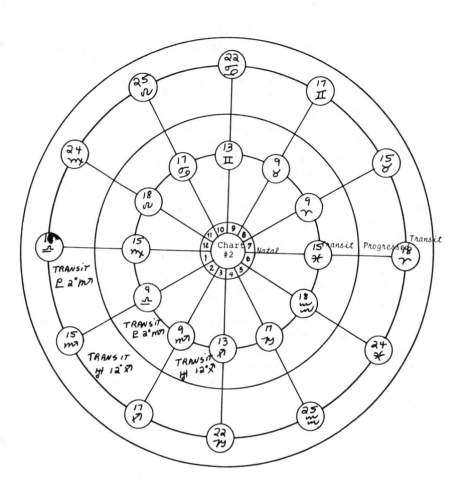

Chart #3
(#1 — Crucial Indicators in the Progressed Chart)

Progressed aspects take precedence over major transits.

Progressed Sun in 22° Virgo squared this gentleman's Natal Saturn in 22° Gemini in the Second House of money. He was forewarned to be extremely careful during the next three years with finances.

This native went bankrupt, divorced, lost his home and his excellent supervisory position. The trend continued throughout the three years that this Progressed Sun/Natal Saturn aspect was in effect. One year while the Progressed Sun was applying to the square from 21° Virgo, another year while exact and then the third year as the Progressed Sun was separating in 23° Virgo from the Natal Saturn in 22° Gemini.

The following year, this gentleman was able to secure a new position, married a second time and the financial picture began to look great. Until, Progressed Sun in 25° Virgo began to approach the square to Progressed Saturn in 26° Gemini. Again, he lost his supervisory position and began another three year trend of financial restriction.

About this time, however, transiting Jupiter, Saturn and Uranus were all in the sign of Libra, trining his Natal Saturn from time to time. Although his Natal Saturn in 22° Gemini was the benefit of three major trines from three major planets in Libra, it was not enough to offset the progressed aspect. The three planets provided assistance from his second wife's parents and through other close associations.

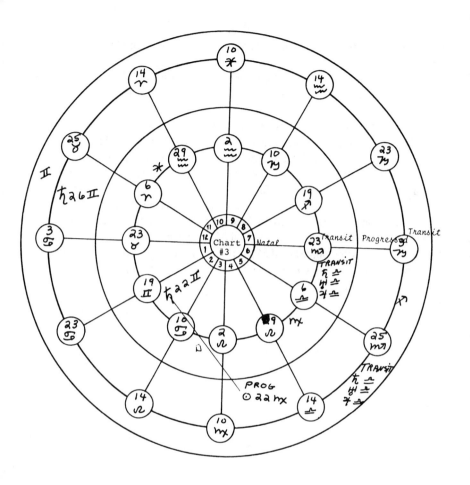

Chart #4
(#6 — Crucial Indicators in the Progressed Chart)

Progressed Mercury 15° Cancer, ruler of this native's Progressed Gemini on the Sixth House Cusp of health squared his Natal Mars 15° Libra, ruler of his Natal 6th.

Notice that both planets, Progressed Mercury and Natal Mars govern the same house and are in square aspect with one another. This gentleman developed a growth in his right lung (Gemini on his Progressed Sixth House Cusp), underwent surgery (Aries on Natal Sixth House), for removal of tumor. The operation was successful and for added protection, he received chemotherapy treatments (Progressed Mercury in trine aspect with Natal Saturn in 15° Pisces).

Not only did this progressed aspect between the two rulers of his Sixth House affect his health, but also his job. It was during this time, that he dissolved a partnership (Natal Mars in Libra squared by Progressed Mercury in Cancer) dealing with wholesale auto parts (Gemini on Progressed Sixth House Cusp).

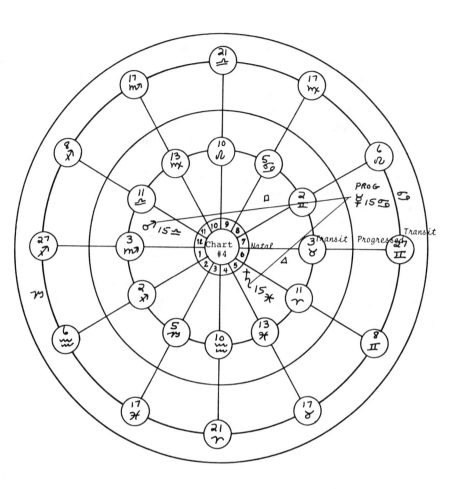

Chart #5
(#7 — Crucial Indicators in the Progressed Chart)

New Moon 23° Pisces squared Progressed Venus 24° Gemini, ruler of Taurus on Natal 3rd House Cusp and Libra on Progressed 6th of Health. Venus also rules the Progressed Ascendant sign in Taurus and the Natal Libra on the Cusp of the 8th House.

This gal owned a book shop (Progressed Venus, ruler of ASC in Gemini) and had to enter the hospital (Pisces New Moon square her Progressed ruler, Venus 24° Gemini), for a kidney stone (Libra on Progressed 6th House of Health). She lost a considerable amount of money because she had to pay a girl friend (New Moon in 11th Pisces square Progressed Venus in Progressed 2nd) to operate the book store in her absence.

The hospital stay was a success, surgery was not required as she passed the stone with the help of medication (New Moon 23° Pisces sextile her Natal Moon 23° Taurus, ruler of her Natal 6th).

Notice that both rulers, Natal and Progressed, of her 3rd House of book shop and her 6th House of health and work were activated by the New Moon in Pisces.

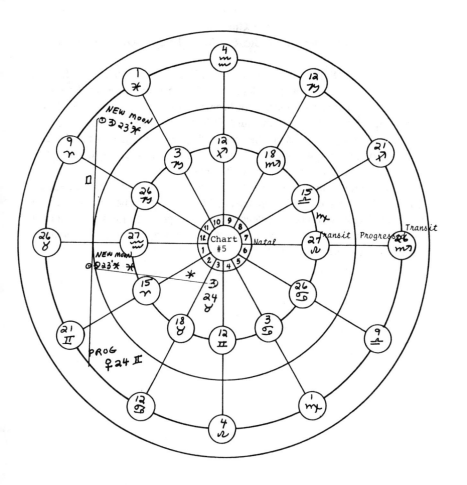

Chart #6
(#10 — Crucial Indicators in the Progressed Chart)

Progressed Sun in 5° Virgo conjuncts Natal Mercury 5° Virgo. In itself, this should not have been considered a difficult aspect. However, Progressed Mercury in 2° Libra was squaring the Progressed 10th House Cusp in 2° Cancer, providing additional force to the Sun/Mercury Progressed aspect.

It was unfortunate that a major transiting planet such as Saturn had to enter the sign of the siblings, Gemini at the same time as the progressed aspects highlighted both Natal and Progressed Mercury.

Transiting Saturn transited 5° Gemini and squared this female's Progressed Sun in 5° Virgo and Natal Mercury in 5° Virgo. Her brother (Progressed Sun conjunct Natal Mercury), became mentally depressed (transiting Saturn in Gemini, mental and squaring the Sun/Mercury conjunction), and committed suicide (Natal Mercury in 12 House).

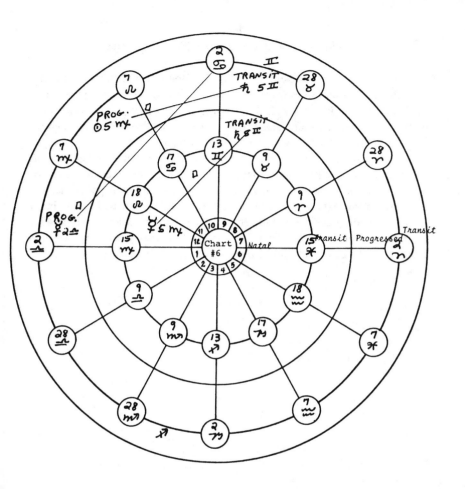

231

Chart #7
(#16 — Crucial Indicators in the Natal Chart)

New Moon 12° Pisces in the Natal 12th House sextile Natal Uranus and Mercury in Taurus in the Natal 2nd House. This native purchased a church raffle ticket (12th Pisces sextile Uranus ruler of 12th), from her sister (Mercury in Natal 2nd and rules her Natal 3rd). Very unexpectedly she received a phone call that her ticket was the winner of a $500 drawing.

The New Moon in 12° Pisces in her 11th House of unexpected circumstances squared her Progressed Mercury, ruler of her Progressed 2nd House of Money. The back end of her car gave out a loud explosive noise while she was driving. No one was hurt (New Moon in Pisces sextile Progressed Uranus in 1st House), however, the damage to her car for a new transmission ran over $400.

The one planet in the Natal Chart brought the unexpected monetary gain while the afflicted aspect to the Progressed Second House planet took most of it away.

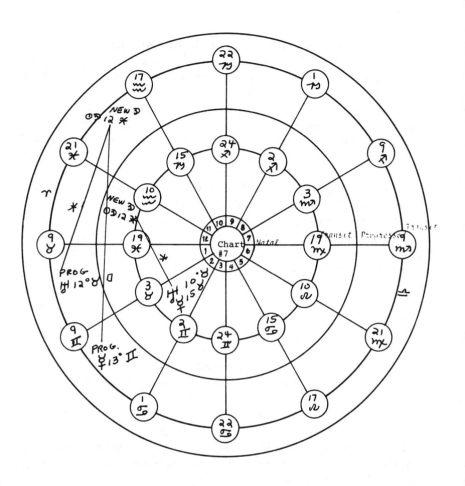

233

Chart #8
(#17 — Crucial Indicators in the Natal Chart)

Notice that the Progressed 10th House Cusp in 6° Aquarius is approaching a sextile aspect with Natal Uranus in 7° Aries.

As the Progressed 10th House Cusp continues to advance to 7° , the aspect will be exact. Ordinarily, its influence would lessen as it reaches 8° and separating. However, Progressed Uranus is now positioned in 9° Aries, therefore, the 10th House Cusp is continuing to enhance careers matters. As the Progressed 10th House Cusp advances to 8° Aquarius, it will apply to a sextile aspect with Progressed Uranus in 0° Aries. One year later, the career will reach its peak as the 10th House Cusp reaches 9° and exactly sextiles Uranus, and still holds its influence while separating in 10° Aquarius.

This gentleman invested in a Computer/Video store at the 1st Natal Uranus/10th House sextile aspect. His business is still prospering and booming beyond his wildest imagination.

Chart #8
(#18 — Crucial Indicators in the Progressed Chart)

Transiting Jupiter and Uranus are positioned in the native's 10th House of Careers in Sagittarius. The rise in one's career begins to climb and culminate when transiting Jupiter and Uranus leaves the sign of Sagittarius, enters the Progressed 9th in Capricorn and finally, reaching its peak when Uranus enters the sign of Aquarius and the Progressed 10th.

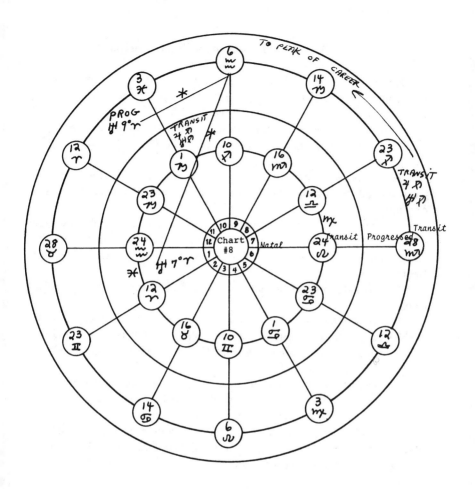

235

Chart #9
(#19 — Crucial Indicators of the Progressed Chart)

Both rulers of the 7th House, Natal and Progressed, are afflicted.
Both rulers of the 9th House, Natal and Progressed, were afflicted.
  (The 9th is the 3rd of accidents of the 7th)
Both rulers of the 12th House, Natal and Progressed, were afflicted.
  (The 12th is the 6th House of health of the 7th)

Progressed Mars in 21° Taurus ruler of the Progressed 7th House, exactly semi-squared Natal Venus in 6° Cancer, ruler of the Natal 9th and Progressed Ascendant.

Progressed Venus 5° Leo (ruler of Natal 9th, 3rd of 7th) is within 1 degree of leaving the square aspect of Natal Mars in 4° Taurus. Mars rules the Progressed 7th. Progressed Venus also is applying to a square aspect with N/P Neptune in 6° Scorpio, ruler of Natal 7th.

Both Natal Mars and Neptune are rulers of the Natal and Progressed 7th House.

Progressed Sun 27 Cancer conjuncts Natal Mercury 28 Cancer, both rule the Natal and 12th House (6th House of Health of the 7th). Two weeks prior to her accident, there was a Solar Eclipse in 11°43′ Sagittarius semi-squaring both Progressed Sun and Natal Mercury.

Notice that the ruler of the 5th House of romance, Saturn has Retrograded to 14° Capricorn and now squaring the Progressed ASC 14° Libra.

This young man was on a snowmobile with his girlfriend. He hit a tree, he escaped with no serious injuries. She, however, suffered serious head injuries (Aries on the Progressed 7th). Remained in a coma for 6 weeks. The doctors' foresee a long recuperation period ahead.

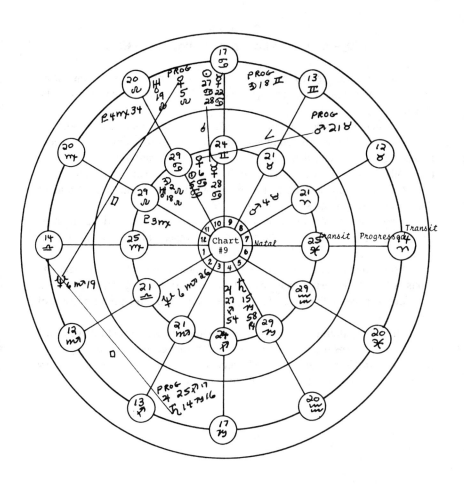

Chart #10
(#20 — Crucial Indicators in the Progressed Chart)

The Solar Eclipse of June 11, 1983 in 19° Gemini 43′ exactly conjuncted Progressed Moon in 20° Gemini in the native's Natal 4th and the Progressed 1st House.

This person lost both her mother and an uncle during the year ahead.

The Solar Eclipse also conjuncted transiting Mars 18° Gemini. Two weeks following her mother's departure, her uncle died of a cardiac arrest. This was her mother's brother, Mars in Gemini (brother) in the Natal 4th (parent).

The Solar Eclipse squared Progressed Mars in 18° Virgo (uncle) ruler of the 12th House of uncles.

Progressed Moon in Gemini in the Natal 4th illustrated the mother. Transiting Mars in Gemini in the 4th was the mother's brother, along with the square to Progressed Mars in Virgo (uncle).

Notice that there are two more confirmations coming from the Natal 8th House of death. Transiting Saturn and Pluto in Libra squaring Natal Mercury in 28° Cancer in the Sixth House of uncles and Mercury also rules the 4th House of parents.

The rule of thumb with Progressed Moon is to keep a watchful eye on the planet that governs the sign position of the Progressed Moon. The Progressed Moon was in Gemini and Natal Mercury received very afflicting and heavy aspects from transiting Saturn and Pluto in Libra.

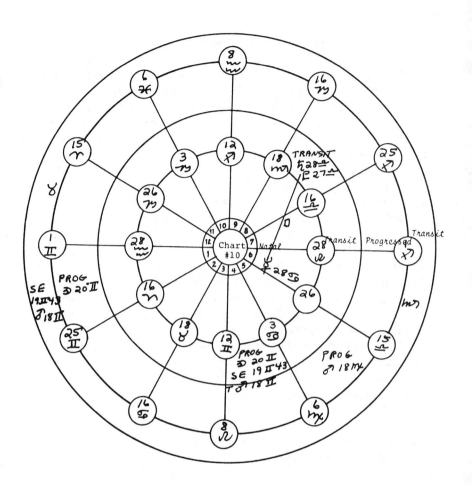

239

Chart #11
(Natal Pisces Ascendant Progressed to Aries Rising)

She was a young woman in her early 20's who has just recently emerged from her Piscean shell. Her friends commented of the remarkable changes in her personality. She was beginning to take full charge of her life. She had just undertaken driving lessons to become more self-reliant with thoughts of purchasing her own car. She had been totally happy in her vocation with the telephone company (Progressed Mars, ruler of her Progressed Ascendant in the communication sign of Gemini).

It was unfortunate that she did not notice a sex fiend observing her daily walk to the bus stop at the same time every morning on the way to work. She was abducted, raped and murdered, by a man who only lived a few doors away from her home (Progressed Mars in Gemini, neighbor).

Progressed Mars, ruler of her Progressed Aries Ascendant had reached 9° Gemini and applied to a semi-square aspect with Natal Uranus in 23° Cancer. Transiting Uranus was position in 23° Libra, squaring Natal Uranus and in sesquiquadrate aspect with Progressed Mars in 9° Gemini. Her Progressed ruler was in afflicting aspects with Natal and transiting Uranus, ruler of her Natal 12th House of secret enemies.

Progressed Mars in 9° Gemini had also formed a T-Square with Natal Ascendant in 10° Pisces and Natal Moon in 10° Virgo.

Neptune ruler of her Natal Ascendant was transiting through her Progressed 8th in 5° Sagittarius, exactly squaring her Natal Venus in 5° Pisces, ruler of her Natal 8th House of death.

Another connotation of her impending death, was transiting Pluto in 5° Libra exactly semi-squared her Natal Saturn in 20° Scorpio in her Natal 8th and Pluto ruler her Progressed 8th.

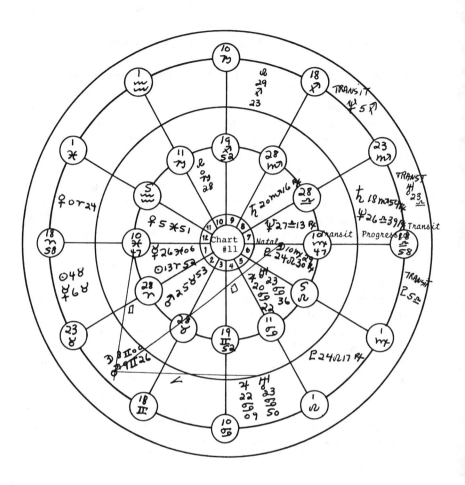

241

Chart #12
(Second decanate of Virgo on the Progressed Ascendant)

Mercury, ruler of his Progressed Virgo Ascendant is positioned in the Progressed 9th House in Taurus conjunct with Progressed Jupiter also in Taurus in the Progressed 9th. During his First decanate of Virgo, he went into the publication business (Mercury in 9th) which he operated from his home (Sagittarius on the cusp of his Progressed 4th, and Jupiter, ruler in the Progressed 9th).

As he entered the Second decanate of Virgo with Progressed Saturn as his decanate ruler, he became involved with clubs and organizations. Progressed Saturn positioned in the Progressed 11th. He also obtained step-grandchildren. His one son married a woman with children by her previous marriage (Neptune in his 11th of daughter-in-law, ruler of his Natal Ascendant decanate and of his Natal 9th of grandchildren).

Progressed Sun in 25° Aries in his Progressed 8th squares his Progressed Saturn in 25° Cancer in his 11th of daughter-in-law. Saturn rules his Progressed 5th of children. His son filed bankruptcy because his son's wife was a compulsive spender, he later filed for a divorce.

It is now a few years later and Progressed Venus in 25° Aries is squaring his Progressed Saturn still in the Progressed 11th of daughters-in-law. Progressed Venus governs the Natal 11th and the Progressed 9th. His son is returning to his former wife and will re-marry her. His former wife's spending habits have not changed. The son's savings account is fast becoming depleted again. If this young man (son of this native's chart) has not learned a lesson, history may repeat itself within another year when Progressed Venus approaches 26° Aries and separates from the square to Progressed Saturn in 25° Cancer.

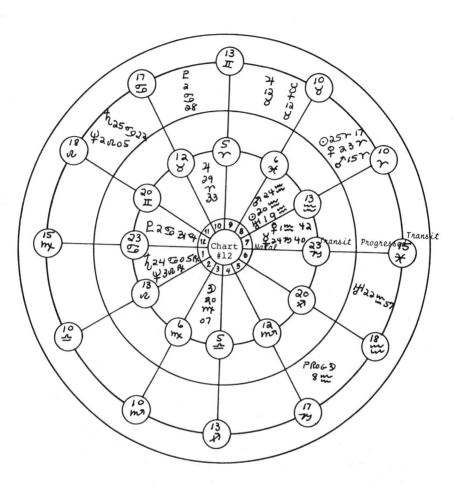

HOUSE CONNOTATIONS

First House Connotation

Chart # 13 is a young woman who, on her way to work in the morning, was abducted by a neighbor, raped and stabbed in the throat. Her murderer is now serving a life sentence. Notice that Natal and Progressed Mars, ruler of her Progressed Ascendant Sign is heavily afflicted. Progressed Mars in Gemini was caught at the tail end of an inconjunct with heavy afflictions to it. Mars in Gemini, governs a neighbor and this is confirmed by Progressed Venus in 0° Aries, ruler of Natal Third House, squaring the North Node. The ruler of the North Node is Saturn, in the Natal 8th House in direct opposition to Natal Mars in Taurus, ruler of the Progressed Ascendant. The one major serious afflicting aspect was Progressed Saturn in 18° Scorpio 59' inconjunct Progressed Ascendant in 18° Aries 58', a Martian ruled sign.

Chart # 14 is a young girl abducted, no body found and no suspect. Notice the similarity in graphic aspects between the two charts. Natally, Saturn in 1° Gemini opposes Natal Neptune in 0° Sagittarius, ruler of her Natal 8th. Her father remarried, and this girl was living with her father and step-mother. Notice that the Progressed Sun in 18° Cancer has just separated from the Progressed sesqui-quadrate (135°) from Natal Neptune in 0° Sagittarius, and is now applying to a semi-square aspect with Progressed Saturn in 2° Gemini. Other afflicting aspects to Venus, ruler of the Natal and Progressed Third and positioned in the sign of Gemini, along with afflicting aspects to planets in the Third in Libra (the marriage partner) and the planet in the Third rules the Seventh, confirming same. I would suspect a relative on the stepmother's side of the family. Someone she calls uncle, out of respect for her elders (Saturn rules her natal 6th of aunts and uncles). Progressed Moon in 28° Aquarius inconjuncts Natal Pluto in Virgo (uncle) and Pluto governs the 4th of parents. A relative of the parent. The Progressed Moon also squares Natal Jupiter in the 4th (an in-law) in Scorpio.

244

Chart #15 is one of the young black male youngsters murdered in Atlanta. Notice the uncanny similarity between this graphic aspect and the ones illustrated in Charts #13 and #14. Both Natal and Progressed Venus, ruler of the Natal and Progressed Ascendant sign, is heavily afflicted. Both Natal and Progressed Venus are caught in an inconjunct aspect with afflictions to both. Through many years of research, it has been my experience, that when there is a heavy overlay of planets in Sagittarius and activity with Natal or Progressed Jupiter plus additional confirmation from the ruler of the Natal or Progressed 9th, that someone of the opposite color or race is involved. In this case, there can be no question in my mind that it was not a black person who murdered this boy, but a white person. Notice Progressed Sun conjunct Natal Mercury in Sagittarius and afflicted. Natal Sun in Sagittarius and Progressed Venus in Sagittarius and afflicting Jupiter in Libra. The confirmation comes through Progressed Saturn in 2° Taurus, ruler of the Natal and Progressed 9th in semi-square aspect with the North Node 16° Pisces. It has been my experience, that a white person with a heavy Sagittarius, Jupiter and 9th House configuration, will have dealings with individuals of a different color and race. A black person with the same configuration, will have dealings with white individuals and persons of a different race.

Chart #16 is a young girl abducted, body never found, no suspect. Notice the two inconjuncts with heavy afflictions to planets at either end.

Chart #17 dealt in drug traffic. Tried to withhold money belonging to the racketeers. Was shot in the head. Notice the double inconjunct, that is heavily afflicted from every angle. Plus the T-Square involving Mars, ruler of his Natal 7th and Mercury, ruler of his Progressed 8th.

Chart #18 was murdered by his friend. Notice the unusual configuration of no inconjuncts, instead, two major oppositions with afflicting aspects to both. Notice the triangular formation in both Charts #17 and #18.

Chart #19 and Chart #20 suffered a massive heart attack. Notice the unusual similarity in the ''Astro-Graphics'' illustration in both charts. An inconjunct with a square on one side and a trine on the other.

Chart #21 and Chart #22 both had a serious motor vehicle accident. Notice the uncanny similarity in the ''Astro-Graphics'' illustrated in both charts. Both had an inconjunct with Progressed or Natal Mars involved with the planet at one tail end and in dire aspect with Uranus.

Second House Connotation

Chart #23 won $5000 in the State Lottery and had the chance to win $100,000. Unfortunately, the Progressed Ascendant in Scorpio (a money sign) was in a semi-square aspect with Saturn, the planet of limitations.

Chart #24 won $15,000 in the State Lottery. Notice how Charts #23 and #24 both had an inconjunct with sextiles or trines to a planet at either end. Chart #24 won more money due to the Grand Trine involving Natal M.C., Progressed Mercury in Taurus and Progressed Moon in Virgo. The Progressed M.C. in 6° Pisces 59′ semi-squared both Natal Sun 21 Aries and Natal Jupiter 21 Capricorn, lessening the chance of winning $100,000.

Although Chart #23 did not have a Grand Trine in the Progressed Chart, it did however, have Progressed Ascendant 10° Scorpio in three Trine aspects with Progressed Sun, Natal Venus and Natal Moon, all in Pisces.

Chart #25 won $5000 in the State Lottery. This native did not have an inconjunct, however, the usual opposition was present. Whenever a major event occurs, whether favorable or unfavorable, an inconjunct appears to be present or its comparable aspect, the opposition.

In the winning of a State Lottery, which is government controlled, the major denominator is the Tenth House Cusp, either natal or progressed. Through Progressions, the ruler of the Tenth, the M.C., or the sign Capricorn is favorably aspected with the ruler of the Natal or Progressed Second House Cusp.

Third House Connotation

Successful Kidney Transplant.

Charts #26 and #27 are brothers. Chart #26 donated a kidney to his brother Chart #27. Notice the uncanny activity in both charts.

Chart #26, the donor, has Natal Moon in Gemini in the 12th House.

Chart #27, the recipient, has Progressed Moon in Gemini also in the 12th House, at time of surgery.

Chart #26, donor, has Pluto and Jupiter in Natal 3rd, ruler of Natal 6th and Progressed 6th.

Chart #27, recipient, had no planet in the Natal 3rd, however, through progression, Progressed Pluto has entered the Progressed 3rd and Pluto governs the Natal 6th and Progressed 6th. Progressed Uranus (the planet of the unexpected) is also in the Progressed 3rd and has just received a sextile aspect from Progressed Moon in Gemini in the Progressed 12th.

Chart #26, the donor, has Progressed Sun in Aries trine Natal Jupiter in the Natal 3rd, ruler of the Progressed 6th.

Chart #27, recipient, has Progressed Ascendant in Cancer trine Progressed Sun in Pisces ruler of Progressed 3rd. Natally, Cancer is on the 3rd House Cusp.

Chart #26 was apprehensive and the decision was a major factor in his life as indicated by the two Progressed Oppositions, with afflictions at one angle and favorable aspects at the other angle. This was his second oldest brother, so the activity lies with the 5th House. Progressed Mercury, ruler of Natal Asc. opposed Natal Neptune in the 5th (second brother) and ruled the Progressed 10th (second brother's 6th house of health). The other Progressed opposition was Uranus in the 1st in opposition to Mars in the 7th.

His brother, Neptune in Libra (kidney) in opposition to Mercury in the 11th, was faced with a decision as well as he, with a 1st and 7th House opposition.

Chart #27, as with his brother, had an unusual aspect configuration. While his brother had two progressed oppositions. This one had two trines involving the same planets. Progressed Mercury in Pisces trines Natal Mars in Cancer. Progressed Mars in Cancer trined Natal Mercury in Pisces. Natal Mars had turned Direct in motion and caught up with Progressed Mercury who had since turned Retrograde in motion. Natal Mercury, was trined by Progressed Mars who had since turned Direct in motion.

Another major configuration was Progressed Jupiter and Saturn in Capricorn conjoined in the Progressed 8th of surgery and both govern the Natal 7th and Progressed 7th House Cusp. This was his *third brother* (7th House) who was donating the kidney. Progressed Jupiter and Saturn inconjunct Progressed Moon in Gemini in the Progressed 12th of Hospitals (Gemini, sibling) and Natal Uranus in Leo in the 3rd of siblings.

Both Charts #26 and #27 have trines involving the Natal or Progressed 3rd House.

Both Charts #26 and #27 have heavy afflicting aspects to Venus, ruler of kidneys. The surgery was serious, delicate, but extremely successful due to the many saving graces between the two charts of these two brothers. This love was expressed through Chart #27, his Sun in 14 Aquarius trines his brother's Moon in 14° Gemini, ruler of his Natal 3rd House. Chart #26 reveals the same devotion, Natal Sun 28 Pisces, ruler of Natal 3rd, trines Uranus in Cancer. Both aspects were exact in orb, which creates a deeper intensity of an emotional bond.

247

Sister has Mastectomy, but is doing fine.

Chart #28 — The planet Mercury is neither female nor male and depends upon other planets to give it a sex. In conjunction with Venus in 28° Aquarius, this indicates the sibling would be a sister. Both Mercury and Venus were in a serious afflicting aspect with Natal Venus in Capricorn, ruler of Natal 3rd in opposition with Progressed Mars in 14° Cancer.

However, both Progressed Venus and Mercury are involved in a trine aspect with Progressed Jupiter, ruler of the intercepted sign of Sagittarius in the Progressed 3rd.

Anytime a Natal or Progressed planet rules a House Cusp and aspects a Natal or Progressed planet in that House, we get a double confirmation. For example, Progressed Venus in 28° Aquarius, ruler of Natal 10th House Cusp, sesqui-quadrates Progressed Mars in 14° Cancer in the Progressed 10th. Two, 10th House configurations. She abruptly quit her job that year.

Progressed Mercury 27° Aquarius, ruler of 12th (she is an RN) trines Progressed Jupiter in her Natal 1st. She found a new job in a nursing home. This was confirmed by Progressed Sun 25°, ruler of Natal 12th trining Natal Jupiter in 25° Libra in her Natal 3rd. Both rulers of her Twelfth House of hospital employment were involved in a progressed trine aspect.

We had two confirmations to her quitting of her present position. Venus, ruler of her 10th and Mars in the 10th.

We had two confirmations of finding employment in an institution, both rulers of the 12th trined.

Fourth House Connotation

Chart #28A purchased a new home and subsequently moved.

When purchasing, selling and moving, Gemini and Mercury are usually activated along with the 3rd House to indicate a new neighborhood, and change of environment. Especially when either the sign Gemini or the planet Mercury is in an aspect with the ruler of the Natal or Progressed 4th House Cusp. In the Chart of #28A, the Progressed M.C. was positioned in 16° Gemini in semi-sextile aspect with Progressed Pluto 16° Cancer, ruler of the Progressed 3rd House Cusp. We now have an aspect between Gemini, the natural ruler of the 3rd and Pluto, Progressed ruler of the 3rd. A double connotation of a new neighborhood indeed.

Progressed Mercury in 15° Leo semi-sextiles Natal Pluto 15° Cancer, fortifying the first aspect. Mercury is the natural ruler of changes and neighbors and aspects the ruler of the Natal 4th of home.

Progressed Mars in 17° Virgo, ruler of the 8th House of mortgages, sextiles Progressed Pluto 16° Cancer. All indications clearly indicate a move for the better.

Chart #28B paid off a large mortgage on her home.

The differences between these two Charts is easy to spot. This chart has no Gemini, Mercury involvement. Indicating a change of neighborhood. Instead, there is heavy emphasis on 8th House (mortgages) matters, and 4th house property.

We have loads of confirmation to this effect. Note that Progressed Sun in 0° Scorpio (mortgages) is sextiling Progressed Neptune (ruler of the Natal 4th) in the Progressed 8th (mortgages) and the Progressed Sun governs the Cusp on the Progressed 8th House of banks and loans.

Whenever a planet rules a house and in turn, aspects a planet within that same house, it is a double feedback. The matter in question will be concerned with the House the planet rules because it is also aspecting a planet within that very house.

Chart #28-C
Death of a father through cancer.

When there is a loss of a parent, especially a male parent, the Progressed Sun and Natal or Progressed Saturn are more than likely involved. The chart also requires a heavy dire aspect involving either the 11th House (8th of the 4th House parent), or the 5th House (8th of the 10th House parent).

Note that Progressed Saturn in 11° Taurus conjuncts Progressed Jupiter in 10° Taurus and both conjoin the Progressed 4th House Cusp. Progressed Jupiter is the ruler of the Progressed 11th House (8th of the 4th). Both Progressed Saturn and Jupiter Sesqui-quadrate (135°) Natal Mars in 27° Virgo and Progressed Neptune in 26° Virgo. Both Mars and Neptune govern the 3rd which is the 12th Hospital of the 4th House parent. There is a double feedback that a parent will be seriously ill and hospitalized. Saturn and Jupiter in dire aspect with Natal Mars (ruler of the Natal 4th and Progressed 3rd) and Progressed Neptune (also ruler of the Natal 3rd). Pisces and Neptune and 3rd House aspects all indicate an ill parent when linked with a 4th House planet or ruler thereof.

Progressed Sun in 13° Scorpio in opposition to Natal Saturn 13° Taurus is difficult by itself. Unfortunately they both were involved in difficult aspects with Natal Mars. Additional feedback comes from an inconjunct from Progressed Jupiter and Saturn to Natal Moon which in turn is afflicted by Progressed

Mercury, ruler of the Progressed 8th House of death. This indicates that this individual will have to deal with matters pertaining to death during the coming year.

Chart #28-D, death of mother, heart condition.

Note that the Progressed Sun does not aspect Natal or Progressed Saturn as appears in Chart #28-C (death of father). There are two inconjuncts, one involves Natal and Progressed Moon, and the other, the M.C. in Cancer with Natal Saturn (a parent). A confirmation of parental concern is proofread by Natal Saturn in 4th and Progressed Moon in 4th. Progressed Mercury, ruler of the Natal 11th (8th House death of 4th House parent) is semi-squaring Natal Sun, ruler of Progressed 11th,

Fifth House Connotation

Chart #29 is the mother who give birth to a child blind at birth through cataracts. The child had corrective surgery six months later and was fitted with contacts.

In a female's chart, the 4th House indicates the first born child. Progressed Mars in 11° Sagittarius inconjuncts Progressed Moon in 12° Cancer in the Progressed 11th (8th of the 1st child in a female's chart). Mars ruled the Progressed 9th, 6th of the first child's health.

Progressed Ascendant in 3° Virgo sesqui-quadrate Progressed Jupiter in Progressed 5th, ruler of Natal 5th. Progressed Asc. also inconjuncts Natal Saturn and Moon in 4° Aries in the Natal 9th (6th House health of 1st child). Saturn now rules the Progressed 5th. We have two confirming aspects to health problems concerning a child.

The ruler of the Progressed Asc. Virgo, is Progressed Mercury in 29° Virgo trining Progressed MC 29° Taurus and sextiling both progressed Pluto 29° Cancer and Progressed Venus 0° Leo. Venus and Pluto are in the 11th and both rule the Natal and Progressed 4th (1st born child in a female's chart), indicating that surgery would be of beneficial help to the child.

With the ruler of the Progressed First House Cusp in a trine and sextile aspect, she would have the ability to cope successfully with the problem.

Charts #30 and #31 both had a child born with Cerebral Palsy. Both charts had the same aspect of Progressed Ascendant in opposition to a Progressed planet conjoined with the 7th House Cusp and afflicted.

Chart #30 had a female child. Progressed Venus 16° Scorpio inconjunct Natal Mars 16° Gemini and semi-squared Natal Venus 29° Virgo. Natal and Progressed Venus rule the Progressed 5th House Cusp and Natal Mars rules the Natal 5th House. A double connotation of concern of a child's health.

Progressed Asc. 3° Capricorn opposes Progressed Mars 3° Cancer and both square Progressed Moon 3° Libra. Progressed Sun 18° Libra squares Progressed Pluto 18° Cancer and also semi-squares Natal Ascendant 4° Sagittarius.

Chart #31 had a male child. In a male's chart, the 5th House is his first child, the 11th would be his 4th child. He had Progressed Venus in 19° Pisces conjunct Progressed Mercury 19° Pisces in his Progressed 8th House of birth, ruler of his Natal and Progressed 11th, in sesqui-quadrate aspect with Natal Neptune 3° Leo and opposition to Natal Moon 20° Virgo. Neptune rules his Progressed 8th House of Birth and the sign containments of both Progressed Mercury and Venus.

Progressed Jupiter, ruler of Progressed 5th of children, in 6° Taurus sesqui-quadrates Natal Moon, ruler of Natal Ascendant.

Progressed Ascendant in 21° Leo opposes Progressed Uranus 21° Aquarius conjoining the 7th House Cusp and both are afflicting the Natal MC in 5° Aries. A birth of a child would make a prominent change in his future life style. Note the trine from Progressed Mars in 24° Pisces to Natal Asc. conjoined with Progressed Saturn, he grew to love the child very dearly.

Sixth House Connotation

Aunts and uncles are governed by the 6th House along with the 12th. Both being the 3rd of the 4th House parent, and the 3rd of the 10th House parent. Health conditions of aunts and uncles activate the 11th and the 5th Houses. The 11th being the 6th of the 6th House aunt and uncle, and the 5th House being the 6th House of health and the 12th of aunts and uncles. Death of aunts and uncles involve 1st and 7th Houses. In this case, one will always find a heavy 1st and/or 7th House influence, 6th or 12th House, planets in Virgo, Pluto activated, or planets in Scorpio and Mercury. Along with the rulers of the Natal or Progressed

6th or 12th Houses and their planetary containments. And, 4th and 10th Houses due to parental upsets.

Charts #32, #33, and #34 are all the same individual who lost three uncles throuth suicide. All occurring at various ages in her life.

Charts #32 and #33 committed suicide by hanging. Chart #34, uncle took an overdose of drugs.

Notice how the planet Jupiter was activated in both Charts #32 and #33 and in the sign of Virgo. Jupiter governs the Natal 6th House offering a double connotation of aunts and uncles. Ruler of the 6th in the sign that naturally rulers the 6th. Natal and Progressed Pluto was also activated along with Uranus, ruler of Natal 8th (a death) and Progressed 7th. The Progressed Sun in 21° Sagittarius square to Jupiter in 22° Virgo (uncle) gave the necessary male sex to the aunt or uncle.

Chart #34 was suicide through overdose of drugs. No indication what so ever of a Neptunian effect in the Natal or Progressed Charts. Except for one major aspect which was in force for some time. Progressed Neptune in 10° Virgo (uncle) squaring Natal Mercury in 6th House (uncle). As mentioned before, Progressions set the stage, but the major transits or an Eclipse lifts the curtains for the play to begin. In this case, it was unbelievable that in January of 1973, transiting Neptune was in 7° Sagittarius conjunct with Progressed Mercury in 7° Sagittarius, setting off the Progressed square aspect between the same identical planets. Other transits in January of that year also gave further bearing. Transiting Uranus in Libra in the Natal 4th opposed Natal Moon, ruler of the Progressed 12th and squared Progressed Pluto in the Progressed 12th. Transiting Jupiter was in Capricorn in the Progressed 6th.

Seventh House Connotation

Chart #34A is a female's chart indicating marriage.

One of the most frequent indicators for marriage is to have Progressed Sun conjunct Natal Venus or favorably aspect the ruler of the 7th House Cusp. Another common denominator is Progressed Venus conjunct Natal Sun or favorably aspect the ruler of the 7th House Cusp. Naturally, the 1st House has to have a part of this action. Either the ruler of the 1st House Cusp, the Ascendant's Degree or planets therein.

Chart #34A was easy to spot with Progressed Sun conjoined with Natal Mercury, ruler of the Natal and Progressed 7th and also conjoined with Natal

Venus (ruler of marriage). Progressed Moon in 29° Sagittarius was trining Natal Neptune in 29° Leo. Unfortunately, Progressed Moon squared all three planets that were indicators of marriage. Progressed Sun and Natal Mercury and Venus in Virgo. Progressed Mars in the Progressed 7th House was in semi-square aspect with Jupiter, ruler of the Ascendant. This woman has remained married over 25 years. Her honest statement to me was, they were the most miserable years of her life, except for the children. Mars in the Natal and Progressed 7th in semi-square aspect to the ruler of the first indicated possible arguments and much bickering (Gemini) over monetary issues (Jupiter in Taurus).

Chart #34-B is also a female's marriage chart.

She divorced him one year later, the divorce chart follows. Progressed Asc. conjoined the Natal Sun in 12° Leo, and trined Natal Saturn in 12° Sagittarius, ruler of the Natal 7th House Cusp.

Progressed M.C. in 1° Taurus (money) was squaring Natal Mercury in 1° Leo, ruler of the Progressed 2nd House Cusp, and both were in semi-square aspect with Progressed Venus in 15° Virgo in the Progressed 2nd House of money. To further confirm serious monetary problems in this marriage state, Progressed Mercury in the Progressed 2nd House of Money in 8° Virgo was squaring Progressed Mars in 9° Gemini. As Progressed Mercury advanced to 10° Virgo (around one year later), it began its trine to Progressed Jupiter in the 10th House. She found a very good job.

Chart #34-C is her divorce chart.

The main problem was Progressed Mercury in 11° Virgo applying to a square to Natal Saturn 12° Sagittarius, ruler of the Natal 7th House Cusp. She felt mentally repressed by her marriage partner and financially restricted. She applied for divorce when Progressed Moon, ruler of her Natal Ascendant formed an inconjunct with Natal Mars, ruler of her Progressed 9th of courts of law and legal matters. The divorce was finalized when Progressed Moon exactly squared her Natal Moon in the 9th House. Progressed Sun in 2° Virgo semi-squared her Natal Pluto in 17° Cancer and she felt her husband has changed and was becoming too possessive and dictatorial which compounded her mental depression (Progressed Mercury square Natal Saturn). Progressed Venus in 17° Virgo trined her Natal Pluto in 17° Cancer in her Natal 12th. Yes, she had a hidden relationship during her divorce proceedings and yes, she married the following year.

Chart #34-D is a female's chart in which her husband had a massive heart attack.

253

Whenever a major planet conjuncts an angular House Cusp, it is a good idea to look closely into the balance of the Natal and Progressed Chart for further indications.

Natal Pluto in 17° Cancer conjoins her Progressed 7th House Cusp. Note, that both Natal and Progressed Mercury, ruler of the Natal 7th House Cusp are in afflicting aspects with the Moon, ruler of the Progressed 7th and Natal Sun, also, ruler of the Progressed 7th due to the intercepted sign of Leo therein.

Progressed Venus is afflicting the 7th House Cusp and Natal Pluto conjoining the 7th House Cusp. Venus governs the Natal 11th House which is the 5th House from the 7th (heart).

Whenever both Natal and Progressed ruler of a certain House Cusp is afflicted, this is serious, a forerunner of an important event. In this case, Mercury, both Natal and Progressed was afflicted, ruler of the 7th House Cusp. The Natal Sun received afflicting aspects (ruler of heart problems) along with Progressed Venus, ruler of the 11th, the 5th House of heart of the 7th House partner. He survived this massive heart attack as Progressed MC in 12° exactly sextiles the Natal Sun in 11° Virgo 56'. Also Progressed Mercury sextiled Natal Neptune in Leo (heart), ruler of the Progressed 2nd House Cusp, which is the 8th House of death of the 7th House partner.

One year later when Progressed Pluto in 18° Cancer conjoined her Progressed 7th House Cusp, her husband suffered a broken back in a car accident.

Eighth House Surgery

Chart #35 had a Laminectomy (back surgery). Surgery of any kind generally involves Natal or Progressed Pluto or the ruler of the Natal or Progressed 8th and the Natal or Progressed 1st House Cusp.

Progressed Ascendant in 26° Virgo was semi-squared by Natal Pluto in Leo (surgery on back). This was confirmed by Progressed Mars in 15° Cancer, ruler of Progressed 8th House of surgery in semi-square aspect with Natal Ascendant in 1° Virgo. Two aspects to First House, self.

The Houses have an uncanny way of confirming the part of the body. Progressed Sun (back) conjunct Progressed Venus in Aquarius in the Progressed Fifth House of back, both inconjunct Progressed Saturn, ruler of the Natal and Progressed 5th House of back.

This was not a life threatening health problem for there were no heavy afflictions to either at each end of the inconjuncts.

It was indeed a serious operation, but one could be assured that all would go well.

Ninth House Connotation — Progressed and Converse

Charts #36 and #37 are the Progressed and Conversed Charts of an individual who moved to the United States with her parents while she was a young child. This is the only example of a Conversed Chart.

Notice that the Progressed M.C. in 11° Scorpio squares her Natal and Progressed Saturn in 12° Leo in the 7th House of grandparents. They were very upset that their daughter and grandchildren were moving to another country.

Natal M.C. was trined by Progressed Sun, Pluto and Mercury in Cancer. The change was a favorable one for the family (Cancer). Progressed Venus, ruler of the Natal and Progressed 9th House was trining Natal Mars in her 8th, indicating a major change and her Progressed Moon in her Progressed First in 27° Capricorn. She had a Grand Trine, from the ruler of her 9th of long distance travels to the ruler of her 3rd, immediate environment and to Progressed Moon in her First, self. A confirmation of moving to another country, was the natural ruler of distant countries, Jupiter was in 26° Gemini exactly conjoining her Natal Sun in 26° Gemini.

Chart #37 is her Conversed Chart to provide some possible insight as to the moving to a foreign country (the United States). In the Converse Chart, we find additional confirmation of relocation to another country, Conversed Sun in 18° Gemini trines her Natal Moon in her 9th House. However, the square aspect from Converse Mars in 24° Virgo in the Conversed 9th to Natal Jupiter in Gemini (sibling) and Mars rules the Natal 3rd of siblings indicated that her brother would not fare too well. Confirmation of this health problem stems from Converse Neptune squaring Natal M.C. 4° Scorpio and Neptune rules the Conversed 3rd. Her brother died at an early age of tuberculosis.

255

Tenth House Connotation

Chart #38-A is a young man who had been out of work for over a year.

It was easy to assure this young man that he would have a job shortly. His Progressed Sun in 14° Capricorn was exactly sextiling his Natal Venus and Neptune in 14° Scorpio. Venus governs his Natal 10th House and Neptune his Natal 3rd and Progressed 2nd.

The Progressed M.C. in 13° is still within 1° orb of sextiling its own ruler, Natal Pluto in 12° Virgo.

Progressed Mercury in 3° Aquarius 48' is semi-sextiling his Natal Mercury 4° Capricorn.

He got a job with a printing company. Their main source of income is derived from printing of raffle tickets, bingo cards for churches and other paraphernalia that deals with a legalized form of gambling. This is all covered under the Venus/Neptune conjunction in his Natal 10th in Scorpio (other people's money). Of course, Progressed M.C. in Scorpio sextiling Natal Pluto assisted in the coloring of his vocation.

Chart #38-B is a young woman who received a large job advancement.

Note that Progressed Mars in 14° Capricorn exactly conjoins the Progressed 10th House Cusp. The planet Mars, is now the ruler of her Progressed Ascendant Aries.

There were no afflicting Progressed aspects, so we are to assume this Mars/10th House conjunction would be a favorable change in vocation.

Progressed Sun in 19° Pisces sextiles Natal Venus and Semi-sextiles Natal Mercury, both rulers of the Natal and Progressed 3rd House Cusp. Venus also governs the Natal 8th. She was a CPA and was made head of her department. When the 10th House Cusp is activated and at the same time both rulers of the 3rd House Cusp, the person will deal with records, and keeping of books that deal with money.

Twelfth House Connotation

Charts #38 and #39 were confined in a hospital for mental depression. Chart #40 is the chart of a native whose brother-in-law is confined in a penitentiary for possession and sales of narcotics.

Through research, it has come to my attention that many cases of mental depression involve the North Node if in the sign of Capricorn or in aspect with Saturn.

Notice in Charts #38 and #39 both had North Nodes activated by a Progressed aspect. Chart #38 had North Node in Capricorn and brought into play through progressions. The other had North Node in Taurus and aspected through a square by Progressed Mars and Natal Saturn. As you will note through the "Astro-Graphics," there were other progressed aspects in force at the same time.

Chart #40 is the brother-in-law confined in prison. There was a lot of activity among planets that govern in-laws. Sagittarius, Libra, Jupiter, Mercury and Gemini. Note Progressed Ascendant in 6° Sagittarius in opposition with Natal Mars in 7° Gemini, a relative. Progressed Venus in 17° Leo in the Progressed 8th and squaring Progressed Jupiter (in-law) in Scorpio in the Progressed 12th. Venus in the 8th and squaring a planet in Scorpio is a double connotation of an in-law accepting money through illegal transactions. The fact that Venus rules the Natal 7th is one indication that the relative may be on the husband's side of the family. Progressed Mercury in 8° Leo ruler of the Progressed 7th of marriage partner is in semi-square aspect with Natal Uranus in the 8th House in the sign of Gemini, brother of the 7th House partner.

In Conclusion

The most important feature is to note when the same two houses are activated through progressions. If that happens, zoom in on the affairs of that house and seek the consequences through the activity of the other planets. For example, Progressed Pluto semi-square Progressed Ascendant. Progressed Mars semi-square Natal Ascendant. Both Natal and Progressed Ascendant Signs are activated indicating that it is possible surgery will be a must that year for the native.

Look for confirmations, you will always find them.

For example, Venus in the 8th House squaring a planet in Scorpio. A double connotation, of money, sex or death problems.

Jupiter in Virgo, ruling the 6th House of aunts and uncles.

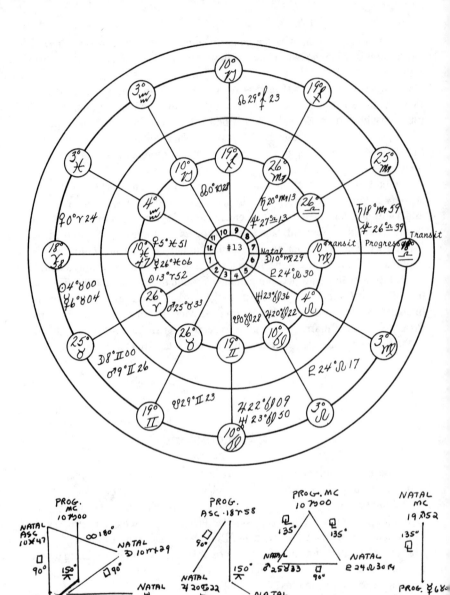

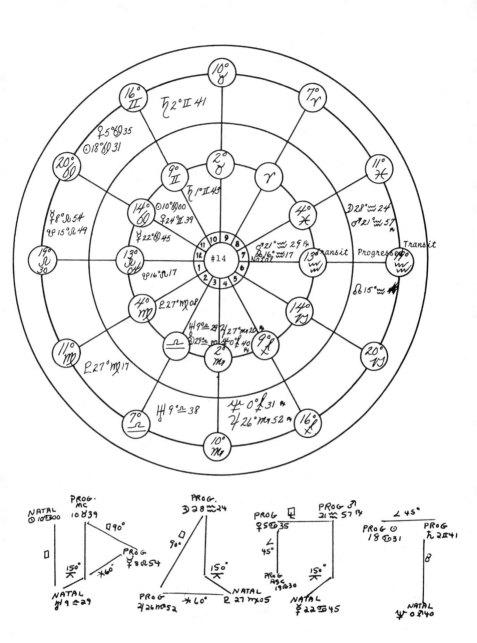

259

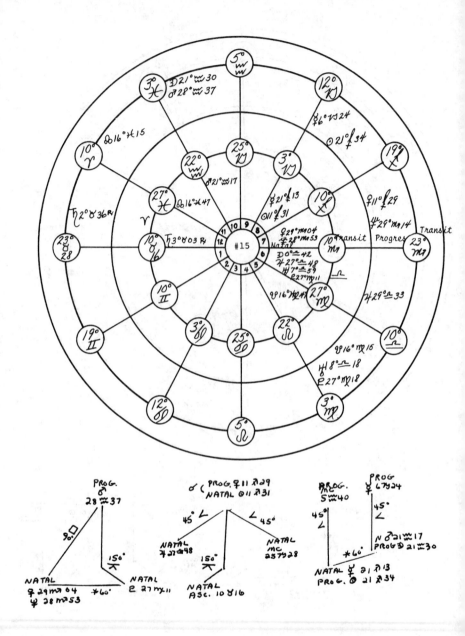

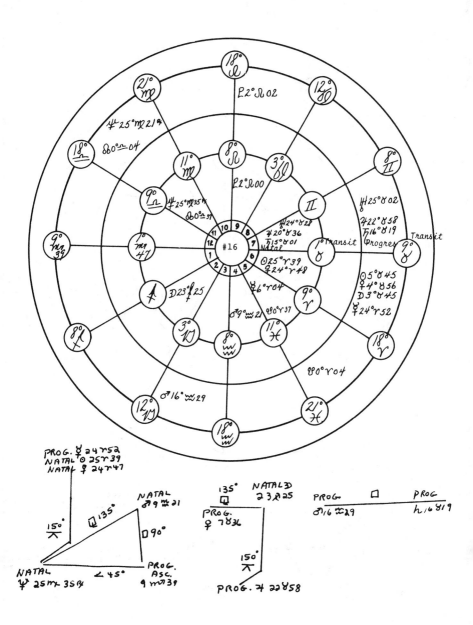

PROG. ☿ 24♈52
NATAL ☉ 25♈39
NATAL ♀ 24♈47

150° ⊼   NATAL
              ♂ 9♒21
□ 135°   □ 90°
              PROG.
              ASC.
NATAL   ∠ 45°   9♍39
� 25♍35℞

135°   NATAL ☽
□   23♌25
PROG.
♀ 7♉36

150° ⊼

PROG. ♃ 22♉58

PROG. □   PROG
♂ 16♒29   ♄ 16♉19

261

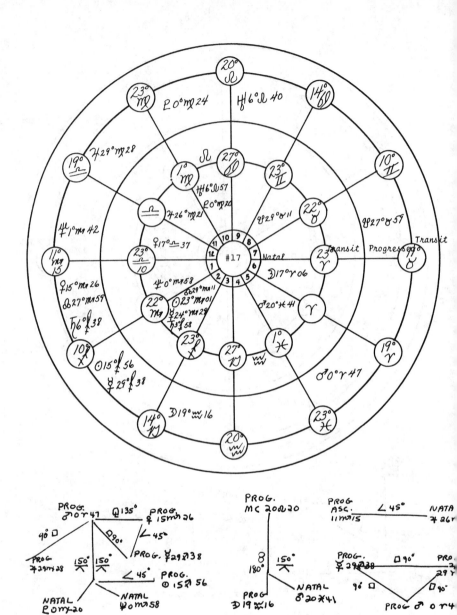

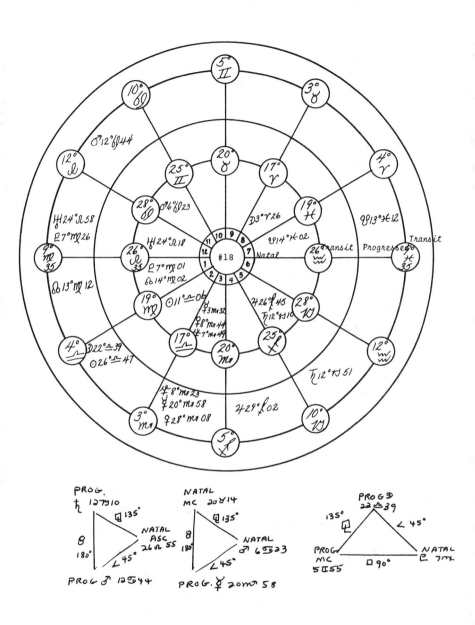

PROG.
♄ 12♑10

△ 135°

8
180°

∠ 45°

NATAL
ASC
26° ♌ 55

PROG ♂ 12♋44

NATAL
MC 20♉14

△ 135°

8
180°

∠ 45°

NATAL
♂ 6♋23

PROG. ☿ 20♏58

PROG ☽
22♎39

135°
⊔

∠ 45°

PROG
MC
5♊55

□ 90°

NATAL
♇ 7♏

263

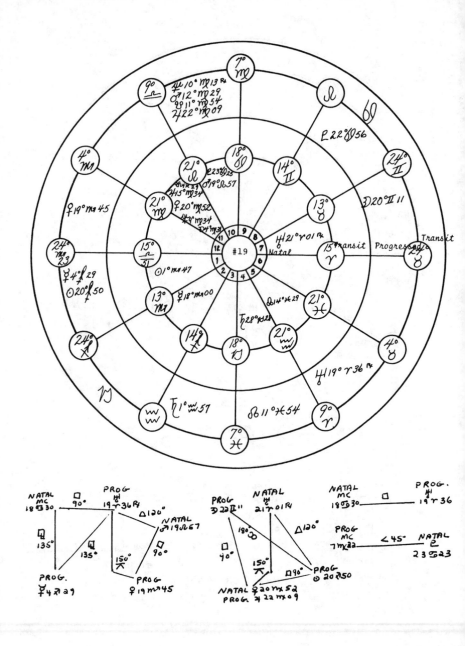

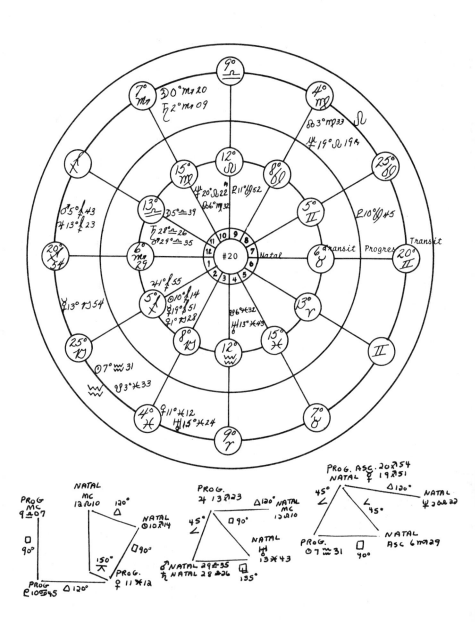

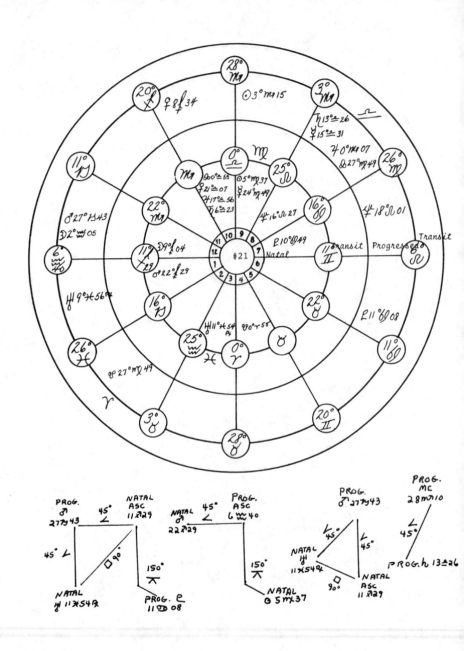

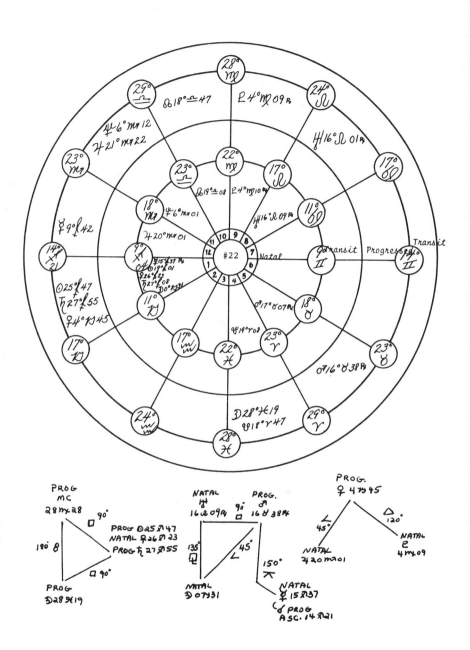

267

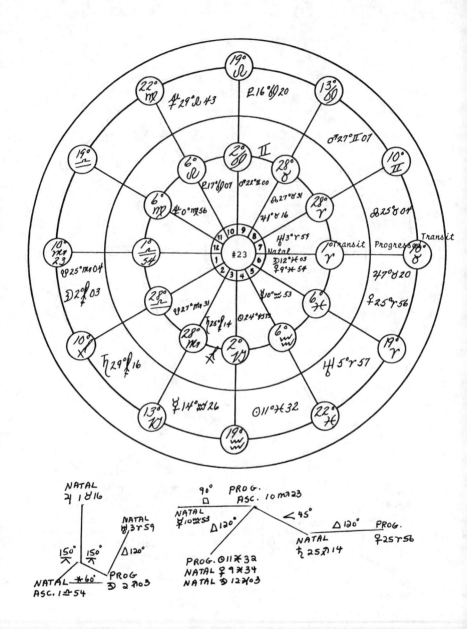

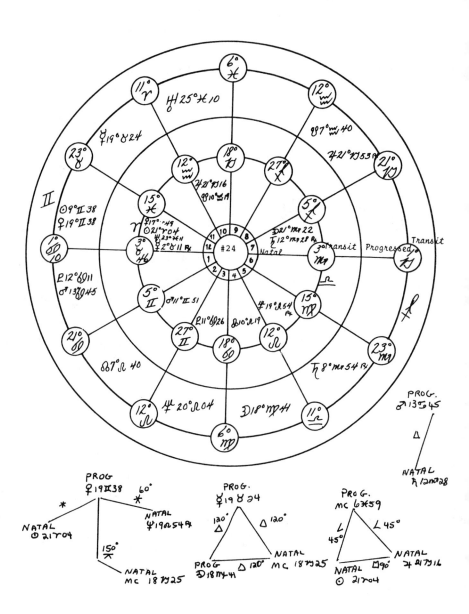

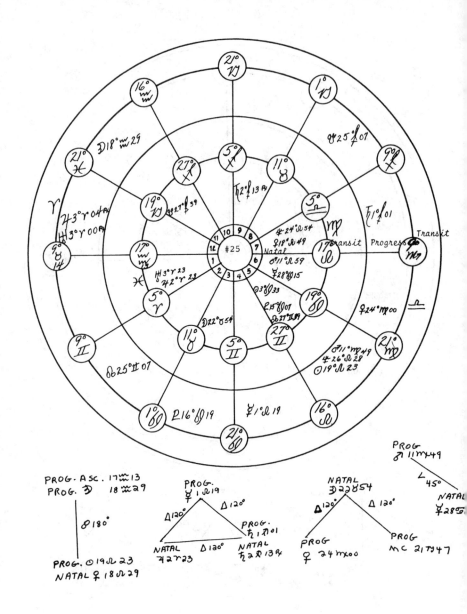

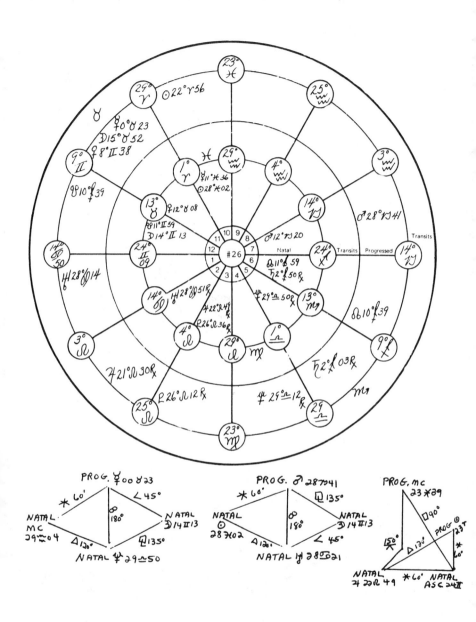

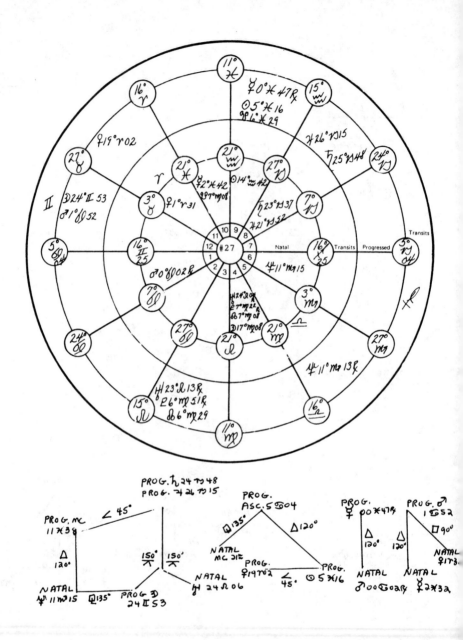

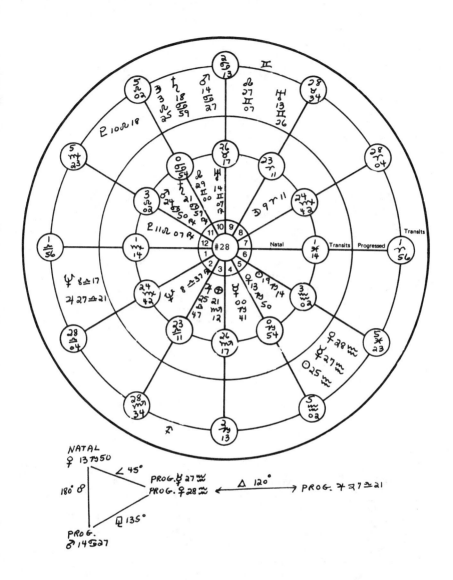

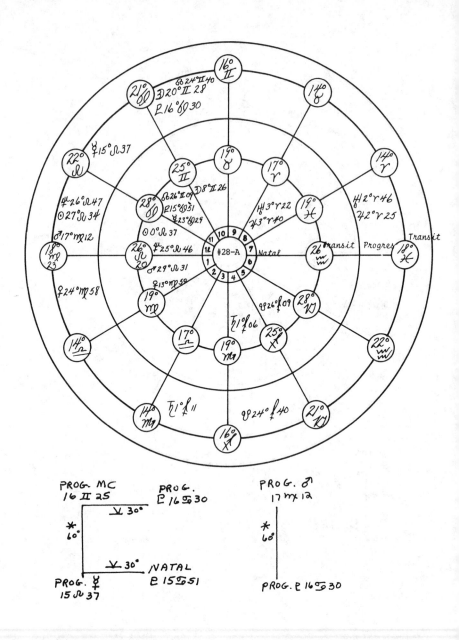

PROG. MC
16 Ⅱ 25

PROG.
♇ 16 ♋ 30

PROG. ♂
17 ♍ 12

⊥ 30°

⚹ 60°

⚹ 60°

⊥ 30°   NATAL
♇ 15 ♋ 51

PROG. ♀
15 ♌ 37

PROG. ♇ 16 ♋ 30

274

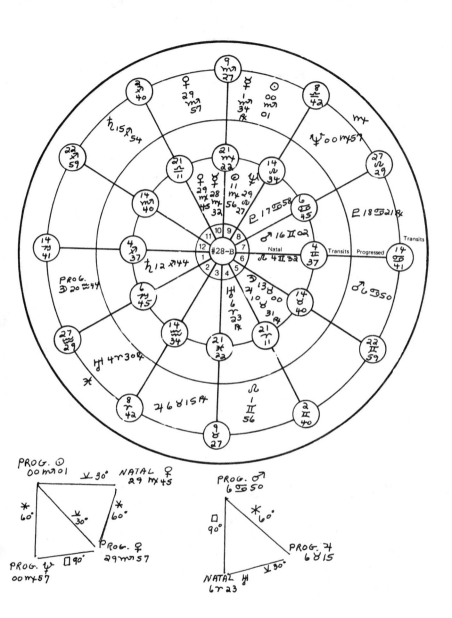

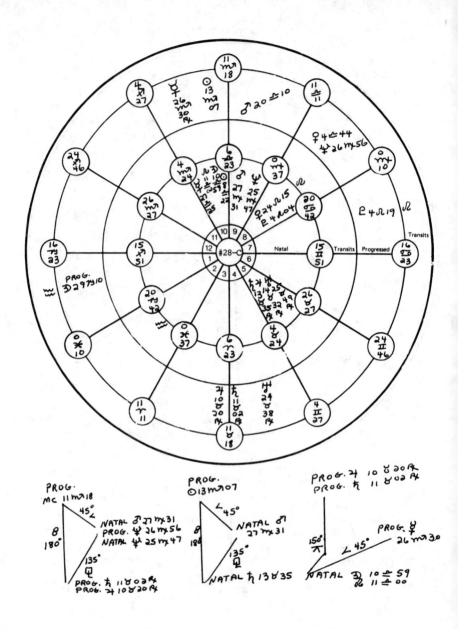

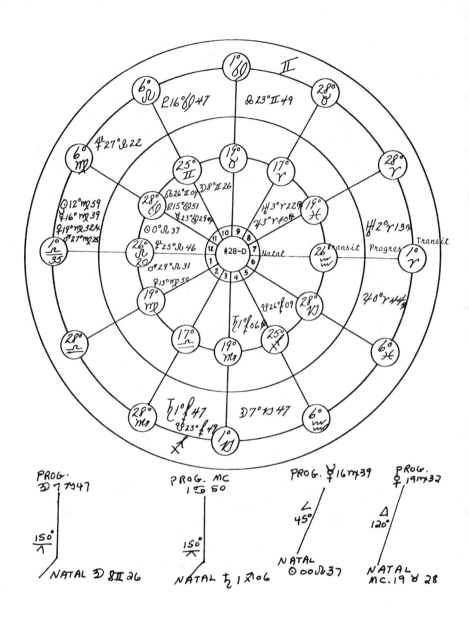

PROG.
☽ 7° ♐ 47

150°
⚹

NATAL ☽ 8 ♊ 26

PROG. MC
1 ♑ 50

150°
⚹

NATAL ♄ 1 ♐ 06

PROG. ☿ 16 ♍ 39

∠
45°

NATAL
☉ 00 ♌ 37

PROG.
♀ 19 ♍ 32

△
120°

NATAL
MC. 19 ♉ 28

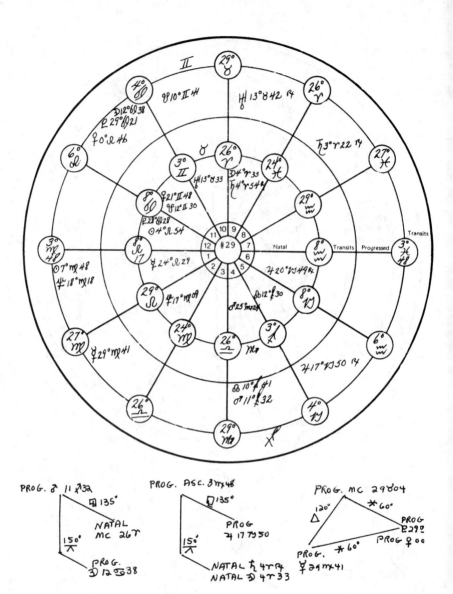

PROG. ♂ 11♐32
⊞ 135°
NATAL
MC 26♈
150° ☌ ⚹
PROG.
☽ 12♋38

PROG. ASC. 3♏48
⚹ 135°
PROG
♃ 17♐50
150° ⚹
NATAL ♄ 4♈℞
NATAL ☽ 4♈33

PROG. MC 29♉04
120° △ ⚹ 60°
PROG
℞29°
PROG ♀ 0°0
PROG. ⚹ 60°
☿ 29♏41

278

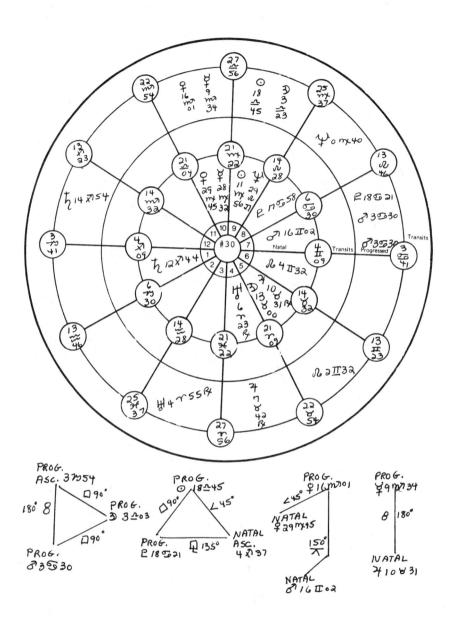

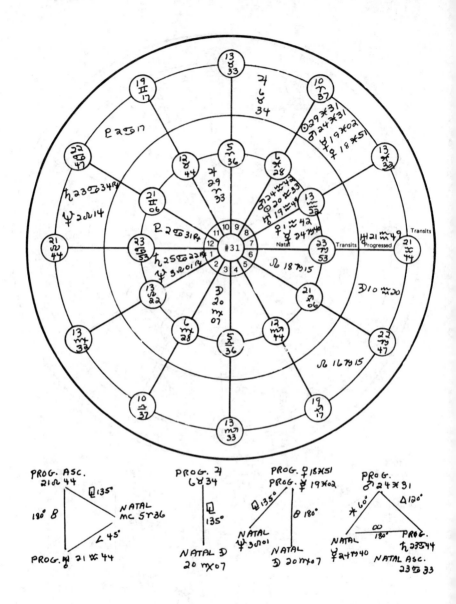

PROG. ASC.
21 ♌ 44

☋ 135°

180° 8

NATAL
MC 5 ♈ 36

∠ 45°

PROG. ♆ 21 ♒ 44

PROG. ♃
6 ♉ 34

♇
135°

NATAL ☽
20 ♏ 07

PROG. ♀ 18 ♓ 51
PROG. ♀ 19 ♓ 02

☋ 135°

θ 180°

NATAL
♆ 3 ♌ 01

NATAL
☽ 20 ♏ 07

PROG.
♂ 24 ♓ 31

✶ 60°

△ 120°

∞
180°

NATAL
♃ 24 ♏ 40

PROG.
♄ 23 ♋ 44

NATAL ASC.
23 ♋ 33

280

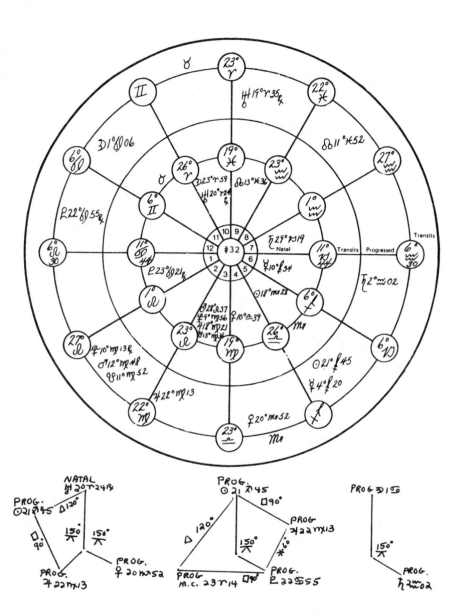

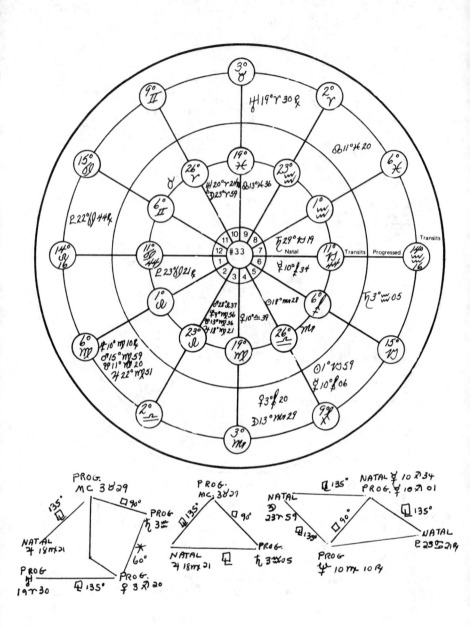

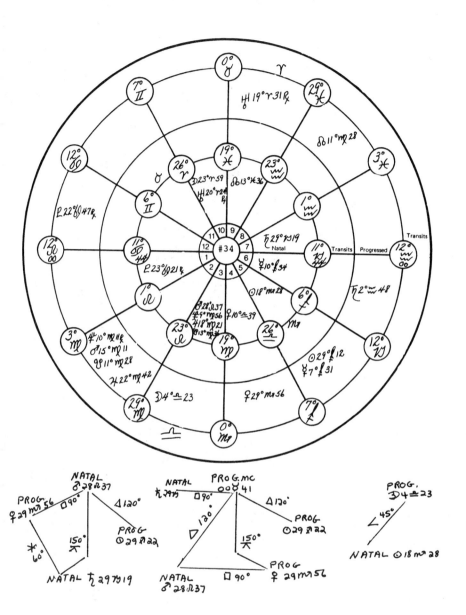

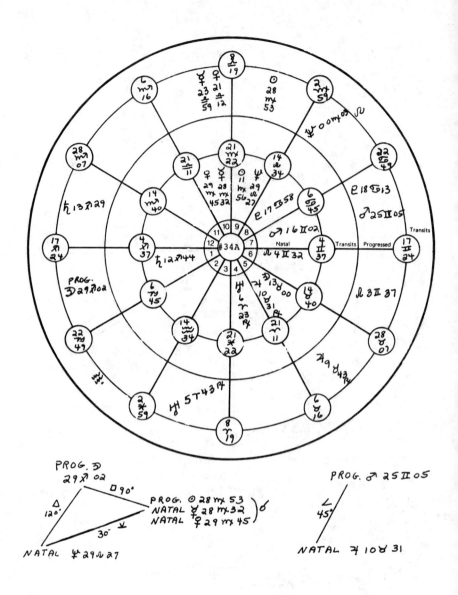

PROG. ☽
29 ♐ 02

△
120°

□ 90°

PROG. ☉ 28 ♍ 53
NATAL ☿ 28 ♍ 32
NATAL ♀ 29 ♍ 45

30° ⚹

NATAL ♇ 29 ♌ 27

PROG. ♂ 25 ♊ 05

∠
45°

NATAL ♃ 10 ♉ 31

284

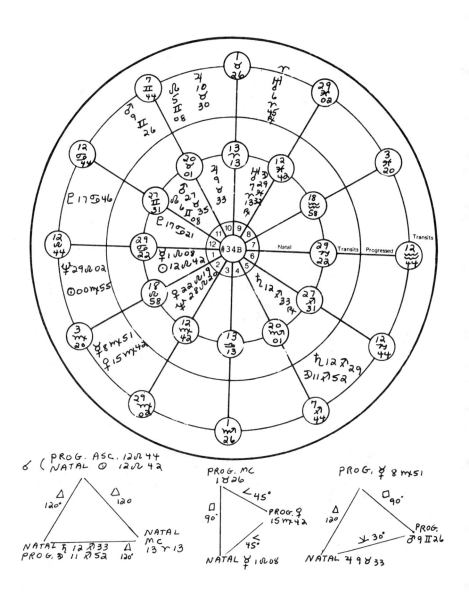

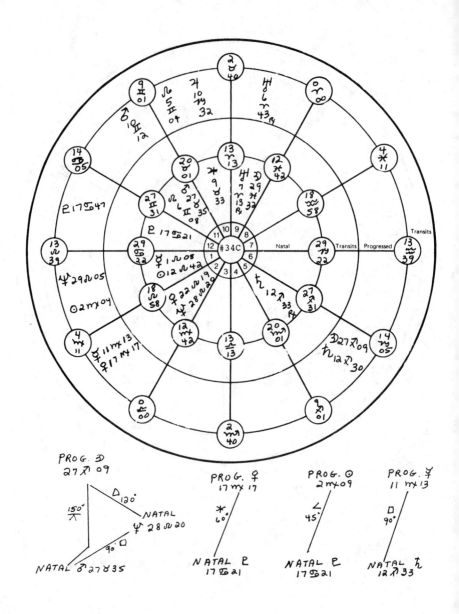

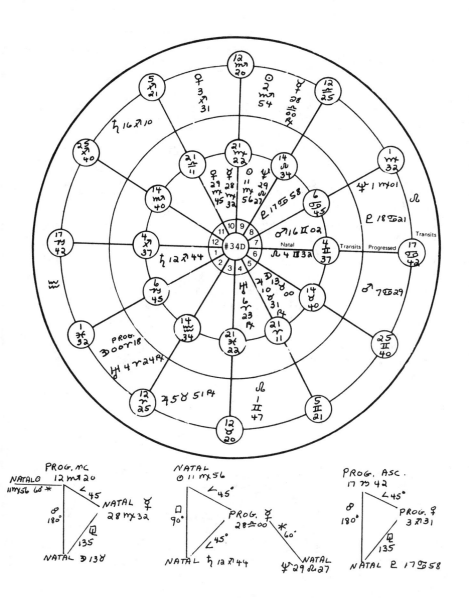

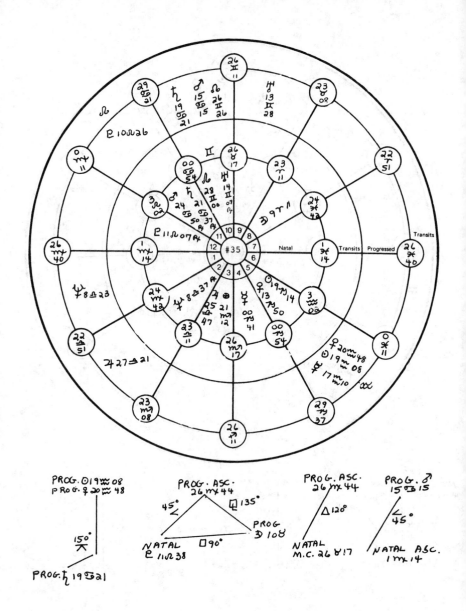

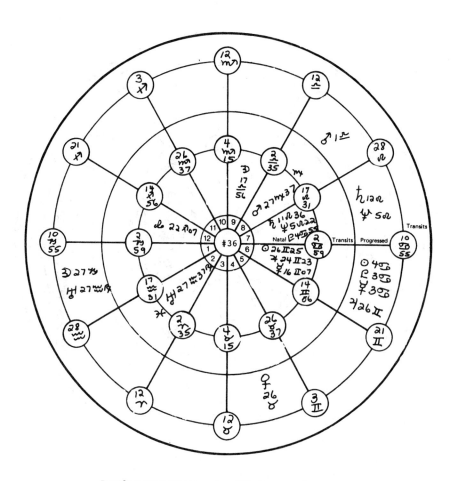

Regular Progressions for 9th House relocation.

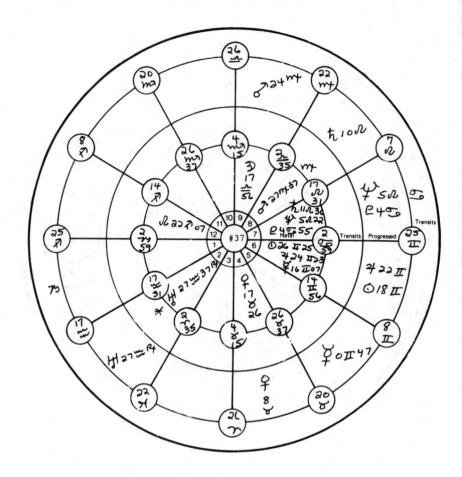

Converse Progressions for 9th House relocation.

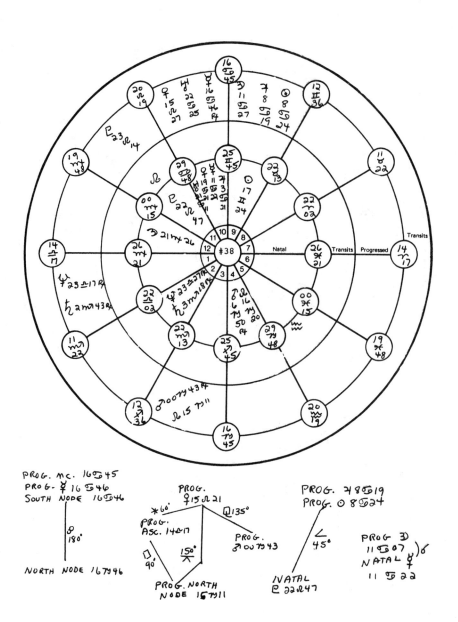

PROG. MC. 16♋45
PROG. ☿ 16♋46
SOUTH NODE 16♋46

⊗
180°

NORTH NODE 16♑46

PROG.
♀15♌21

✱60°

PROG.
ASC. 14♎17   ⚻135°

□,   150°   PROG.
90°   ✕   ♂00♑43

PROG. NORTH
NODE 15♑11

PROG. ♄8♋19
PROG. ⊙ 8♋24

∠
45°

NATAL
♇22♌47

PROG ☽
11♋07
NATAL ☿   )☌
11 ♋22

291

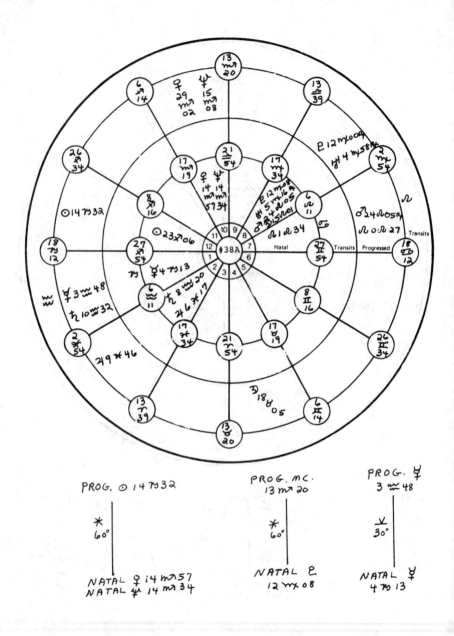

PROG. ☉ 14♐32

✶
60°

NATAL ♀ 14♏57
NATAL ♇ 14♏34

PROG. MC.
13♏20

✶
60°

NATAL ♇
12♏08

PROG. ♄
3♒48

⊻
30°

NATAL ♇
4♐13

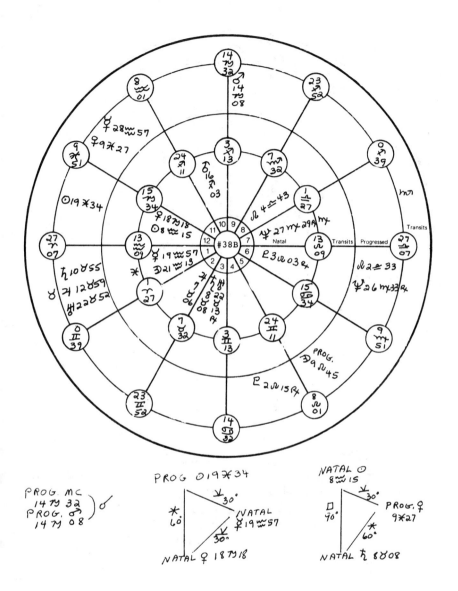

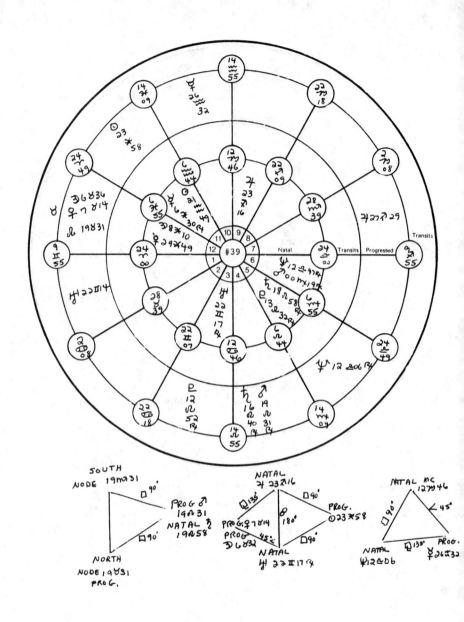

294

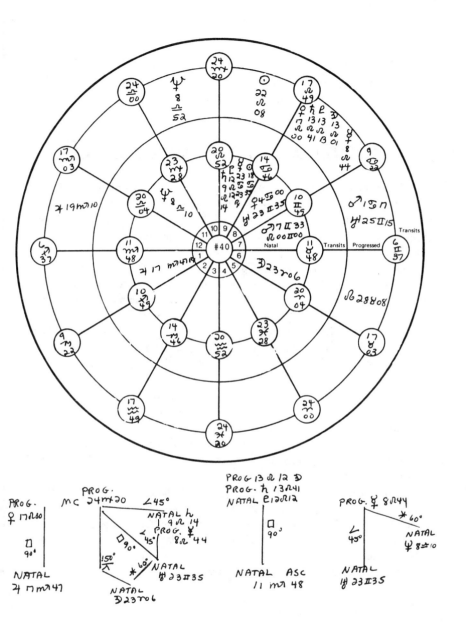

MATHEMATICS OF PROGRESSIONS

The response to my article, "Tips on Utilizing Your Progressed Chart" (Volume 45, Number 3) in the AFA *Bulletin* resulted in numerous requests for the "Mathematics of Progressions." This came as a real surprise for I had assumed that computers were vastly replacing the desire for knowledge of the mathematical procedures.

Computers are not infallible. They are capable of errors. It may not be due to the software as much as the individual feeding the information to the computer. With this in mind, I am offering one very easy method that only takes a few seconds of your time to calculate. This method can be used as an excellent source of proofreading your computerized chart, although it may be off by 1 or 2 degrees. This short method can also be applied to progressed charts of children and young adults up to 20 years of age with a great deal of accuracy. This will be explained and illustrated later in the chapter.

The second illustrated method cannot be beat for accuracy and will be equal to any computerized progressed chart, except perhaps, for a few minutes difference. I use Secondary Progressions which is "A Day for a Year." Should a progressed chart erected for any given year indicate a major event and you are having trouble determining the event, then you should erect a "Conversed Progressed Chart."

It makes no difference whether we progress a chart forward or backward in time. Conversed Progressions can provide us with additional insights and information that often fill in the gap that our Progressed Chart is trying to tell us.

Before we venture into any method of calculations, we should learn the "Basic Figures" of each sign. This will enable us to properly subtract or add when working with more than one Zodiac sign.

BASIC FIGURES FOR EACH SIGN

Aries is	0 or 360 Degrees	Libra is	180 Degrees
Taurus	30 Degrees	Scorpio	210 Degrees
Gemini	60 Degrees	Sagittarius	240 Degrees
Cancer	90 Degrees	Capricorn	270 Degrees
Leo	120 Degrees	Aquarius	300 Degrees
Virgo	150 Degrees	Pisces	330 Degrees

As you can see, the figures are merely a multiple of 30 degrees. This should enable one to memorize them with little effort.

"The Easy Method"

Adding your present age to your Natal 10th House Cusp. That is all there is to the "Easy Method."

Example: 18 Deg. Capricorn 21 Min. on the Natal 10th House Cusp, and we are progressing a chart for 10 years of age.

	Deg.		Min.
Natal 10th House Cusp	18	Cap.	21
Add the age	+ 10		
	28	Cap.	21

                      is on the Progressed 10th House Cusp for age 10.

Find 28 Cap. 21 Min. on the 10th House in the Table of Houses for your Latitude of Birth. You now have your new progressed Ascendant and Progressed House Cusp.

(Note: Always be sure to add your age to the "Degrees" on your Natal 10th House Cusp.)

Another Example: 18 Deg. Capricorn 21 Min. on the Natal 10th House Cusp for a Progressed Chart of the 58th year of birth.

	Deg.		Min.
Natal 10th House Cusp	288	Cap.	21
with Basic Figures added			
Add present age	+ 58		
	346	Deg.	21 Min. on Progressed 10th House Cusp.

Refer to the "Basic Figures" for each sign. Note that 346 Deg. is lesser than the 360 Degrees of Aries. Immediately this tells us that we have the sign Pisces on the Progressed 10th. Subtract the "Base Figure" of Pisces to get the exact Degree.

	Deg.	Min.
On Progressed 10th	346	21
Minus the Base Fig. for Pisces	330	

16 Pisces 21 Min. is on the Progressed 10th House Cusp for 58th Year.

"The Easy Method with Converse Progressions"

Same example for Progressed 10th year with 18 Deg. Capricorn 21 Min. on Natal 10th House Cusp.

	Deg.	Min.
Natal 10th House	18 Cap.	21
Converse Prog. year for age −	10	

8 Cap. 21 Min. is on the Converse Progressed 10th House Cusp for 10th year of birth.

Another Example: 18 Deg. Capricorn 21 min. on Natal 10th House Cusp applying Converse Progressions for the 58th year.

	Deg.	Min.
Natal 10th House Cusp with Base Figures added	288 Cap.	21
Converse Prog. year for age −	58	
	230	21 on Converse Progressed 10th House Cusp.

Refer to the "Base Figures" for each sign. As 230 Deg. is lesser than Sagittarius's 240, we know immediately that our Converse Progressed 10th House Cusp will be in the sign of Scorpio. Subtract the "Base Figure" of Scorpio to get the exact degree.

	Deg.	Min.
On Converse Prog. 10th	230	21
Minus the Base Fig.		
for Scorpio	− 210	

20 Scorp. 21 min. on Converse Prog. 10th House Cusp for 58th year of birth.

Find 20 Deg. Scorpio 21 min. on the 10th House Cusp in your Table of Houses for your Latitude of birth. You now have your Converse Progressed Ascendant and House Cusp.

"The Exact Method"

This method uses the Mean Motion of the Sun. The difference between the Natal Sun and the Progressed Sun is added to the Natal 10th House Cusp. Be sure to use the noon position of both Natal and Progressed Sun when subtracting. In other words, if you have a natal computerized chart, the Sun's position has been adjusted. Subtracting this Sun's position taken from a computerized chart rather than the noon's position from an Ephemeris can alter the calculations. Always take their noon position directly from the ephemeris for your day of birth, your progressed date and conversed progressed date.

Never use a computerized chart and attempt to use your Natal Sun to subtract from the noon position of your Progressed Sun.

Before we can subtract the Natal Sun from the Progressed Sun, we must first determine the progressed birthdate.

Step #1: Determining the progressed birthdate by adding the present age to the DAY of birth.

	Month	Day	Year
	4	11	1925
Progressed year is age		+10	
	4	21	1925

is progressed date for the native's 10th year of birth.

Step #2: Take the Progressed Sun's noon position of 4/21/25 and from it subtract the Natal Sun's noon position of 4/11/25.

| | Deg. of Sun | Min. |

4/21/25 Prog. Sun with
Base Figures added ...... 30 Deg. Taurus 52
Minus Natal Sun of 4/11/25 ...... 21 Deg. Aries 05
                                    9 Deg.   47 min. is added to Natal
                                                    10th House Cusp.

Step #3: Natal 10th House Cusp is 18 Deg. Capricorn 21 min.

| | Deg. | Min. |

Natal 10th House Cusp ...... 18 Cap. 21
Difference from Natal Sun
and Prog. Sun ...... + 9 47
                      28 Cap. 08 is on Progressed 10th House
                                 Cusp.

Note that the degrees on the Progressed 10th House Cusp for the 10 year old child is the same for both the "Easy Method" and the "Exact Method." The Sun's DEGREE moves at the same rate of speed through the Zodiac as does the 10th House Cusp. It is the MINUTES that we either accumulate or lose as we advance with age that makes up the one or two degrees gain or loss on the Progressed 10th House Cusp. This is clearly illustrated as we do the "Exact Method" (the "Exact Method" is really just Solar Arc Progression), for the native as he enters his 58th year of birth.

Step #1: Determining the progressed birthdate by adding the present age to the DAY of birth.

| | Month | Day | Year |

Birth date 4 11 1925
Progressed year for age ...... +58
                              4 69 1925 (the 69 days has over 2
                                        months in it.)

Subtract 30 days of April
and add to the month ...... −30
                            5 39 1925 (Still another month)

Subtract 31 days of
May and add to month ...... −31
                            6 08 1925 is Progress Date for 58th
                                      year.

300

Step #2: Take the Progressed Sun's noon position of 6/8/25 and from it subtract the Natal Sun's noon position of 4/11/25.

Deg. of Sun Min.

	Deg. of Sun		Min.
6/8/25 Prog. Sun with Base Figures added	77	Gemini	10
Subtract Natal Sun of 4/11/25	− 21	Aries	05
	56	Degrees 05	minutes is added to the Natal 10th House Cusp

Step #3: Natal 10th House Cuspis 18 Deg. Capricorn 21 min.

	Deg.		Min.
Natal 10th House Cusp with Base Figures added	288	Cap.	21
Add difference from Natal Sun and Progressed Sun	− 56		05
	344	Deg.	26 min. on Progressed 10th House Cusp

Refer to the "Base Figures" for each sign. As 344 Degrees is lesser than the 360 Degrees of Aries, we immediately know that our 10th House Cusp will be progressed into the sign of Pisces. Subtract the "Basic Figures" of Pisces to get the exact degrees.

	Deg.	Min.
On Progressed 10th	344	26
Minus Base Fig. of Pisces	330	
	14 Pisces	26 min. is on the Progressed 10th House Cusp

If you go back and check the individual's progressed chart for the same age of 58 with the "Easy Method," you will note there is a discrepancy of 2 degrees, between the two.

As this native advanced with age, he lost 2 degrees on his Progressed Tenth House Cusp by adding the Solar Arc to his Natal 10th House Cusp rather than his age.

"The Exact Method, Converse Progressions"

Converse progressions works the same way as Solar Arc Progressions, except we reverse the process.

Step #1: Determining the Converse Progressed Birthdate by subtracting the present age from the DAY of birth.

	Month	Day	Year
Birth date	4	11	1925
Converse. Prog. year for age		−58	

The only way we would be able to subtract the age 58 from 11 days is to borrow the past two months of February and March and change them into days and then add them to the 11 days.

Bear in mind with regular progressions, whenever the age was added to the DAYS and exceeded over 60 days, we knew there were over 2 months that had to be extracted, beginning with the month in which we were born.

However, with Converse Progressions we do not begin with the month of which we were born to begin subtracting but rather the previous months.

	Month	Day	Year
We borrowed 31 days of March and the 28 days of February and add them to the days and subtracted these two months from the four months.	2	70	1925
Converse progressions for age		−58	
	2	12	1925

is Converse Progressions for age 58

In conclusion, some individuals may become confused when they try both methods and still come up with the same degree on their Progressed Tenth House Cusp. This is possible, even when they reach the age of 30 or 60. There are several months a year that the Sun's Mean Motion moves at a steady pace of one degree a day which is equal to one year in progressions. Natives born during these months have a Natal Sun that has the same rate of motion as the 10th House Cusp. The following graph should give some insight.

Month of Birth	Degrees as they advance on the 10th House	
	By age 30	By age 60
January	1 deg. gain	2 deg. gain
February	0 deg. gain	0 deg. gain
March	0 deg. loss	1 deg. loss
April	1 deg. loss	2 deg. loss
May	1 deg. loss	2 deg. loss
June	1 deg. loss	2 deg. loss
July	1 deg. loss	2 deg. loss
August	1 deg. loss	2 deg. loss
September	1 deg. loss	2 deg. loss
October	0 deg. loss	1 deg. loss
November	0 deg. loss	0 deg. loss
December	1 deg. gain	2 deg. gain

These figures are by no means conclusive but merely illustrates the Sun's Mean Motion varying speed from 57 minutes to 1 degree 1 minute at different times of the year. These extra minutes gained or lost, depending upon the month in which you were born, can add up to one or two degrees by the time one reaches 30 or 60 years of age.

In keeping with the main purpose of this text book "Delineation of Progressions," there are no further illustrations on mathematical calculations. The "ACD," planetary adjustments of the progressed moon and planets can be found in many of the popular publications on the market.